A DICTIONARY OF KASHMIRI PROVERBS & SAYINGS

A DICTIONARY OF KASHMIRI PROVERBS & SAYINGS

Explained and Illustrated from the rich and interesting Folklore of the valley.

REV. J. HINTON KNOWLES, F.R.G.S., M.R.A.S., &c.

GYAN

Published by

GYAN

Gyan Publishing House
5, Ansari Road
Daryaganj, New Delhi-110002
Phone: 011-47034999, 9811692060
E-mail: books@gyanbooks.com

Distribution Network
gyanbooks.com
India, USA, Canada, UK, Australia, France

ISBN : 978-81-212-9522-2 (PB)
First Published, 1885

2nd Impression 2023

Printed at: Gyan Press, Delhi.

A DICTIONARY OF KASHMIRI PROVERBS & SAYINGS
Author: REV. J. HINTON KNOWLES

A

DICTIONARY

OF

KASHMIRI PROVERBS & SAYINGS

Explained and Illustrated from the rich and interesting Folklore of the Valley.

BY THE

REV. J. HINTON KNOWLES, F.R.G.S., M.R.A.S., &c.,

(C. M. S.)

MISSIONARY TO THE KASHMIRIS.

A wise man will endeavour "to understand a proverb and the interpretation."—*Prov. I. vv.* 5, 6.

1885.

PREFACE.

THAT moment when an author dots the last period to his manuscript, and then rises up from the study-chair to shake its many and bulky pages together is almost as exciting an occasion as when he takes a quire or so of foolscap and sits down to write the first line of it. Many and mingled feelings pervade his mind, and hope and fear vie with one another and alternately overcome one another, until at length the author finds some slight relief for his feelings and a kind of excuse for his book, by writing a preface, in which he states briefly the nature and character of the work, and begs the pardon of the reader for his presumption in undertaking it.

A winter in Kashmír must be experienced to be realised. The air is most invigorating, and the quiet is sublime. Even an ordinarily busy missionary enjoys much leisure through such a season in this beautiful country.

I have now spent two long quiet winters here, and this "Dictionary of Kashmírí Proverbs and Sayings" is the result of many hours of labour, study, and anxiety, during these leisurable months. As a missionary, on arriving in the Valley, I at once devoted my attention to the study of the language; and believing that Proverbs taught "the real people's speech," discovered "the genius, wit and spirit of a nation," and embodied its "current and practical philosophy,"

I quickly began to make a collection of them.* This book, I believe, contains nearly all the Proverbs and Proverbial sayings now extant among the Kashmírí people. They have been gathered from various sources. Sometimes the great and learned Panḍit instinctively uttered a proverb in my hearing; sometimes I got the barber to tell me a thing or two, as he polled my head; and sometimes the poor coolie said something worth knowing, as carrying my load he tramped along before me. A few learned Muhammadan and Hindú friends also, have very materially helped me in this collection and its arrangement; and here I again heartily acknowledge their kind and ready service.

Actum est. It is done; and now the manuscript has to be sent to the publishers, and notices have to be posted to the different papers and journals interested to advertise the work as "in the press." What will the little world say, into whose hands it may chance to arrive? How will the philologist, the ethnologist, the antiquarian, the student of folklore, and the general reader regard this which has cost some considerable time and study. Dear reader, in order that your criticism may not be so hard as it might, perhaps, otherwise be, please permit me to remind you that Kashmír proper is but a small country, a little vale surrounded by snow-capped mountain ranges, about eighty-four miles long from north-west to south-east, and from twenty to twenty-five miles in width, with an area of about 1,850 square miles; that the Kashmírí

* "The genius, wit and spirit of a nation are discovered in its proverbs."—*Bacon.*

"Proverbs embody the current and practical philosophy of an age or nation."—*Fleming.*

"Proverbs teach the real people's speech, and open up the hitherto sealed book of the native mind."—*John Beames.*

language is virtually *minus* a Dictionary and Grammar, and that besides one or two very unimportant works* written in the Persian character, all true Kashmírí books are printed in a kind of mongrel-Devanágarí character called Sháradá, which only a very small proportion of the population can properly read; that the Kashmírí language itself is very difficult, and is spoken differently by different persons—the Hindús and Muhammadans, especially, speaking distinct dialects; that information from books of travel, &c., like Vigne's, Hügel's, Knight's, Drew's, Bellew's and others, is very crude, scanty, and contradictory, concerning the manners and customs of the Kashmírí; and that this individual is not naturally so communicative as might be expected from his cheery look and humorous disposition.

Horace says somewhere "*Nonum prematur in annum*;" and perhaps it would have been better to have kept by me what I have written, for nine years before publishing it. But other work demands much of my leisure time,—the preparation of a Kashmírí Dictionary, of which these proverbs, and the words that contain them, form but a stepping-stone, and the translations of the "Psalms of David" and "Proverbs of Solomon," which have been deferred only because of the non-appearance as yet of the revised edition of the Old Testament. However, I trust the reader will accept my various excuses and forgive any error, whether in the romanizing, or the style, or the information, as the case may be.

The Proverbs and Sayings have all been translated as literally as possible; and with a fairly-trained ear I have honestly tried hard to render correctly in the Roman character what

* A short interesting account of the origin of this character is given in Dr. Elmslie's Kashmírí Vocabulary, p. 149.

I heard ; but the different dialects made this very confusing work ; and there were some sounds which could not possibly be written like Roman-Urdú, except with the following additional vowels :—

An *o* as the German *ö*, but short.

An *o* as the German *ö*, but long and drawling. These two vowels, I believe, exist in Hungarian.

An *u* as the German *ü*.

An *u* as the German *ü*, but long and drawling.

In addition to these there is a sound which is something like a very short *i*, to which I have given the name of *khiyálí zer ;* it is frequently the sign of the instrumental case as *hún*, a dog, *húni* by a dog, &c. This sound, I believe, is to be found in Russian, and is in that language written as *j*. In the Roman character this sound will be represented by the simple letter *i*, and in order that this *i* may always appear, I have always written the final *he* (*há,e mukhtafí*). With the exception of this *i* or *khiyáli zer*, I have, however, avoided introducing any diacritical points. The following is the Roman-Kashmírí alphabet with the powers of the letters :—

A a pronounced as *a* in wom*a*n.
Á á ,, *a* in *a*rt.
Ai ai ,, *ai* in *ai*sle.
Au au ,, *au* in *our*.
B b ,, *b* in *b*ut.
Ch ch ,, *ch* in *ch*urch
D d ,, *d* in *d*ew, the point of the tongue is pressed on the upper fore-teeth.
Ḍ ḍ pronounced as *d* in ba*d*—the point of the tongue is struck back on the palate.
E e ,, *e* in there.
Ĕ ĕ ,, *e* in pet.
F f ,, *f* in *f*ind, the English *f* is only sounded, and then very badly, in the

middle or at the end of a word. If it occurs at the commencement of a word it is most distinctly and invariably turned into *ph*.

G g pronounced as *g* in *go*.

The Arabic letter <u>*hgain*</u> *gh*, with its peculiar guttural sound is seldom heard in pure Kashmírí.

H h pronounced as *h* in *house*.

I i is a kind of half *i*. I hear that there is something analogous to this to be found in Russian and is written as *j*.

Í í pronounced as *i* in pol*i*ce.

J j ,, *j* in *just*.

K k ,, *k* in *keck*le.

<u>Kh</u> <u>kh</u> ,, *ch* in the Scotch and Irish lo*ch*, or the final *ch* of the German scha*ch* and bu*ch*.

L l pronounced as *l* in *lane*.

M m pronounced as *m* in *man*.

N n ,, *n* in *noon*

Ṅ ṅ ,, *n* in the French words sa*n*s, bo*n*.

O o pronounced as *o* in n*o*.

P p ,, *p* in *p*aint.

Ph ph ,, similar to *ph* in *ph*legm. The Kashmírís turn the Persian ف *fe* into *phe*, *e.g.*, phakír and phaṭah for fakír and faṭh, except perhaps when this letter, or rather sound, comes in the middle, and at the end of a word.

R r pronounced as *r* in *r*an. A Scotchman's *r* is perhaps not met with in pure Kashmírí.

The euphonic *r* is very common, *e.g.*, boṅṭh and broṅṭh, byor and bror, &c. The Muhammadans generally omit the *r* in these and similar words.

S s pronounced as *s* in sin.

Sh sh ,, *sh* in *sh*ine.

T	t	pronounced as *t* in *t*ake, the point of the tongue is pressed on the upper fore-teeth.
Ṭ	ṭ	„ *t* in *t*ub, the point of the tongue is pressed back on the palate.
Ts	ts	pronounced as *ts* in ge*ts*.
U	u	„ *o* in top.
Ú	ú	„ *u* in r*u*le.
V, W	v w	„ both having a power between the English *v* and *w*.
Y	y	„ *y* in *y*ear.
Z	z	„ *z* in zeal.

Note.—Bh, chh, gh, kh, ph, th, ṭh and tsh are respectively the aspirates of ch, g, k, p, t and ṭ, and ts, and are pronounced as one letter.

With regard to the "point" of the different proverbs and sayings, I have been through them all, as here written, with a little council of learned Muhammadan and Hindú Kashmírí friends, and not allowed one to pass, until I got their full and undivided sanction to my explanation of it. The notes and facetiæ, &c., are such as cropped-up in the course of writing, and have been jotted down in the hope that they will be interesting to some readers.

And lastly, but by no means of the last importance, I trust that if any reader is pleased with this book, and thinks fit, he will kindly recommend it to others, as the whole profits of the work are to be devoted to the sorely-strained funds of the "Medical Mission Hospital," Kashmír.

J. HINTON KNOWLES.

Kashmír, *February 7th*, 1885.

KASHMIRI PROVERBS.

A

Ab tih ṭoṭh bab tih ṭoṭh.

I love myself and I love my father.

The reply of a very covetous man to a friend, when that friend said that he would give him only one out of the two things which he coveted.

A grasping disposition.

Ábah tali shrák.

A knife in the water.

A traitor in the camp.

Áb is the word generally used by Muhammedans in the valley. The Hindús invariably say *páni* or *poni*.

Ábas andar kranḍ.

A big basket in the water.

A man, who *ex officio* is a person of some position and influence, is like a kranḍ in the water. So long as he retains his employment, he retains his authority, but as soon as he is dismissed, he loses that authority and honour. The basket as long as it floats in the stream is filled with water, but immediately you take it out of the stream it is emptied.

Achh káni ján tah wat káni nah.

Better that the eye be blind than that the way be blind.

He that goes a-borrowing goes a-sorrowing.

Achh watshah tah gáshah ratshah.

May your eyes be opened but see nothing.

A Kashmírí curse.

Achhin ungujeh ṭhukanih.

To strike the eyes with the fingers.

To tease, to bother.

Achhuv andarah riyih surmah kaḍit.

He'll take the (very) antimony out of your eyes (and you'll not know it).

A sharp fellow, Beware ! . . .

Surmah is black sulphuret of antimony, used for pencilling the eyes.

Adal tah wadal zanánah chhai pashich zadal tshai.

A contrary woman is like bad grass on the roof.

Grass not fitted for thatching does not set well, but lets the rain through the roof. Cf. Prov. xxvii. 15.

Aḍi dadi yĕtshih tah aḍi dadi rĕtshih.

Half (the people) are burnt with wishing and half are burnt with scandal.

The struggle for popularity and place.

Aḍi Lár tah aḍi Dár.

Half at Lár and half at Dár.

A man of large and scattered property; but who cannot get at it or obtain anything from it.

Aḍin khash tah aḍin ash.

To half (the people) wretchedness and to half happiness.

Admi bastan andar chhuh sir.

A secret is (concealed) under the skin of man.

Man is a make-up of mystery.

Aḍui umr tah baḍuí balái.

Half-life and great misfortune (be to you).

A Kashmírí curse.

Aḍyav khĕyih chinih aḍyav khĕyih ṭákí.

Half (the people) ate from the large dishes and half from the small dishes.

A badly-arranged dinner.

Ágah boḍ paharas naukar boḍ waharas.

The master is great in three hours, the servant is great in a year.

Some people earn as much in three hours as others do in twelve months.

Ágah karán nethar tah parzun nah mánán.

The master gets married, but the servant does not agree to it.

A contrary servant.

Agar Khán tsáyov gagar wáji, talih no míjis kum-yúji.

Agar Khán entered into a rat's hole, and there he did not get, even, a bran-cake.

In extremis.

Once Agar Khán was reduced to such distress that he was glad to take shelter in a little broken-down hut and sleep there.

Agar Khánun hustú luslú tah lustú; lustú nah tah khústú.

Should Agar Khán's elephant live, it lives; and if it does not live, then never mind.

Some people are so little respected, that it does not much matter whether they live or die.

Agar Khán was one of the old Paṭhán governors of Kashmír. In his time affairs arrived at a crisis. The army had rebelled, and the treasury was empty. To support his family and servants he parted with his jewels and other treasures, and yet all through this time of the direst distress he was keeping a favourite elephant. When he could no longer feed the pet beast, he let it go to wander whither it pleased.

Agar tser karih jald yiyih, agar jald karih tsír yiyih.

If he delays he will come quickly, but if he hastens he will come slowly.

More haste, worse speed.

Ahalamarí ratah-kharí.

The quarrelsome people of Ahalamar.

Ahalamar is one of the chief divisions of the city of Srínagar. In olden days it was the regular thing on every Friday for the young people of one division to challenge in fight the young people of another division. A certain place and hour would be arranged, and the youths armed with sticks and slings, &c., would assemble on their respective sides. At a signal from their leaders they would join combat, and generally there were several broken limbs and sometimes deaths, resulting from these fights. His Highness the late Maharájah Guláb Singh put an end to these disgraceful proceedings.

The youngsters of Ahalamar were very pugnacious, and especially so respecting the people of Suth, a neighbouring division. Perhaps this was because they generally "got as good as they gave." At any rate these two divisions had many fights with one another. The Ahalamar youth would march in a crowd shouting :—

Suthĕn zachih tah kuthĕn nár
Ahalamariav ganḍak lár.

"Ragged clothes to the people of Suth, and may their bundles catch fire.
The people of Ahalamar gave chase to them."

Then the crowd from Suth would meet them shouting :—

Ahalamarí ratah-kharí ;
Lĕjan chhik nah batah phalí ;
Chandan chhik nah hárah nalí.
"The quarrelsome people of Ahalamar
They have not a rice-grain in their pots.
They have not a cowrie in their pockets."

One is reminded of the English custom of "beating the bounds" on Holy Thursday, when the parish school children, accompanied by the clergyman and parish officers, used to walk through their parish from end to end. The boys had willow wands with which they struck the lines of boundary, (and sometimes the boys of the adjoining parish).

"*Ai hák tsah katih ák ?*"
"*Az khánai Mumah Ṭák.*"
"*Nah tsah nún nah tsah pák.*
"*Birav binshín bálá-i-ták.*"
"O cabbage, whence came ye ?"
"From the house of Mumah Ṭak."
"You are neither salted nor cooked.
"Heugh ! go and sit on the window."

Hák sometimes called Hák-wák, or (as in Persian) Ság, a cabbage or any edible vegetable.

Whenever the hák is badly cooked the above lines are sure to be quoted.

Mumah Ṭák was a great greengrocer in Srínagar city.

Aib panun máshok.
A man loves his own fault.

"Oh, wad some power the giftie gie us
To see oursels as others see us."

Aibo pĕyiyo gaibuch balái, mandachhih patah chhai khijálat.
O sin, let Heaven's misfortune fall upon you—to you is shame upon shame.

"Be sure your sin will find you out."

Ák ai tah untham kyah ? Yimah ai tah khyáwaham kyah ?
If you have come, what have you brought ? If I come, what will you give me to eat ?

A mercenary individual.

Ak bánah, bĕyih pánah, bĕyih talabánah, bĕyih koriadilh gánah.

First (they seized) my dish, then myself, then (I had) to pay the witnesses, and then (they abused me, calling me) the eater of my daughter's hire, and the keeper of a brothel.

A poor prisoner in the hands of the policeman.

Ak bará,e Khudá tah bĕyih hastis khasit.

A man begs and then gets up on an elephant.

"*To mount an elephant*" is an expression for becoming proud or angry.

Ak buḍih tah meṭhih, byák buḍih tah ṭĕṭhih.

One man is old and sweet, another old and bitter.

Ak chhiwyov masah byák hákah rasah.

One man is intoxicated with the juice of the grape, another with the juice of vegetables.

Pride dwells in every one, be he rich or poor.

"Kashmír is the only part of India where wine is made from the juice of the grape, a fact to be attributed rather to its acescent quality than to any scarcity of the fruit."

Ak gav jáni yár, byák gav náni yár.

One is a thorough friend, another is a "loafer."

Náni yár, a bread friend.

Persian—Yár-i-ján o yár-i-nán.

Ak gub nerih, ak khár kuchih, pĕtsih gásah, wafáí nah kĕnh.

One sheep in a meadow, one kharwar (of grain) in the house, and the bulrush (these three) do not last.

The sheep and the kharwár are but "as a drop in the ocean," soon swallowed up, and the bulrush quickly rots.

Khár or *Kharwár*, is a dry measure, containing lbs. 192. The literal meaning of the word is an ass-load. *Khar* is the Kashmírí word for an ass (like the Persian).

Ak khojas suĕt baṭah khyun, bĕyá sinis kun athah nyun?

When a person is dining with a great man, will he stretch out his hand towards the dish (to help himself)?

Give him a yard, and he'll take an ell.

Ak koṭ tah bĕyih kátis garawani.

First there's the gallows, then there's the trouble of making the gallows.

A difficult and losing game.

Ak lĕwán graṭṭas byák lĕwán graṭṭawáli sunzih chinih.

One licks the mill-stone, the other licks the miller's dish.

As fast as one earns, the other spends.

Ak nyuv Yaman tah byák khyav braman.

Death took one and the other was seduced from his own country to another country in hope of gain.

A man of large family, but not one child left to him, all scattered. *Yama* is the Hindú god and judge of the dead.

Ak ráfiz tah bĕyih gámah ráfiz.

A Shí'a and also a village Shí'a.

There are Shi'as and Shi'as.

The village Shi'as are much more superstitious and bigoted than the city Shi'as. Altogether there are about six thousand Shí'as in the valley. They are found chiefly at Zaḍibal, a few miles to the north of Srínagar, and at Hasanábád near to the city lake, where their principal mosque is.

Great bitterness of feeling exists between the Súnís and the Shí'as, the rival sects of Muhammedanism, which occasionally manifests itself in open fights ending in loss of life and great destruction of property. In 1874 the Maharájah's troops were obliged to be called out to quell the rioters. During the Paṭhán rule in the valley the Shí'as were forbidden to celebrate the Muharram. About the time when the country was annexed to the Durrání empire (1753-1819 A.D.), the Shí'as determined to enact this sacred feast; and acordingly compelled a Súní boy to eat salt; then tantalized him with water; and just as he was about to drink it they shot him to death with arrows, so, that he might perish like Husain, who was killed by Yazid near Kúfa, in the desert, of thirst. When 'Abdu'llá Khán, who had just conquered this country, heard of this, he was much enraged and immediately gave the order for the collecting of all the Shí'as in Srínagar, that their noses might be pierced, and one line of string run through the whole of them, and that, thus fastened together, they might be conducted through the principal thoroughfares of the city. Nothing daunted, however, they very soon again tried to celebrate their sacred festival, and notably in the time of the Sikh governor Bamá Singh (1830 A.D.) There was a great Súní living in Kashmír in the fifteenth century, whose name was Muqaddam Sáhib, He had a large number of followers, amongst whom was Shams-ud-dín, a Persian Shí'a, who managed to conceal his religious views and to ingratiate himself into his master's favour, though all the time he was really proselytising. He thus made many converts to the Shí'a faith, and in consequence is much respected by the Shí'as, for these people have a principle of religious compromise called takía, whereby the Shí'a thinks that he is perfectly justified in lying and deceiving to save himself from religious persecution. It appears that during the year or so of Bamá Singh's governorship in Kashmír, the Shí'as when celebrating the Muharram purposely spat in the direction of the Muqaddam Sáhib's tomb, and this so enraged the Súnís that they fell upon them then and there and slew fifteen of them, besides doing much damage to their property. Since then Persian traders have kept at a distance from Kashmír.

Ak tah ak gav kah.

One and one are eleven.

Two heads are better than one.

Ak wonán wagivi byák pilanáwán chhus pěts.

One weaves the mat and another holds out to him the reed.

The mat-maker could work much better alone. Hence the above is quoted when unnecessary help is received.

Ak wukur běyih trakur.

First, you are unfortunate; secondly, you are proud.

Pride without reason.

Ak zálih bachhih tal bihit toh, tah byák zálih tumul.

One will sit by the fire-place and burn chaff, while another will burn rice.

Economy and extravagance.

Ak zanánah chhai daulat, byák zallat.

One woman is wealth to you, another is ruination.

Ak zanánah chhai hat lanjih búní, byák chhai bar tal húní hish.

One woman is (like) a hundred-branch plane-tree to you, another is like a bitch at the door.

The *búní* or chinár (*Platanus Orientalis*) of Kashmír is one of the finest and most shade-giving trees. It was introduced by the Muhammadans from the West, and under the fostering attention of royalty this splendid tree with its palmate leaves and spreading branches, has reached the greatest age and attention in Kashmír.

Akhá gomut yírah tah wirih mangán ṭang.

A man is confused and asks for pears from the willow tree.

Akhá khut hastis biyákhá khastan dusih.

One man rode upon an elephant, another mounted the wall.

High and low; rich and poor.

Panjábí.—*Hik pinne, te díyá ghore ghinne.*

Akhá lasin sásas maras.

Let one man live for the sake of a thousand houses.

God spare the public benefactor.

Akhi laṭik khasih nah guris, bĕyih laṭih pakih nah piyádah.

At one time he will ride on a horse, at another time he will go on foot.

Díruit ædificat mútat quadráta rotundis.

Akhi waktah pránah-kuj tah bĕyih waktah pránah-dyal.

At one time the onion-plant, and at another time the onion-skin.

Good and bad times.

Aki sund dazih áb tah bĕyih sund dazih nah tíl.

One man can burn water, where another cannot even burn oil.

A matter of luck.

Aki sund dyárah chanḍah bĕyih sund katá.

One man's pocketful of money (is no more than) another man's word.

Aki t̲s̲at sum tah sás gav kuliḥ.

One man cut the bridge, and a thousand people fell into the river.

Punishment visited upon many because of the iniquity of one.

This is a saying derived from a true story (so a native friend says). A very long time ago a large crowd of people were travelling together;—perhaps they were going on a visit to some popular shrine. In the midst of the crowd there was a very wicked man who did not seem to be able to think, or say, or do, anything except that which was evil. On seeing a swift and deep stream in front, this wicked man ran on ahead and crossed the ordinary plank bridge built over it; and no sooner had he himself crossed over, than with his big hatchet he hacked and hewed away at the supporting beam of the bridge, until it broke into two pieces and the whole structure fell down, and was soon carried away by the angry waters. Now what were the people to do?—go they must to this place, concerning which they had been making preparations many-a-long-day before. At length two or three of the bolder spirits among them determined to wade the stream; and the others encouraged by their example resolved to venture also. They all started together, but, alas! when they reached the middle of the water the swiftness and depth proving too much for them they all lost heart, gave themselves to be carried away by the waters, and were drowned.

Aki t̲s̲onḍ dunyá tah bĕyih aki ímán; dunyá tah ímán chhih nah donawai athih yiwán.

One man sought the world and another sought for faith; the world and faith both do not come into the same hand.

"Ye cannot serve God and mammon."

Akis chhĕh dazán dár tah byák chhus wushanáwán athah.

One man's beard is on fire, and another man warms his hands by it.

To be glad at another's misfortune.

Panjábi.—*Kisí ká ghar jale, koí tápe.*

Akis gom zah; mĕthar gám shĕthar; káwas gáyam kukil.

One became two; friends became enemies; the crow became a dove.

An old man's answer to a friend, who had sent to enquire how he was. The meaning is that a staff was now "part and parcel" of him; that his teeth had deserted him; and that his raven-black hair had turned grey

Aklah chhání gará chání tah gará myáni.

Aklah, the carpenter's wife, sometimes yours, and sometimes mine.

A stupid, garrulous, unfaithful woman.

Akuí abur tah Mág zan; kunuí phákah tah drág zan.

A single cloud, and it is as the month of January; a single fast, and it is as though a famine.

Au jour le jour.

Al Kashmir murdah-pasand.

The Kashmírí people are fond of the dead.

To "never speak evil of the dead" is a prominent good feature in the Kashmírí's character.

Alagaḍih buḍán tah malagaḍih wotalan; Wĕtha hukhan; hĕnar grazan; tĕlih, há málih, ási wándur ráj.

The great man will sink; the base man will rise; the river will dry up; the sewer will roar (by reason of the much water); then, O Father, will be the monkey rule (*i.e.*, a time of utter irreligion and great oppression).

A saying of Shekh Núr-ud-dín, who was a very famous Muhammedan saint in Kashmír about six hundred years ago. His shrine is at Tsrár, a village about fifteen miles from Srínagar; and every October there is a great melá there in his honour.

Wĕtha is the Jhelum river in its course through Kashmír. Hindú priests call it Vetasta.

Alah kulis tulah kul.

A mulberry tree from a pumpkin plant.

A mountain from a mole-hill.

Alah ruwuni wángan kaḍuni.

To sow pumpkins, and reap egg-plants.

To begin a thing and not finish it.

Wángún is known in Hindustán by the name of brinjál (*solanum melongena*), the egg-plant. The Kashmírís dry it, and eat it during the winter.

Álan chhuh phal tah nindan chhuh dánih.

There is fruit to the plough, and rice for the raking.

Thrift brings its own reward.

Albailas nah chhas akl tah nah maut.

Neither understanding nor death to a fat man.

"Fat paunches have lean pates."—Shaks.

Áli ángun sambúle ; fakír auye damále.

O Álí, prepare your garden ; the fakír has come to dance.

Quoted as a warning to prepare for any person's coming.

"*Fakír has come to dance.*" Fakírs stamp upon the ground, gesticulate, and in other ways annoy people, if their demands for largesse are not quickly complied with.

Áli ditsáv tálih gyav zuwav kurus lyav tah lyav.

Álí oiled her head with ghí, and the lice licked and licked it all up.

Money in the hands of a worthless person.

Álih drás tah tálih logum tsĕl.

In the moment of birth my head was squeezed.

Man commences his troublous career as soon as he is born.

Álikánini dándah hawar ; ak nah atsan garah, tuh byák nah nerán barah.

One-eyed 'Alí's yoke of oxen,—one will not enter the house, and the other will not come out of it.

A poor man with a refractory family.

Most people in the valley will remember one-eyed 'Alí and his two troublesome bullocks.

Álond tsánḍun

Seeking to get at a thing which is hanging out of reach.

Clavam Hercŭle extorquére.

Amal gav gulih mal.

Employment is like dirt upon the wrist.

Employment is uncertain ; like dirt upon the wrist, it quickly comes and goes.

Amánatas khiyánat.

To embezzle a deposit (is a tremendous sin).

The height of dishonour.

Ámanuk ṭoṭ.

Áman's pony.

A bad, lazy fellow who requires a lot of urging before he will do anything,

Áman is a small Kashmírí village. A man once purchased a pony from this place, and was setting forth on his way home, when the beast suddenly stopped. and nearly threw the rider over his head. Any little ditch or such like place caused the pony to thus stop. Eventually the purchaser got off the animal, and asked a passer-by to mount it. The other man being a good horseman was not afraid to hit the pony; and so for the rest of the journey, and ever afterwords, the pony went splendidly.

Ámas suĕt har gayih khámas suĕt garah karun.

To quarrel with the common people is like keeping house with a stupid, untaught person (which is misery).

Amí phukah chhuh dazán tsoṅg tah amí phukak chhuh gatshán pati.

With this blow of the breath the lamp is lit, and with this blow it is extinguished.

"Out of the same mouth proceedeth blessing and cursing."

Amí yárabalan chhih kátiyáh naṭi phuṭarávamati !

How many water-pots this ghát has broken !

A source of much evil.

Ámin gogalan tíl zan pherun.

Like mixing oil with raw turnips.

Treasured wrath.

The oil will not settle, but runs all over and about the turnips. In this way anger spreads over the breast of an unforgiving man.

Ámin naṭán mál.

A desire for raw flesh (is it?)

Cited to a man who is impatient for his food, &c.

Ámis dudas suĕt dabadab.

To wrestle with uncooked milk.

To strive with the weak.

Ámis panas darah dar.

To pull raw thread.

To fight, or bully, a weak fellow.

An mana, kar fana ; rachhun chhuí boḍ gunah.

Bring a maund, and spend it. It is a great sin to store.

. Jogís sometimes quote those words,

An Wĕth, dis dúm, adah buḍin gámi gám.

Bring the Jhelum, drink it, and then let the whole village be drowned.

An unprincipled man who has no care for others, as long as he can accomplish his own selfish ends.

Anawune, zenawune.
Ranih hinde madano.
Thakamute, losamute.
Májih hinde gubaro.
At the time of earning and bringing,
A wife's friend you are ;
But when you're tired and weary,
A mother's son you are.

Ánchár-nuṭ akis khut tah beyis hut.

A pickle-pot,—one man's (pickle) turned out splendidly, another man's (pickle) went bad.

The same concern, &c., may turn out well for one, but adverse for another man,

Andah kanih manzbág.

Being outside or on the edge, to sit in the midst.

The monkey, who would fain use the cat's paw to pull the chestnuts out of the fire.

Andarah dazún pánah tah nĕbarah dazún lok.

Inside he himself burns, and outside the people burn.

The genteel poor man. Poverty and cold are burning him within, whilst outside, owing to his wearing nice clean clothes, the people burn with envy, supposing that he has money.

Andarah gom wírih hund dudur tah nĕbarah rodum tserih hund rang.

Within me is the rottenness of the willow, but without continues the colour of the apricot.

Andarah tshunihas thukah tah nĕbarah dupun "Gumah ám."

Inside somebody spat upon him. Outside he said, "It is perspiration."

Salvá dignitate.

Andari, andari, wot Tsandari gom.
Secretly, secretly, he reached the village of Tsandar.
"In truth, he is in great distress."

Andarim dádi no mashinam marit
Nĕbarim shádi kyah barah wúini buh?
I shall never forget the pains of my heart, even after death.
Shall I wish then for outside happiness?
Refusing to be comforted.

Andarim nah tuts tah nĕbarim nah pats.
No strength within, and no respect without.

Anĕtis ai yiyih ladanah tah mantis wátis.
If the cover be filled then it holds one pound and a half.
Think before you leap.

Anhaharin armán tah haharimuti pashemán.
The bachelor wishes (to get married), the married man regrets (that he got married).
Marry in haste, and repent at leisure.

Ani chhur lam tal tah kúnsih dyuthus nah.
A blind man sat down behind a pile of stones, and thought that nobody had seen him.
The ostrich hides his head in the sand, &c.

Ani sunz kulai Khudáyas hawálah.
A blind man's wife is in God's keeping.

Anigatih guli álawuni.
To show affection in the darkness.
Kind to the unthankful.

Anim suí, wavum suí, lajum suí, púnasuí.
I brought the nettle, I sowed the nettle, and then the nettle stung me.
Ingratitude.

In olden times there was a famous fakír in Kashmír, who punished himself in the following way. He uprooted a nettle, and fixing some mud upon the palm of his hand, planted the nettle therein. All the day and all the night for several years he held out his hand with the palm uppermost, and the nettle in it. The plant grew and was strong and by reason of this, thousands of Hindús used to visit the fakír, and give him alms.

The fakír had a disciple, who eventually became very jealous of the honour which his master received; and one day in a fit of anger, he hit the nettle, earth and all, out of his master's hand. The fakír then spoke the above saying concerning both the nettle and his disciple, whom he had brought up and nourished from his infancy.

The sting-nettle is a plant sacred to Shivá, who is said to have first planted it. Hindús pluck the leaves, and throw them over the god's favourite symbol, the lingám.

Anin manz káni sundar.

An one-eyed woman is beautiful among blind women.

Anis háwán sári wat be-aklas nah kanh.

All men show the blind man the way; nobody can show the man without understanding.

Anis musht háwuni, nah chhĕh gunah, nah sawáb.

To show the thumb to a blind man is neither a sin nor a virtue.

Advice is lost on some people.

"*To show the thumb*" is a vulgar act amongst children and stupid people in Kashmír.

Anis rát tah doh hĕhui.

Night and day are the same to the blind man.

Anit natsanáwuni!

(Enough) to make a cover dance!

A great trouble or surprise.

Ánkár tah mál, nakár tah kasam.

Confess and property, refuse and oath.

One man charges another man with a debt. The other man denies. Then the matter is carried into court, where the judge and people sometimes cite the above proverb, which means "Confess and pay, or refuse and swear to it."

Antan tah háwanai.

Bring it to me and I'll show it to you.

An angry retort when a man expresses surprise that his friend has not seen, or heard of, a certain person or thing.

Apárih sanduk; yapárih sandúk; duhúli kháwas yaḍ bandúk.

On that side a box; on this side a box; and a gun to the stomach of him, who breaks the fast (of Ramazán).

Apárih tárum gáḍih han, yapárih hurmas ras, sál kurum Makkah Madínas.

From the other bank of the river I brought a small fish, and here I made soup, and then invited all Mecca and Medina.

Apárimav mun dánih yapárimin gayih athan haṭh.
A man on that side pressed the grain, but to a man on this side a gall became.

One does the scath, another has the harm.

Apih hund gyav.
A foolish woman's ghí.

A foppish person.

Apih is a term applied only to a woman, whose one care is dress, &c.

Kashmírí people, both wealthy and others, rub their hair with fresh ghí. Scented oil is never used.

Apuzis goḍ kyah?
A lie has no beginning.

Ari ái sári tah ur gav nah kanh.
All people came (*i.e.*, were born) in good health, but not one became (*i.e.*, continued) healthy.

Árimi kaḍih nah múj tah phakíran dáras kisht.
The gardener had not dug out the radish, when the fakír held the alms-bowls in front of him.

Aris pánas drakah.
A leech to a healthy body.

Suffering for others.

Asan ai tah lasah kitah páṭhi?
If I laugh not how can I live?

Ride si sapis.

Ásas gatshih phulai ásuni, adah gayih phulai wuchhuni.
One's mouth must blossom before he goes to see the flower-blossoms.

The different pleasure-gardens around the Ḍal Lake are constantly and largely visited by the natives, and especially, when the plum-trees and roses and lilacs are in full bloom. They take their dinner with them, and spend the greater part of the day on the excursion.

The expression "*one's mouth must blossom*" refers to eating and drinking.

The natives have also got a proverb in Persian with the same meaning.—*Áb i Ḍal átash numáyad chún na báshad tabbákh.*

Ásas kuṭáh tsáiyo áhí wádáh dráiyo.
When food had entered your mouth, blessing came forth therefrom.

The guest flatters and blesses his host.

Ásas mazah tah yad dazah-dazah.
A taste in the mouth and a burning in the stomach.
Just enough to whet the appetite.

Asawai tah gindawai koryav, khyun chyun chhuh yih.
Let us laugh and play girls. This (thumb) is eating and drinking.
Some people are very mild in speech and witty in manner, but they are not very liberal in their dinner arrangements, or in the matter of largesse.
'*This thumb*'' refers to the vulgar Kashmírí custom of holding up the thumb as an answer in the negative, when asked if there is anything in the house.''

Áshnav gav páshnáv.
An acquaintance (or kinsman) is like a dung and refuse boat, (*i.e.*, a nuisance).
"Save me from my friends."

Ashráf gav suí yas ashrafih ásan.
The man with the gold is the gentleman.
Another version of this proverb cited by those, who are of another way of thinking, is:—
Ashráf gav suí yas ashrafí ásih.
He, who is gentle, is a gentleman.

Ásmánah pyav tah zamínih logus dab.
He fell from heaven to earth and is wounded.
High towers fall to the ground with greater crash.

Asmánah watsh balai tah khana i gharíb kujást?
Misfortune descends from heaven, and where is the poor man's house.
From hand to mouth.

Ásun chhuh hĕchhináwán nah ásun chhuh mandachháwán.
To be (wealthy) teaches, not to be (wealthy) makes ashamed.

Asun chhuh kharas khasun.
It is a shame to laugh (immoderately).
"And the laugh that spoke the vacant mind."—Goldsmith.
Kharas khasun, *lit.*, to mount an ass, which, according to the natives, is *infra dig*.

Átá Muhammad Khánin gaḍih begári.

Impress for the work of Átá Muhammad Khán's (fort).

The present fort of Harí Parbat was built by Átá Muhammad Khan about sixty years ago. On Fridays, until the work was completed, every citizen, whether rich or poor, young or old, was forced to take up one stone to the top of the hill.

Oppression.

Áth gai sheṭh gai.
Yim pánṭsh pĕṭh gai.

Eight gone, sixty gone.
These five besides gone (what are they ?).

What is a little more trouble to a man already overwhelmed with it?
Persian—*Ábe ki az sar guzasht chi yak neza o chi hazár neza.*

Ath shúbih zú kút lúbih ?

Will the soul desire this beautiful thing ? No.

"It is naught, it is naught, saith the buyer."—Prov. xx. 14.

Athachan pánṭshan ungajan andar kis lukuṭ; muhr chhih melán kisí.

The little finger is the smallest of the five fingers of the hand; and yet the signet-ring is worn upon the little finger.

The humble shall be exalted.

Athah chhuk balih tah kathah chhuk balih nah.

A wound in the hand is well, but to be wounded by (unkind) words is not well.

Athah chhul tah mĕtrut tsul.

As soon as the hands were washed friendship ran away.

After a native dinner an ewer of water is brought round, in which the guests wash their hands.

Athah ditam bronṭhah yitam.

Give me your hand and come in front of me.

To lend a hand.

Áthan waryan puch nad sheṭhan waryan puk srĕh.

For eight years the river ran, and for sixty years (after the waters had disappeared) the ground remained damp.

Men die but their deeds live.
Panjábí—*Ádmí nahín rahindá, par ádmí dí al ráh jándí hai.*

Athi bánas khyun tah athi bánas chharun.

To eat out of a vessel and then defile it.

To receive a man's hospitality and then slander him.

Aṭyuv bulah-baṭ.

An image made from flour.

A weak man.

Bulah-baṭ are the little images, horses, &c., which children play with. A sugar toy.

Auḍ khákí auḍ phúkí.

Half dust, half blowing.

A fool and his money are soon parted.

Audur tah mudur.

Wet and sweet.

Spoken concerning bázár food.

Auṭ gatshih nerun yá talimih tsakajih yá pĕṭhimih.

The flour must come out either by the lower or by the upper stone.

By hook or by crook.

Áv ai tah yeruv, gav ai tah gásuv.

If it has come then it is like wool, but if it has gone then it is as grass.

Indifference.

Áv tah jáv chhus barábar.

Coming and going are alike to him.

A happy-go-lucky individual.

"Awah," layih pántsáh tah "Nah" layih lachh.

"Yes" is worth Rs. 50 and "No" is worth a lakh.

No of some people is more esteemed than the Yes of others.—"Oraculo Manual," Balthasar Gracian.

Áyas wate tah gayas tih wate;
Sĕmanz suthe losum doh;
Wuchhum chandas tah hár nah athe.
Náwah táras kyah dimah buh?

I came by a way (*i.e.*, I was born) and I also went by a way (*i.e.*, I died).
When I was in the middle of the way (*i.e.*, when my spirit was between the two worlds) the day failed.
I looked in my pocket, but not a cowrie came to hand.
What shall I give for crossing the ferry?

A saying of Lal Dĕd, who was a very holy Hindú woman.

The Kashmírí Hindú belief is that during the sixth month after death the spirit of the deceased has to cross the waters of the Vaitaraṅi; but it is impossible to get to the other side of the river except by special means, as the waters are so deep and stormy and the opposing powers, preta, yamadut, matsya, and kúrma are so strong. Accordingly about this time the bereaved relations call the family Bráhman, who repeats to them the portions appointed to be read on this occasion. Among other things the departed spirit is represented as standing on the brink of the river and crying "Where is my father? Where is my mother? Where are my relations and my friends? Is there no one to help me over this river.?" This is sometimes recited with much feeling, and great are the lamentations of the bereaved, who now with sobs and tears present a little boat and paddle, made of gold, or silver, or copper, according to their position, to the Bráhman; and in the boat they place ghí, milk, butter, and rice. The boat is for the conveyance of the spirit across Vaitaraṅi, and the provisions are for the appeasement of the contrary powers preta, matsya, and others, who will try to turn back the boat, but who on having these, ghí and rice, &c., thrown to them, will at once depart their own way.

The Hindús believe that if this ceremony is performed in a right manner, a boat will be at once present upon the waters, close to that portion of the bank of the river, where the spirit is waiting and praying for it, and that the spirit getting into it will be safely conveyed to the opposite side. The gift-boat, however, is taken home by the Bráhman, and generally turned into money as soon as possible.

At the moment of death amongst other things a paisá is placed within the mouth of the corpse, wherewith to pay the ferry.

The belief here expressed is common in one shape or another to all nations and peoples, but especially to all Indo-European nations. In Grecian mythology it was the river Styx, Acheron, or Cocytus; and Charon rowed the shades across in his little boat. A small piece of money, too, was placed in the mouth of the dead, to pay the fare to the Stygian ferryman. In Scandinavia bodies were buried in ships and boats under the belief that the dead crossed the waters in them. Coleman, p. 319, mentions that among the Garrows of Bengal also, "the dead are kept for four days; burnt on a pile of wood in a dingy or small boat, placed on the top of a pile," &c. In the old French romance of Lancelot du Lac the demoiselle d' Escalot orders that after death, her body richly dressed should be placed in a ship, and that the ship should be let go to find its own way before the wind and waves. In Grimm's Deutsche Mythologie, 3te Ausgabe, 791, a story is told concerning some monks crossing the Rhine at Spires. In former times the Rhine, the political boundary of Germany, was also regarded as the boundary between the upper and lower world; and "to go to the Rhine" and "to die" were mutually equivalent expressions:—"A drowsy boatman is roused up one stormy night by a monk, who put some money into his hand, and asked to be ferried over the river. At first six monks get into the boat, but no sooner is it started than a great company press in, to the great inconvenience of the boatman.

With much difficulty the river is crossed; and the passengers having disembarked, the boat is immediately carried back by a strong wind to the place whence it started. More passengers are waiting there, and they, too, embark directly the boat touches the bank; and as they enter the foremost of the strange company puts the fare into the ferryman's hands with his icy-cold fingers. Some readers may not know that the Germans in olden times thoroughly believed that our own little island was the island of souls, and that to this day remnants of this belief are still to be found among them." For more particulars concerning traditions about the dead, their world, and the way to it, &c., cf. Kelly's most interesting book on "Curiosities of Indo-European Traditions," Ch. IV.

Áyih wúnis gayih kóndris.

She came to the baniyá's but arrived at the baker's.

To miss the mark.

This saying has its origin in a story well-known in Kashmír. Lal Děd, whose name has been mentioned before, used to peregrinate in an almost nude condition, and was constantly saying that "He only was a man, who feared God, and there were very few such men about."

One day Sháh Hamadán, after whom the famous mosque in Srínagar is called, met her, and she at once ran away. This was a strange thing for Lal Děd, to do; but it was soon explained. "I have seen a man," she said, to the astonished baniyá, into whose shop she had fled for refuge. The baniyá, however, turned her out. Then Lal Děd rushed to the baker's house and jumped into the oven, which at that time was fully heated for baking the bread. When the baker saw this he fell down in a swoon thinking that, for certain, the king would hear of this and punish him. However, there was no need of fear, as Lal Děd presently appeared from the mouth of the oven clad in clothes of gold, and hastened after Sháh Hamadán. Cf. Note 743, Part XX of "Panjáb Notes and Queries."

The Kashmírí Muhammedan will tell as many and long stories concerning this Sháh Hamadán, or Saiyid 'Alí as the Kashmírí Pandit will tell about Lal Děd—how that when Timur Lung slew all the saiyids in his country, he accused that monarch of impiety and said that he would not stay in his country, but by virtue of his holiness would transport himself through the air to Kashmír; and how that he alighted in the very spot, where now the famous mosque stands in the midst of Srínagar, and within a few days after his arrival here converted so many Hindús to Islám that two-and-a-half Kharwárs of Yonís or Bráhmanical threads were delivered up to him.

Sháh Hamadán's mosque is one of the most beautiful as well as one of the most famous in the Valley. Over and beside the entrance and upon the wall of the first of the five divisions of the building are these three Persian inscriptions:—

Ai dil agarat matlab i faiz e dú jahan ast.
Rav bar dar i shahanshah i Sháh e Hamadán ast.
Makrún i ijábat ast zi dare aust du'á rá.
'Arsh ast dar ash balki azú' 'arsh nishán ast.

* * * *

Har faiz ki dar sábikay e har-dú jahán ast.
Dar pairauí e hazrat i Sháh e Hamadán ast.
Sháh e Hamadán ańkí Shahanshâh e jahán ast
Ai Khák barán dída ki dar raib o gumán ast.

* * * * *

Ín Hamadán Hamadání dihad.
Ma'rifat e sirr i nihání dihad.
Ya'ne agar báshidat ín árzú ;
Az dar i Sháh e Hamadání bijo.

Az gav begáh wuini wulah pagáh.

To-day is not the time. Now (is not the time). Come to-morrow.

Ad Græcas Kalendas.

Az nah tah, adah kar.

Not to day,—when then?

To-morrow is no day.

B

Bábah Ádamas zúi zah gabar, aki rat áwareni bĕyih rat kabr.

Father Adam had two sons. One was burnt and the other was buried (*i.e.*, one became a Hindú and the other became a Muhammedan).

Bábah, budatham tah khidmatah kartam.

O father, become old and serve me.

The old parents are very often the slaves of the family.

Bábah matyov tah dĕd tih mateyih.

The father has became mad and the mother also has become mad.

A kingdom or city in a wretched plight.

During a certain king's reign the gods determined that the people should become mad from drinking the ordinary water. Now the king's wazír being versed in astrology discovered this matter and at once told the king of it privately. "O, king," said he, "after one month all your subjects will lose their reason from drinking the water of the country." "What shall we do?" said the king, "that we two, at all events, may be saved." "Procure water at once," replied the wazír, "and store it up in skins." The king did so, and the result was that at the time appointed, when all the people were raving mad, he and the wazír were perfectly sane. It happened, however, that the whole country being quite beyond governing, the people were murdering one another and doing the most strange acts. At length some determined to slay the king and his wazír, and so in order to save themselves these two also drank of the diseased water and became mad. Then it was that the father and mother were mad, and the above saying was first spoken.

Persian—*Áb-i-diwánagí.*

Babah nethar zih hamín súat.

O father, let me be married thi moment.

Impatience.

Bábam Ríshín kaṭi.

Bábam Ríshí's child (*i.e.*, disciple).

A stupid fellow.

This good saint's followers were most ignorant and stupid people. People gave alms to them only for the sake of their saint and leader.

Bábam Ríshí died about the year 1474 A. D. His shrine, and a convent attached to it, lie on the road from Báramula to Gulmarg, and are amongst the richest, as well as the most frequented, places of pilgrimage in the valley.

The Ríshís must not be confounded with the Rishis, a sect of Muhammedan peasants, nor with the seven Rishis (also Rikhis), or ancient Hindú sages, Vashishṭa and others. They are Muhammedans, and did not marry or eat meat, or show themselves to men as Ríshís; but used to wander about the jungles, and by the highways, and live on whatsoever they might find. Now, however, customs have changed with the times, and the true Muhammedan tells you with sorrowful countenance, that there is not one real Ríshí in the country, and has not been since Akbar's days, when large land and house property were given to these people, and they became spoiled and got worse and worse, until now they are so degenerated as to sometimes marry and eat flesh and amass money, and do other things equally, and even more, contrary to the spirit and pattern of their predecessors in olden days. Abú'l Fazl in his book remarks that in Akbar's time "the most respectable people of Kashmír were the Ríshís, who though they did not suffer themselves to be fettered with traditions, were doubtless worshippers of God. They did not revile any sect, or ask anything of any one. They planted the roads with fruit trees to furnish the traveller with refreshment," &c. The Muhammedans believe that it was in response to these holy Ríshís' intercessions that Akbar was thrice defeated by the Chak kings, when he attempted to take the country. According to their account, also, a fakír called Khwája Uwys was the founder of this sect; and he lived during Muhammed's life time at Kurun, a little village of Yemen in Arabia; and that the Prophet would never march to this place because a savour of holiness went up thence on account of this holy fakír's residing there with his mother.

There were about two thousand Ríshis in Kashmír during Akbar's time. Now-a-days there are perhaps five thousand, but they are not revered by the more educated and respectable Muhammedans in the valley. Cf. Col. Yule's "Travels of Marco Polo," Vol. I., p. 179.

Bachhih ásih animah kátsah machhih lárunas!

If there should be a little rice-water on the edge of the fire-place how many flies will congregate to it!

Ubi mel, ibi apes.

Bachih dod chhuh lachih dod.

A child's pain is a hundred thousand pains.

Badas sir báwun chhuh bĕbih andar saruf rachhun.

A wicked man may as well place a snake in his bosom as tell out his secrets; (he dare not do it).

Baḍis chhai baḍuí nazar.

High looks to a great man (but not to a mannikin).

Baḍis khor tal marun ján tah lúkis nah shándas pĕṭh.

It is better to die under the foot of a great man, than upon the shoulder of a man of small degree.

Better to be an earl's slave than to go partner with a small shopkeeper.

Búgih bog tah nánih ṭok.

(After receiving his) share in the distribution of the dinner (he asked for) a dish for his grandmother.

A greedy, unsatisfied, fellow.

Bahlol, jandah, tah kashkúl.

Bahlol, a ragged habit, and an alms-bowl.

A very poor man.

Bahlol was a genuine fakír. According to my informant, he was a brother of Áli Mardán Khán, governor of Kashmír under Sháh Jahán, about 1650 A.D., but he did not care for the pomp and show of palace life, and so laid aside the court dress for the jandah and kashkúl.

This voluntary fakír life of one so high in learning and position was not pleasing to the governor, or to his ministers and attendants; and various devices were resorted to for getting Bahlol to accept some distinguished office in the service of the State. At last they succeeded, and Bahlol was appointed Deputy-Inspector. All things went happily for a while, until one day it happened that in the course of his office Bahlol had to ascertain whether the bankers', baniyas', and others' weights were correct or not; and while fulfilling this duty he discovered so much distress and fraud and trickery, &c., that he determined to know no more of it, went back quickly to his house, and doffed the grand dress of a Deputy-Inspector for the jandah kashkúl and the fakír life again.

"*Bajih mashídih hindyav thamav, yut kithav páṭh wátiwah?*"
"*Pananih sĕzarah.*"

"How did the pillars of the great mosque get here?"
"By their own straightness."

The way to accomplish a difficult work.

The roof of the cloister surrounding the open square in the centre of the great mosque in Srínagar is supported by wooden pillars, each formed of a single deodár tree about thirty feet high, and resting upon a plain stone base. There are three rows upon the north, south and west sides, but only two on the east side.

Bajih mashídih tsalyá kunj nerit?

"Will the corner of the great mosque tumble out?"

The whole country or concern is not going to ruin, simply because "So and-So" has died. There are plenty as good and clever as he to prosecute the work.

Bakhtas bud chhih khidmatgár.
Understanding is butler to success.

Bálah korih wálanai.
Dishonour to a beloved daughter
A terrible wrong.

Balái dúr tah khair kabúl.
May misfortune be far from you and prosperity nigh.
A Kashmírí blessing.

Báli wuchhithai záli wáñkah ḍáḍi díṭhmak kundaluí.
O woman, you have plaited your hair very nicely, but I see you always a kunḍal.
Fine clothes do not make the lady.
Kunḍal is the inner earthenware part of a kángar, the Kashmír portable fire-place. The outer part is generally of very pretty basket-work, which conceals the kunḍal's faults.

Bánah hatas dizih ṭhánah hat tah ásah hatas kyah dizih ?
A hundred covers for a hundred vessels, but what shall be given (to stop) a hundred mouths.

Bánas andar nar tah dánas andar har.
Arm in the pot (for serving out food) and wood under the oven (for cooking it).
Panjábí.—*Hun tán tuhádá ghio bich ramba hai.*

Band bandas mangih, ágah bedár tah naukar shungih.
For one acquaintance, or relation, to ask from another, is like a master awake, whilst his servant sleeps (*i.e.*, the one is as much a matter of shame as the other).

Band kus ? Zih chandah.
Who is (your) friend ? (Your) pocket.

Bángis chhĕh báng dapun.
It is the work of the bángih to cry the báng.

Another version is :—

Bángis chhuá báng dapuni matih kih nah neh anini ?
Is the bángih to call the báng, or to bring the people (to prayer) ?
Every man to his own work.
Báng is the Muhammedan call to prayers.

4

Bápárich kúṭ chhai sudarah káñz pov hish, yút tsunahas tyút kaḍahas.

A tradesman's shop is like an earthenware vessel, as much as is put into it, so much is got out of it.

Tradesmen are frequently bankers, also, in Kashmír.

Bar dit achh tovranih.

To shut the door and put on a terrifying look.

A coward.

Bar dit khar natsán.

The ass shuts the door and dances.

A man very spirited and full of words in his own house, but outside he does nothing.

This is also a Kashmírí riddle, of which the answer is, a mill-stone.

Bastah tshunit núl khakaráyih mandachhun.

To wear sheep's skin and be ashamed of its rustling.

Don't be ashamed of your real position.

Bastih sún dahĕr.

Three sers with the skin. (The swindler had weighed the skin in as well).

A swindle.

Batah badyos chhánih tah garah zúnai nah wath.

I am the better because of your dinner, but I do not know the way to your house.

Hopes unfulfilled.

In hope of receiving something from you I have contracted a debt here and there, but now I perceive that I hoped in vain; so henceforth I shall not know the way to your house (*i.e.*, will not see you).

"*Batah, batah,*" *tah piyádah patah.*

Having no food and a peon after you (because of some debt).

Great distress.

Batah dag chhai Kártikin súrah dag.

Earning one's living is (as hard to bear) as the pain of hoar-frost in the month of October.

Natives suffer terribly in their feet from walking out early on a frosty October morning.

Baṭah gajih ruhun.

As garlic upon the hearth of a Panḍit (so your presence is to me).

Hindús of the valley will not touch garlic (or onions). These are eaten only by the Muhammedans. Hindús say that their ancestors would not eat them because of their aphrodisiac effects, which they did not wish to experience, as they had devoted themselves to religion.

Batah gardan.

To behead another with hospitality.

To heap coals of fire on an enemy's head.

Baṭah gav graṭṭah.

The Hindú is a mill.

Muhammedans quote this jestingly of their Hindú neighbours.

Batah lĕlis chhih pĕṭhah kanih wuchún.

Men look into the rice-pot from the top part (to judge whether the food is cooked properly or not).

Men are judged by their speech.

Batah lukharih hír tah pránah kujih shrúk.

A head from the portion of rice, and a knife from the onion plant.

There was a very holy man, who prayed unto God for justice. He had too high an opinion of himself to ask for grace also. "Only give me my deserts," he said, "and I shall fare all right."

This good man once dined with a friend, and according to custom placed the remainder of his dinner within his tsádar, or wrap. On the way home it happened that the rice and vegetables were changed into a human head and a knife, both of which were saturated with blood, that dropped upon the road as he walked along. A policeman noticed this, and at once enquired what was in the tsádar. The holy man without any hesitation opened out his wrap, and, lo! there was a human head and a knife.

Of course the poor man was immediately marched off to the prison-house. On the next day the court was assembled and the prisoner brought forth. The excitement was intense.

The case was tried, and the whole evidence was against the man. The judge considered much and long, but at last, finding no way by which he could possibly acquit the prisoner, he was about to pronounce the sentence of death upon him, when there came from heaven the sound of a voice saying, "The man is not guilty, let him go free."

Ever afterwards this good man asked for grace also, when he prayed.

Baṭah miskín, nah dunyá tah nah dín.

The poor Hindú has neither the world nor religion.

The Muhammedans quote this saying.

Batah mod shenkih.

The Pandit died from hesitation.

Once upon a time a Pandit and a Muhammedan were travelling together. In the middle of the way ran a swift stream which they had to wade. The Muhammedan crossed at once without the slightest hesitation; but the Pandit cried out: "Stop, stop, let me first look at my Nechi-puter to see whether it is an auspicious time for me to cross or not" He consulted the kalendar and discovered that it was not a good time. However, as he had to travel a long distance, and the day was already far spent, he dared to step into the waters; and commenced to wade. But when he had reached the middle of the stream his heart failed him, and his legs began to tremble, so that he fell; was carried away, and dashed about by the fierce waters, and died.

Batah nah tah batás chhiṭ nah tah atlás.

No food in the house, yet he wishes for sugar; not even a ragged cloth to his back, yet he wishes for satin.

A poor man with great desires.

Batah páwih tal chhĕh aibah khár gaib.

Beneath half-a-pound of rice a khár (lbs. 192) of sin is concealed.

Riches cover a multitude of sins.

Baṭas baṭah káwĕh baṭah.

One Pandit with another Pandit is like a mountain-crow.

If one crow caws the whole flock caws. If one Pandit is in difficulty, all the Pandits take up the case, &c.

Baṭas boḍ doh tah phákah;
Musalmánas boḍ doh tah shrákah;
Ráfizas boḍ doh tah bákah.

On his big day the Hindú fasts;
On his big day the Muhammedan feasts;
On his big day the Shí'a weeps.

Baṭas tsĕd Musalmánas yaḍ, tah ráfizas huḍ.

To the Hindú endurance, to the Musalmán (*i.e.*, the Súní) stomach, and to the Shí'a weeping.

An allusion to the Hindú's much fasting, to the Súní's eating capacity, and to the profound lamentation of the Shí'a during the days of the Muharram, when he commemorates the death of 'Alí, Hasan and Husain.

Batav andarah toṭh kyah, zih tahar?
Howarih andarah toṭh kyah, zih hahar?
Among dishes which is the favourite? Tahar.
In the wife's house who is the favourite? Brother-in-law.
Tahar—a kind of boiled rice coloured with turmeric.

Báts̱an ízú tah putalĕn púzá.
For the family distress, but for the idols an offering.
Charity begins at home.

"*Báyih myánih kalandarai;*
Yih nerih tih nerih khalah andarai."
"My brother monk, what will come, will come from the harvest" (*i.e.*, will be the result of honest toil).
The gods give everything for labour.

Bázigaras chhĕh bázigaras.
A deceiver deceives himself.

Be-akl nah kañh tah garah patah kah kah.
"Not one ignorant man?"—Why there are eleven in every house (*i.e.*, the world is full of such people).
Ce monde est plein de fous.

Bĕbih andar phánsi tah athas kĕt tasbíh.
The noose (of the executioner's rope) under the arm, and the rosary in the hand.
Hindustání.—Háth meñ tasbíh, aur bag̱hal meñ phánsí.

Bechán tah guris khasit!
Begging and riding upon a horse!
A proud beggar.

Bechanas bánah kámuni.
The beggar's pot (in which he collected food) is broken.
The last straw gone.

Be-hayáhas sharm dúr.
To the shameless shame is distant.

Be-kár chhuh bĕmár.
The unemployed, or idle man, is sick.

Be-kár chhuh wakíli har darbár.
An unemployed man visits every darbăr.

Be-káras chhih trah kăr.

To the idle man there are three works (viz., sleeping, quarrelling, and eating).

Bemah haharav chhuh sah mormut.

Two brothers-in-law killed a lion (between them).

Union is strength.

The tale is, that a sister's husband and a wife's brother, who are naturally the greatest enemies to one another, were walking along together one day, when a lion chanced to cross their path. They did not run away, but each stood his ground firmly, and backed-up the other, and the result was that by their united efforts the lion was killed.

Be-málas ailah.

Cardamoms for the man, who is not hungry.

" *Bemáro ás kyut chhui ?*" " *Nah tsuk tah nah mudur.*"

" O, sick person, how is your mouth?" " Neither bitter nor sweet. "

The answer is equivalent to our English reply, " O, thank you, I'm middling."

Be-murawat mahnyuv chhui zan ; phakíri ba-ṭamah rahzan.

An unmanly fellow is a woman, and a courteous fakír is a robber.

Be-suṅmb chhuh dapán " Mĕh suṅmb nah kaṅh. "

The unequal man says " I have not an equal "; (but the really great man thinks himself less than the least).

Bĕyih sund amánat chhui khárawánuk nárah tungul hyuh.

Another's belongings in your charge is like a live coal from the blacksmith's shop.

Bĕyih sund dod chhui be-máne ;
Yas akhis banih tai sui záne.

Another's pain is without meaning.
Only he, who suffers it, knows what it is like.

" It is impossible for any man to form a right judgment of his neighbour's suffering."—Addison.

Bichis parutsuk, " Wandas kunah chhuk nĕbar nerán ?
Dupanak, " Rĕtah kălih kyah kurum hásil ? Haradu lánat hishí."

Somebody said to the scorpion, "Why do you not come out in the winter?" He replied, "What did I get in the spring-time?" Both times alike are a curse to me.

Either miserable oneself or making others miserable.

The scorpion lives under the ground during the winter and spends a miserable time of it, according to the natives; and when he does come forth from his temporary grave, it is only to give trouble to others.

A translation from the Gulistán:—*Gaj-dum rá guftand ki "Chirá ba zamistán?" "Birom na miáyí guft; ba tápistánam chi hurmat ast?"*

Bihĕh pĕṭhai rihĕh tráwán.

Sitting down in one's chair at home and throwing out a flame.

Every cock crows loudest on his own dunghill.

Bihĕhwani tsarih.

A sitting sparrow.

On probation.

The sparrow must keep a good look-out, or some boy with a caterpault, or perhaps a cat, will notice it and kill it.

Bihit wani poni tolyá?

Will the grocer sit and weigh water?

Nothing better to do?

Bíkh mangán tah puṭ rangán.

Asking for alms and dyeing his coat.

A helpless man's wish.

Bír Balan puruts Akbaras, "Jangah wizih kyah siláh?" Dupanas "Yih bronṭhah peyih."

Bír Bal asked Akbar, "What weapons they should fight with, when the time for fighting arrived?" He replied, "Whatever you find at hand."

Bír Balanih korih puruts Akbar pádsháhan, "Kyah mahnyuv chhuá parasán?" Dupanas, "Dánd chhuá dud diwán?"

Akbar, the king, asked Bír Bal's daughter, "Can a man give birth to a child?" She replied, "Can an ox give milk?"

A Roland for an Oliver.

Bír Bal was Akbar's great minister. The Muhammedan ministers hated him and tried to get rid of him. Bír Bal was often punished on account of what they said. One day a Muhammedan minister said to Akbar: "Will your Majesty please get some bullock's milk from Bír Bal." Akbar promised that he would give the order, and on the following morning there was the paper signed and sealed by the king, spread out before Bír Bal, ordering him to procure some bullock's milk within fifteen days, or else die. Bír Bal was overwhelmed with fear and astonishment. The minister's daughter seeing her father in this wretched state at once devised a scheme. She went off straight to the butcher's shop, and there soaked her tsádar, or wrap, in some blood lying about, and then went and washed it in the part of the river opposite the king's palace. Akbar noticing this, enquired the reason of the blood. She replied: "No, I have not murdered any one; but yesterday Bír Bal was delivered of a child in the house." Akbar said: "Can a man bear a child"? The girl answered: "Can a bullock give milk?"

Bír Bal was exalted to still greater honor and power on account of this shrewdness of his daughter.

Readers will probably be disgusted at the ridiculousness of this story, but at Basle so late as the fifteenth century great excitement was caused by the announcement that a cock had laid an egg. I may be pardoned, perhaps, for quoting the following from "Chambers's Book of Days":—

"At Basle, in 1474, a cock was tried for having laid an egg. For the prosecution it was *proved* that cocks' eggs were of inestimable value for mixing in certain magical preparations; that a sorcerer would rather possess a cock's egg than be master of the philosopher's stone; and that in Pagan lands Satan employed witches to hatch such eggs, from which proceeded animals most injurious to all of the Christian faith and race. The advocate for the defence admitted the facts of the case, but asked what evil animals had been proved against his client, what injury to man or beast had it effected? Besides, the laying of the egg was an involuntary act, and as such, not punishable by law. If the crime of sorcery were imputed, the cock was innocent; for there was no instance on record of Satan having made a compact with the brute creation. In reply, the Public Prosecutor alleged that, though the devil did not make compact with brutes, he sometimes entered into them; and though the swine possessed by devils, as mentioned in Scripture, were involuntary agents, yet they nevertheless were punished by being caused to run down a steep place into the sea, and so perished in the waters. The pleadings in this case, even as recorded by Hammerlein, are voluminous; we only give the meagre outlines of the principal pleas; suffice it to say, the cock was condemned to death, not as a cock, but as a sorcerer or devil in the form of a cock, and was with its egg burned at the stake, with all the due form and solemnity of a judicial punishment."

Bír Balun kaṭ.

Bír Bal's ram.

One day in reply to some ministers who were slandering Bír Bal, Akbar said: "Never mind, if Bír Bal is a Hindú, he is a wise and clever man, and worthy of the confidence, which I have in him Shall I prove to you his wisdom and shrewdness? Call all the ministers." Akbar then gave to each minister a ram, and ordered them to feed each his ram for the space of two months, and to take care that at the end of that period, they should not be heavier or lighter than they were then at that moment. He also caused the name of each minister and the weight of his ram to be written down.

Bír Bal took his ram and fed it in the usual way, but constantly kept a dog near it. The consequence was that the poor ram from very fear did not become any fatter or thinner, but was altogether *in státu quo* at the end of the allotted time. Some of the other ministers gave their rams grass in the morning, and not at night; and some fed their rams one day and not the next day; and in various other ways they tried to keep them in the same condition; but at the end of the two months, when all the ministers and their rams were again assembled before Akbar, only Bír Bal's ram was found to be the right weight. "Did I not tell you," said the king, "that he was wiser and better than you all?"

"*Bír Bal's ram.*" These words are quoted, when any person counteracts whatever good he may have done, by performing some evil work, *e.g.*, a Kashmírí would cite these words against a man who was especially liberal to a servant one day, and flogged him severely in a fit of temper on the following day.

Biṭhis gásah diyár.

Money for cutting grass to an idle man.

Wages to a servant, who has very little work.

Boḍ ai ásih auḍuí totih chhuh boḍuí.

If a great man becomes half (*i.e.*, comes down in the world) still he is great.

Fortúna nón mútat gĕnus.

Boḍ baḍih jágír kaḍih; aup baḍih tah ṭup kaḍih.

If a man of good family becomes great, he will give pensions in land (to the people); but if an ignoble man becomes great, he will take out the very hairs of their heads.

Boḍ kamac kurhak? zih modyav.

"Who made you a great man?" "Death" (*i.e.*, Relations died and left you their position and money).

Persian.—*Kas na mánad dar sará mosḳ gardad kat-Khudá.*

Boḍ myunḍ gatshih khyun tah baḍ kath gatshih nah karani.

You must eat a big mouthful, but you mustn't do much work. (Oh, no!)

Spoken sarcastically to a lazy dependant.

Boí gar kani binih gayih thani.

Brother is (hard like) a stone, and sister is (soft as) butter.

Bor chhuh jahannamuk por.

A burden is one of hell's storeys.

This saying is rather against the idea that the coolie thinks his load a trifle.

Bozit zur tah díshit un.

Be as the deaf man hearing and the blind man seeing.

A little paternal advice to a child—"Be as if you had heard and seen nothing."

Bragas dapyuk, "Tuṅth chhai haj." Dupanak, "Nah tah kyah chhum syud?"

They said to the heron, "Your bill is crooked." He replied, "Am I not all crooked?"

Bhojpurí.—"*Haṅsuá ne túṅ terh káhe?*" "*Ato apná gauṅ se.*"

Brári hindi gyav khĕnah chhum nah lagan tyút, yút brári hindi luṭ gilahwanah.

I am not so angry at the cat eating the ghí, as I am at her shaking her tail.

"'Twas not the loss that I minded so much as the man's rudeness and impenitence."

Persian.—*Zi roghan khurdan e gurba na nálam, zi dum jumbídanash áshufta hálam.*

Brári hund hal hyuh, athih nah yiwán kánsih.

Like the secundine of a cat, no one can get it.

A man here, there, and everywhere—no finding him.

Hindús think that whoever succeeds in obtaining the after-birth of a cat will become exceedingly rich and prosperous. Only three or four persons in the whole city have been known to get it, and they all are very wealthy. As soon as this precious treasure is obtained it is put into a jar well covered over and kept in the house. Blessed are the people in whose dwelling it is placed.

Brári zún.

The cat's moon.

"Such excitement, as that I could not sleep or do anything." Natives say that cats are fond of the moon, and get more and more excited as she increases. They remain out all the night and disturb the whole neighbourhood with their shrieks and depredations.

The *London Review* says:—The Egyptians worshipped the cat as a symbol of the moon, not only because it is more active after sunset, but from the dilation and contraction of its orb, symbolical of the waxing and waning of the night-goddess.

Bráris nah "bishtah," tah húnis nah "durah"? týut chhuh nek!

He has not even a "bishtah" for the cat, nor a "durah" for the dog—so good is he!

He would not hurt a worm.

Bishtah is a sound for driving away cats.

Durah is a sound for driving away dogs.

Brárisai pakah yĕhan saran rozahan nah pachhin.

If the cat grew wings, the water-fowl could not live in the lakes.

A cunning tyrannical fellow checked from doing much harm by sickness or poverty, &c.

Persian.—*Gurba e miskín agar par dáshte, tukhm i gunjishk az jahán bardáshte.*

Brimjih chhántih Walur púzun!

Sweeping away the waters of the Walur Lake with the branches of the Brimij!

Prendre la lune avec les dents.

Bror márun.

To beat the cat.

Pour encourager les autres.

Tirhuti.—*Dhí márún putoh le taras.*

A father on the occasion of his son's marriage gave him a little special advice. "You are going to be married, my son; and you will wish that your wife should be quiet and submissive to you in all matters. Follow the advice, which I now give you. Procure a cat, and one night after your marriage so arrange that the animal shall be in the sleeping room at the time, when you and your wife retire to rest. You will go to the room as usual, and on entering it you will pretend to be very much surprised and annoyed that the cat, should be found there, and you will draw your sword at once and slay it. Your wife, of course, will be terribly frightened, and from the sight of the slain cat, and a hint from you that she will fare likewise if she is not very careful over herself, you may depend upon it that she will be the proper, dutiful wife that she should be."

Bror wuchhit gatshih "bishtah" khasun.

When he sees a cat, he must cry "bishtah."

"Why don't you say this before the man's face? What is the good of threatening him, when he is absent?"

Buchih phuharih tah nindarih pathur.

Burnt bread for the hungry and the bare ground for sleep.

Appetite is the best sauce and tiredness the best bed.

Buchis húni máz halál.

It is lawful for a hungry man to eat the flesh of a dog.

Necessitas non habet légem.

Buḍah ashak mohari mushak.

An old man's love is worth a guinea a pinch.

Mushak, a pinch (of snuff or tobacco, &c.)

Buḍah káwah jugah jugah.

Dancing an old crow (on the hand).

Fussing about anything unworthy.

Buḍun tah lokatĕn hunz khidmat gatshih nah karuni.

Do not enter the service of the old or the young (because the old will soon die, and the young do not remember).

Buḍun tah wadun ; buḍun tah mashun ; buḍun tah nashun.

To become old and to cry ; to become old and forget ; to become old and decay.

"Yet is their strength labour and sorrow."—Ps. xc. 10.

Buhogunas chhih bah guan.

The Buhogun has twelve attributes.

Buhogun or *Bhogun* is a small brazen vessel, with a wide mouth. In it the tea is made, rice is cooked, ghí is prepared, &c.

Bujih buthis kanahwájih.

Earrings upon the face of an old woman.

"An old lady with a hat on !"

Bujih gabih chhĕh litsan hanzan bastan nún sárán.

The old ewe takes salt out of the skin of a weak sheep.

It is the custom to carry salt, flour, &c., about in skins. Salt is constantly given to animals.

Bujih gayih tsil tas áv hit.

An old woman tumbled down, and she got excused.

A person full of excuses.

Bujih labyav kujih tal tsuṅṭ ; adah gayih phut hit.

An old woman found an apple under the tree, and afterwards she (always) went (to that tree) with a basket

Give once, and they always expect ; and very often expect more.

Bujih nyúk bar tami nyúv mashídih hund.

An old woman's door was taken away ; so she went and took the door of the mosque.

It is a habit of the Kashmírí tradesman to make up for his losses by plundering other customers.

Bujih tah brárih tsuweyih har tah wanakin hápatan tsáyih lár.

An old woman and a cat fought with one another, and fear came upon the bears of the wood.

Punishment visited upon the wrong persons.

There was a poor old helpless woman, who used to beg for her food by day and cook it at night. Half of this food she would eat in the morning and the other half in the evening. After a while a cat got to know of this arrangement and came and ate the meal for her. This old woman was very good and patient, and so she continued for many days without saying or doing anything to the thief. But one night she could not endure the cat's impudence, and so laid hold of it. She argued with herself as to whether she should kill it or not. "If I slay it," she said, "it will be a sin; but if I retain it alive, it will be to my heavy loss." Accordingly she determined to only punish it. She procured some cotton-wool and some oil, and soaking the one in the other tied it on to the cat's tail, and then set it on fire. Away rushed the cat across the yard—up the side of the window—and upon the roof, where its flaming tail ignited the thatch, and set the whole house on fire. The flames spread to the other houses, until after a short time the whole village was in one mighty blaze. The news spread far and wide, and the governor of the city sent the soldiers; but they only increased the damage by shouting and in other ways exciting the people, so that they ran about wildly, not knowing what they were doing; and many received very serious burns.

The governor, who now had reached the village, seeing these poor sufferers, at the advice of the doctor, ordered the soldiers to march at once for the jungle and kill as many bears as they could, and bring their fat to him; for the doctor had said, that if for the space of two days bear's grease were applied to the burns, they would perfectly heal. The soldiers were rather afraid to venture their lives in this work, and not a few of them ran away, when they saw the bears. The score or so who kept their ground were slain; and one poor fellow, whilst dying, spoke the above words, which have long since passed into a proverb.

Eventually many bears were slain. Hence the bears as well as the poor soldiers were killed, and all because of the quarrel between the old woman and the cat.

Bukchih halál tah hár harám.

Bundle lawful, but cowrie prohibited.

Straining at a gnat, but swallowing a camel.

Bukhári gayih násúr-i-khána.

The fire-place is the ulcer of the house (*i.e.*, eats up the expenses, and sometimes burns the whole place down).

Bukhári, a fire-place in shape like our English stove, built of dried mud, and used only by the few wealthier classes for warming the house, but never for cooking purposes. Wood only is burnt in the bukhári.

Bumasínui zánih satuti sunz dig.

The worm will know the pecking of the lapwing.

Bun kun wuchhit tsun kun nazar.

(Apparently) looking below, but (really) seeing in every direction.

A shrewd, careful master.

Buth wuchhit bog tah tsakij wuchhit tsáńgij.

The face sees the dinner and the backside sees the tsáńgij.

Suum cuique tribuito.

Tsáńgij is a round piece of matting for squatting upon.

Buzi buzi gáḍah khĕwán ásmánas suĕt.

He cooks his fish by the sun and eats.

A man so full of himself, that he listens to nobody.

Buzun bror kámuni, kahan garan kuní thov, buzun bror kámuni.

A cat for roasting is obtained with difficulty; only one frying-pan for eleven houses; a cat for roasting is obtained with difficulty.

Hard times.

These words are said to have been first spoken in the time of 'Azím Khán, one of the old Paṭhán conquerors, whose reign of terror and oppression will long be remembered in the valley. The Hindús are especially bitter against his memory, as he used to fine them so much a head, and so much extra for the tíká, the religious mark, which they wear on their foreheads.

C

Chái kam yá yits lekin tats.

It does not matter whether the tea is less or more, but it must be hot.

Two kinds of tea, and two ways of preparing it, are met with in the valley. There is the *Surati chái*, something like our English tea, which is imported from the Panjáb and Ladák; and the *Sabz chái*, the celebrated brick tea, which reaches Kashmír *viá* Ladák. The first way of preparation is called the Mughal method, *Mugul chái*. Here is the receipt :— For every *tola* or rupee's weight of tea in the pot put five cups of cold water, boil for half-an-hour, then add more cold water together with sugar and condiments, and allow to boil for another half-an-hour. Then add milk, stir well, and serve round hot to the guests *ad libitum*. The second *modus preparandi* is called *Shiri chái*, of which this is the recipe :— Place the required quantity in the tea-pot together with a little soda and cold water and boil for half-an-hour. Then add milk, salt, and butter, and allow to boil for another half-an-hour, when it is ready for drinking. The salt used in the infusion of tea is called phul. It is found in the Nubra valley in Ladák, and contains the carbonate and sulphate of soda, and a little of the chloride of sodium.

Chakih-khor chhuh mirás-dár.

An old servant is an heir (*i.e.*, you must make some provision for his old age).

Chíni barándah kam chhai nah sĕz.

Your doorstep is not straight.

Something wrong with the wife.

There were two friends, one of whom was wise and the other foolish. Upon a certain day, as they were strolling along the same path together, the wise man remarked to his less acute companion that his "doorstep was not straight." The stupid friend replied in a somewhat aggrieved tone, "Why, my doorstep is as straight as yours. I paid five rupees for it. Yours is a common stone. Why do you boast over me that 'your doorstep is not straight?'" The wise man noticing that his friend was a little disconcerted offered to waive the argument, until they both should ascertain for themselves the truth of his statement. After some few days the wise friend took the other friend to his dwelling; and no sooner had he arrived there then with a voice of authority he ordered his wife to bring down a melon from the upper storey of the house, and to get some milk as well. This done he further commanded her to throw some ashes into the milk. The good wife without any questioning either by speech or look at once obeyed. The sage then said to his friend, "I wonder if your wife will do what my wife has done, as readily and unquestioningly?" The foolish friend answered, "Come and see."

The two friends then went together to the house of the foolish man, who on arrival, like the other man, ordered his wife to go to the top of the dwelling and bring down a melon and to bring some milk also; and to sprinkle some ashes over the milk. But he issued his order in a doubting, trembling manner, as was also manifest in his countenance. He evidently had not been accustomed to rule in his home; his wife had rather waved the sceptre of authority. Consequently at this time, as on many other occasions, which were well-known to the dwellers, in the neighbourhood, she most decidedly refused. "Why, I can not; I will not," she said. "Go and bring it down," roared the husband. At last the woman was frightened into obedience But there were further remonstrations before the milk appeared. "I do not know why you are giving me all this trouble," she cried, "why don't you go yourself?" The foolish man now tried entreaties, and at length all the things were brought. Some more time was wasted before the woman, weeping very bitterly, threw the ashes into the milk, her only consolation being the thought that her husband had become mad.

The trial being now concluded the two friends put on their shoes and walked out of the house. When they got outside, the wise friend said to the other, "Was I not correct when I told you that your doorstep was not straight?"

Chánis dahánas guláb.

May roses be to your mouth.

A nice reply to any nice remark made by another.

Chánis hákas chhuh neh pák dinuk hájat.

There is no need to cook your cabbage.

"Now, don't talk nonsense. I am certain you can not, and will not, do what you say?"

Cháyih tah láyih gatshih augun ásun.

A flame is necessary for cooking (both) tea and Indian corn.

Tea here stands for the great man and Indian corn for the man of small degree. Flame here means money, which all classes need according to their rank.

The Kashmírís say "*Turuni chái tah lái chhĕh nah khĕnas láik,*" *i.e.,* Tea and roasted Indian corn are not worth eating cold.

Chhalanah mal chhuá atsán kih nah nerán?

Does dirt come or go by washing?

Does knowledge come from studying or not, &c.?

Chhánah kíj.

The carpenter's wooden nail.

A carpenter was once in very straitened circumstances and obliged to sell his little house. After he had disposed of it, and although the buyer was living in it, the carpenter went every evening when his work was over, and hanged his wrap upon a wooden peg, which was fixed over the front door. He did this for ten days, when the owner of the house remonstrated, saying that the house was his.

The carpenter replied: "Yes, the house is yours, but not this wooden nail." Accordingly the owner had to settle the matter by giving a few more rupees to the man.

Carpenters are constantly omitting a nail here or some other work there, in order that they may be recalled, and be able to make a two or three days more job of it. When the master detects some fault in the work. and sends again for the carpenter, he invariably says to the man, "Look here; what is this? 'Chhánah kíj,' you rascal."

Chhánah thuk chhuh nah bastih rozán.

The sound of the carpenter does not remain secret.

Truth will out.

Chhánah thukas chhul ras taiyár.

Soup is ready at the sound of the carpenter.

Honoured men get well treated wherever they go.

A good carpenter is much flattered and pampered by the people in whose employ he is working—of course with a special reason.

Chhánas tah bázigaras tah shahsawáras chhai aḍúi umr.

A carpenter, tumbler, and horse-breaker (these three) only live out half their days.

Chhánas yĕlih piwán pánas pĕṭh yíkilih kanih lágán wostah-hákah nal.

When the carpenter has to do anything for himself, he uses a cabbage-stalk instead of a large beam (*i.e.*, he does work at the smallest expense possible).

Chháv yit batah tah dáv yit kathah.

When it boils dinner is ready, and when opportunity offers speak and act.

A word or work in season.

Chhĕli chhĕli zun zálun.

He washes the wood before he burns it (because it *may* be unclean).

A particularly scrupulous conscience.

Chhĕní muṭ chhĕh wazán.

Empty vessels sound.

Hindustání.—*Adhjal gagarí chhalkat jáe.*

Chhĕtin pátsin márán gatai Gwásh Shodah patai lárán chhus.

Gwásh Shodah runs after the man who walks (in a pompous fashion) throwing his clothes from side to side.

It is related that a certain man borrowed five rupees from Gwásh and went and bought clothes with the money. No sooner were the clothes made, and the man was walking with great display in the bázár, then Gwásh came running after him asking him to pay his debts.

Shodah is a lazy, smoking, drunken fellow.

Chon muṅgah trak son sun ak.

Your twelve pounds of muṅg is only one of my meals. (My expenses—my family, are so great).

Your gift was but as a drop in the ocean.

Muṅg is a vetch or kind of kidney bean.

Chuṅkaras cháṅkar tah píntskánih naukar.

Servant to a man of humble situation and servant to a small-eyed man.

Amongst other cases quoted, when one servant passes on to another and lower servant the master's order to him. The lower servants in an establishment are "fagged out of heir lives" sometimes.

D

Dab chhuá bab?
Is falling-down a father?
Why should I trouble about that fellow?

Dab lug tah rabih pĕṭh, dil lug tah hilih pĕṭh!
Tumbled into the mud, the heart set upon water-weeds!
A man "smitten" by an ugly, ill-shaped woman.

Dachh ai khĕzih tah ápaimán, kachh ai khĕzih tah zyur.
If a man will eat grapes, then let him eat ápaimán kind; and if he will eat grass then let him eat zyur.
Apaiman.—There are at least six varieties of grape growing in Kashmír, among which ápaimán is said to be the best.
Zyur is a kind of caraway-seed.

Dachh kamawú khĕyí zih paradĕv, mĕh há dup pananĕv.
Who ate your grapes? Strangers. O! I thought your relations (would have had some of them).
He that neglects his own is worse than an infidel.

Dachhun athah chhuh chhalán khowaris, tah khowur athah chhuh chhalán dachhinis.
The right hand washes the left, and the left hand washes the right.
"If the plowman did not plow,
The poet could not write."

Dah báts kahi záts.
Ten wives but eleven dispositions.
"As many tastes as heads and as different."—"Oraculo Manual." Balthasar Gracian.

Dah chandas; dah wandas; dah shúndas.
Ten in the pocket; ten in the heart; ten in the pillow.
No finding out what the man's opinions really are.

Dah gaz hyur kyah tah dah gaz bun kyah?
What is the difference whether it is ten yards up or ten yards down?
A regular ninny-noddy.
Once upon a time a man fell into a well. As luck would have it there was another man passing by that very moment with some rope

in his hand. Of course he threw one end of the rope to the man, who had fallen into the well, and told him to fasten it round his loins, which the man did; and so was pulled up and saved.

On another occasion this man, who had saved the other from drowning, was passing by a high tree, when somebody shouted to him from the topmost branches, that he was fixed up there and could not possibly descend; whereupon, having the same coil of rope hanging upon his arm, he said, "Don't fear, wait a moment. Here—catch hold of the rope," and he threw one end of the rope up to the man. The man caught it, and no sooner had he done so, than he was jerked most violently from the branch and pulled to the ground, dozens of yards below. Of course he died instantaneously; and when the passers-by gathered round the corpse and enquired whether the man, who had done this deed, was mad or a murderer, he replied: "I have pulled a man up out of a well and now I have pulled a man down from a tree. What is the difference whether it is ten yards up or ten yards down as long as you save the man."

Dah thurungi dit tah pathkunui.

Ten dancings-round and yet behind.

Vain struggling against misfortune.

There is a children's game in Kashmír called Tsihul. One boy holds a piece of rope in his hand, and the other end of the rope is fastened by a stake into the ground. The other boys go around him and beat him, when they can, with sticks. Should this boy touch one of the other boys without letting go the rope, that other boy has to catch hold of the rope and take his chance. And so the play continues.

Dahan dah manuṭi gatshan nah tah kunis manuṭ poshih nah.

Ten manuṭs are not required for ten men, but one manuṭ is not sufficient for a single man.

One or two more in a big family does not make any difference in the expenses.

Manuṭ is a weight equal to three pounds.

Dahan thawán sai tah akis nah tsunán wai.

He gives promise to ten, but does not give food to one.

Dahi wahari Dashahár.

Dashahár after ten years.

Long enough about it.

Dashahár or *Dasahrá* or *Das.hará*, is the tenth of Jaith shukl pakeh, which is the anniversary of Gangá's birthday. On this day, also, Ráma marched against Rávana, for which reason it is, also, called Vijai Dasamí.

H. H. the Mahárájah of Kashmír, like other Hindú rájahs, celebrates this day with great pomp and rejoicing. Three immense cardboard figures stuffed with gunpowder are made to represent

Rávana, Kumbhakarna and Mígunád, and these are placed at the proper time in the centre of a large open space without the city. To represent Ráma, Sítá and Lakshman, three little boys are splendidly dressed and carried in a beautiful palanquin to the same place. Crowds of people gather there, and His Highness sends all the troops with the guns, &c. It is a most exciting occasion. Excitement is at the fullest pitch, when at a given signal one of the little boys, who is supposed to be Ráma, steps forth from the palanquin, attended by the two other little boys, and fires a small arrow at the big figure representing Rávana, while the other boys discharge their arrows against the other two figures. Of course at this moment the three monsters, Rávana, Kumbhakarna, and Mígunád explode with a tremendous noise; and then the guns rattle and the cannon roar, and the people shout until they are hoarse, and eventually retire. Cf. the Rámáyana for an account of Ráma and his adventures.

Dai ai diyih tah barah nyásai ; Dai nai diyih tah krúhah sásah tsatit kyah ?

If God intends to give, He will give at the door ; but if God will not give, then what is the good of going a thousand kos (*i.e.*, about 2,000 English miles) for it.

Four men, ambitious to become rich, determined to leave Kashmír for some other country, where they could obtain greater wealth than it was possible for them to amass in "the Happy Valley." They arranged a certain day and started altogether, taking with them four thousand rupees for the purpose of trading. Each of the little company had an equal share in this sum of money, and they all set forth full of hope that they would prosper and become exceedingly rich.

On the way it came to pass that God, according to His mighty power and wisdom, caused a full-grown golden tree to spring up suddenly, and to bring forth at once rich clusters of gold. Seeing this magnificent tree, the four travellers were so surprised that they hardly knew what to say or to do. However, they soon changed their minds about travelling into a foreign country, and resolved to return back to their homes, carrying with them the tree of gold. They were reminded of their own Kashmírí proverb, "*Dai ai diyih tah barah nyásai; Dai nai diyih tah kruhah sásah tsatit kyah?*" which being interpreted is, "If God intends to give, He will give at the door; but if God will not give, then what is the good of going two thousand miles for it?" and therefore they said to one another "we have happed upon this golden tree and must take it home with us and be glad for ever."

In this proposition they all agreed; but how could they so arrange it? The tree was high and large; it must be felled and cut up into bundles, which they could carry. Accordingly it was determined that two of the party should go to the nearest village and procure axes and saws, while the other two would remain to guard the precious treasure.

Presently the two selected started for the tools. The other two, who were left to watch the tree, then began to take counsel together as to how they might kill their partners. "We will mix poison with their bread," said one, "and then when they eat thereof they will die, and we each shall have a double share of the treasure." And they did so.

However, the other two, who were going for the tools, had also plotted together by the way as to how they might get rid of the two partners left behind by the tree. "We will slay them with one stroke of the axe," said one, "and thus shall we each have a double share in the treasure."

In the course of a few hours they returned from the village with the saws and axes; and immediately, on arriving at the tree, they slew both of their partners; each slew one with a single blow from the axe. They then commenced to hew down the tree, and this done they soon cut up the branches and fastened them into bundles for carrying away; and then thoroughly wearied with excitement and their great exertions they laid down to eat and to sleep. Alas! they ate of the poisoned bread, and slept a sleep, the fatal sleep, from which they never woke again.

A short time afterwards some other travellers passing by that way found the four corpses lying stretched out stiff and cold beneath the golden tree. Cf. "The Orientalist," Vol. I., Pts. II. and VII., pp. 47, 165, where incidents in the Arabic account of the Virgin Mary and Jesus, and in the Vedabbha Játaka of the Buddhist Tripiṭakas, are described, which bear a striking resemblance to this story.

Daman bastih dito dil, damanas yitah damn khár.
Shistaras sun gatshí hásil; wuni chhai sul tah tsándun yár.
Sudaras no labí sáhil, nah tat sum tah nah tat tár.
Par kar paidah parwáz tul; wuni chhai sul tah tsándun yár.
Gáfilo hĕk tah kadam tul hushyár roz tráv piyádil.
Tráwak nai tah chhuk jáhil; wuni chhai sul tah tsándun yár.

Give the heart to the bellows, like as the blacksmith gives breath to the bellows,
And your iron will become gold. Now it is early morning, seek out your friend (*i.e.*, God).
The sea has not a shore, neither is there a bridge over it, nor any other means of crossing.
Make to yourself wings and fly. Now it is early morning, seek out your friend.
O negligent man, put on power, be on the alert, take care, and leave off wickedness.

If you will not then you are a fool. Now while it is early morning seek out your friend.

A few lines from Lal Děd constantly quoted by the Kashmírí.

Piyádil—the work of a chaprássí, a bad lot, as he generaly makes his money by oppression, lying, and cheating.

Damas suĕt chhuí namaskár.

"Good day" to the rich or honourable man.

Dambih ai zĕn kore tah ḍaurih ai bowan hachai.

If from the womb a daughter should be born, and if from the fields but an indifferent harvest should be gathered (still he is happy. For a little is better than nothing).

Damí ḍiṭhum nad pakawuní, damí ḍiṭhum sum nah tah tár.

Damí ḍiṭhum thar phollawuní, damí ḍyuṭhum gul nah tah khár.

Damí ḍiṭhum páṅtshan Páṅḍawan hanz máj damí ḍiṭhum krají más.

One moment I saw a little stream flowing, another moment I saw neither a bridge, nor any other means of crossing.

At one time I saw a bush blooming, at another time I saw neither a flower nor a thorn.

At one moment I saw the mother of the five Páṅḍavas, at another moment I saw a potter's wife's aunt.

"Nothing in this world can last."

Quotations from Lal Děd's sayings, the whole of which will probably soon be in print.

The history of the Páṅḍavas, and how their mother was reduced by misfortune to profess herself a potter's wife's aunt, are fully explained in the Mahábhárata.

Dán diwán tah prut harán.

The generous person gives and the miser is sorrowful.

Dáná dushman chhuí nádán metharah sandih khutah ján.

A wise enemy is better than an unwise friend.

Persian.—*Dushman i dáná ki pay e ján buwad bihtar az án dost ki nádán buwad.*

The story is, that there was a prince, who had two ministers, one a friend and the other an enemy. The friend happened to be most weak and stupid, while the enemy was a very cute and wise fellow. One day his friend thought within himself "I will kill the prince and become a great king." Accordingly he ordered some men to dig a ditch and to cover over the top of it with grass. They did so. Then the stupid minister one day asked the king to go for a walk with him; and passing by the way of the ditch he pushed him into it, and ordered the attendants to cover him over with earth. But the other minister was at hand, and the king saw him, and cried unto him, " O minister, let me not die. The country will be ruined." The wise minister knowing that such would be the case, revoked the order of the other minister, and had the king pulled out. On the following day the stupid friend was executed, and the wise enemy was promoted to very great honour. (This story is evidently taken from the Makhzan i Asrár, a Persian work).

Dánah-míran kari júnah-mír barbád.

The big fire-place destroyed the great man.

There was a Pandit of the name of Nand Rám, and belonging to the Tíkú sect. He was indebted to the Pathán, Ázád Khán's goverment to the extent of five lákhs of rupees. The goverment wanted this money, but Nand Rám could not pay it, and so soldiers were stationed around his house, and the order was given for his eyes to be taken out. When the man arrived to execute this cruel order, Nand Rám begged that he would wait, and said, " There is money under the big fire-place. Now Nand Rám's custom had been to feed two hundred people every day—the poor, the sick and the distressed, who thronged his house.

The soldiers according to directions well searched beneath the fire-place, but found nothing. They told the matter to Ázád Khán, who sent for Nand Rám and enquired what he meant. He answered " My big fire-place has ruined me. In it has been absorbed all my wealth." Ázád Khán then repeated the order for his eyes to be taken out. (Ázád Khán, 1783, A.D., is the tyrant of whom it was said that he killed men as though they were birds.)

Danah sumbrun chhuí kani der súrun; danah sumbrun chhuí rázah sund mál;

Danah dú darmas tí chhuí lárun Sáhib gárun din kiho rát.

Gathering money is like gathering a heap of stones, gathering money is as the king's property; (*i.e.*, is appropriated by the state after death).

Giving money in alms, you keep it. Remember God day and night.

" There is that scattereth and yet increaseth; and there is that withholdeth more than is meet, but it tendeth to poverty."—Prov. xi. 24.

Dandah khokhur hammám gaje; dand trávit lubar paje.

O toothless man (your mouth is like) a hammám's fire-place; go and put your teeth at the bottom of a cow-dung basket.

Hindú adults sometimes, but nearly always the children, when a tooth has been extracted, place it at the bottom of a basket of cow-dung, or else throw it into a rat-hole, saying, "*Gagari bá gagaro chon dand mĕh tah myon dand tsĕh*, which means :—

"Rat, O brother Rat, you take my tooth and give me yours."

Muhammedans keep their teeth in a little box, which is buried with them when they die.

"*Dándá phuṅkán kiho, zih chhuk zih madhá chhum.*"
"*Chhor kiho zih chhui, zih darhá chhum.*"
"O bull, why are you bellowing?" "I am proud."
"O bull, why have you diarrhœa?" "I am afraid."

A coward.

Dándas chhiá hĕng gobán?

Are the horns too heavy for the bullock? (No).

No matter how large the family the father would not willingly part with one of his children.

Dándas lov tah watshis gĕd.

A good handful of grass for the bullock, but six handfuls for the calf.

Injustice.

Dándan khĕjih patuj, panuni khĕyan manduj.

The ox who ate the matting ate his rump (*i.e.*, he got whacked for it).

Consequence of evil deeds.

Dandán muyov tah dupuk "Asán chhuh."

A man with projecting incisors was about to die, and the people said "He is laughing."

Dándih sust wáyán dohalih.
Dándih rust wáyán rátalih.
The owner of an ox ploughs in the day.
The man who hasn't an ox ploughs at night (*i.e.*, he plans things in his bed, but forgets them with the morning light).

Dangí suh.

A tiger in the stable.

A tyrant in his house.

Dapahas ai ábas gatshun gatshih khushkas.
Dapahas ai khushkas gatshun gatshih ábas.
If I tell him to go to the water he will go to the land.
If I tell him to go to the land he will go to the water.

A good-natured fellow, but who invariably misunderstands anything and executes it accordingly.

Dapayai húr, kih nah parí ráhat-i-ján chhahamai káñgrí.
O káñgrí, what shall I call thee, a celestial virgin or a fairy! You are the balm of my life.

Persian.—*Aí kángrí, ai kángrí, qurbání tu húr o parí, harchand wasfat míkunam kaz wasaf azán bálá tarí. Tu az parí názuk tarí o az barg i gul ra'ná tarí. Haqqá ajá'ib dil barí.*

Dár yĕlih dudareh yár gatshih pánas, mitsiwis bánas mitsih tal jái.
When the body (lit. wood) becomes old (lit. dry and rotten) the spirit (lit. friend) goes his own way. The place of this earthen pot is under the earth.

Daram Dásini kotrí.
Daram Dás's chamber.

A small room.

Daram Dás was a very celebrated character among Kashmírí Jogís. He lived in Srínagar near to the entrance of the Lake, and died in 1877 A. D. He built several small houses, the biggest of which was sufficient for only two persons.

Darbár garih ai tíl melih tah halam gatshih dárun.
If from the master's house some oil be given, then one must hold up the skirt, wherein to take it.

Although the present may be a mean present, and of as much benefit to the recipient as oil in a cloth, which all runs out and is spoilt, yet it is the duty of the servant to take it humbly and readily. Kashmírí beggars receive alms in this way.

Dard chhĕh gard.
Love is as dust (*i.e.*, must show itself).

Daryawik malkh ganzrani.
To count the waves of the river.

An impossible task.

Persian.—*Mauj i daryá shumardan.*

'Alí Mardán Khán (cir. 1650 A. D) was a governor under the Emperor of Kashmír Sháh Jahán. He had two especial servants, one a Muhammedan and the other a Hindú. The Muhammedan worked all the day, but the Pandit, who worked only for one hour, received more salary than the Muhammedan. The latter petitioned the king, that he would at least give him an equal salary. The king promised that he would do so if the Muhammedan would go and count the waves of the river and tell him how many they were. The Muhammedan went away at once, but soon found that he could not oblige the king. On his return, when the king asked him how many waves there were, he replied, "I have forgotten." Then the king ordered the Pandit to go and count the waves. The Pandit consented on the condition that the king would allow him two thousand rupees and one hundred soldiers for this purpose. The king gave him what he asked for, and away went the Pandit to his task. At every turn or passage of the river he placed four soldiers and a toll house, and ordered them to take four rupees from each boat which went up or down. The excuse to the boatmen, when they demurred, was that they had hindered the Pandit in counting the waves of the river, and therefore they were thus fined. In this way he obtained a lákh of rupees, and then went to the king. In reply to the king's question how many waves there were, the Pandit threw down the bags of rupees at the ruler's feet, saying "One lákh, your Majesty."

This Pandit was promoted to a very high post, whilst the Muhammedan was debased.

The natives say that 'Ali Mardán Khán introduced custom-houses into Kashmír at this Pandit's advice.

Dúshtam, dúshtam chhuh nah bakár ; dáram, dáram chhuh bakár.

What I had, what I had, is not wanted; but what I have, what I have, is necessary.

Quoted to the man who is constantly speaking of his great relations, or previous wealthier state.

Dastár chhih gandán izzatah khátirah wushnerah khátirah nah.

Men bind on their turbans for honour's sake, not for warmth.

Dastárah badalah chhas kalas pěṭh raz.

In place of a turban rope is on his head.

A disreputable person.

Dastáran chhuh nah mul, darbáran chhuh.

No worth is attached to turbans, but to professions.

Not what a man seems, but what he is.

Dastáras dab tah nálas trit chhuh múlis tah mójih pěṭh maranih wizih ján.

To dash one's turban upon the ground, and to tear one's cloak into two pieces at the time of a father's or mother's death is good.

This is principally a Hindú custom. They remain thus with uncovered head and torn cloak for ten days after their parent's death; and if they are rich they then give the turban and cloak away, but if they are poor they keep them.

Daulat jama karuni chhai zallat. Hár hún sár nah káńsih hanz.

Amassing riches is destruction. A piebald dog is not faithful to any one.

The Kashmírí calls many things *hár hún*, but especially these three, viz., the world, health, and money.

A certain wealthy merchant, famed for his goodness and almsgiving, died, and his immense wealth was distributed among all his sons, except the eldest, who did not get a cowrie of it. There was great lamentation in the city, and especially among the poor and sick people when they heard of this good man's death. What were they to do? To whom should they go now? "Perhaps," said some, "the sons will continue their deceased father's liberality, that their name may live and be great in the land." So crowds of the poor and distressed wended their way to the sons' houses. The sons, however, who had come into their father's property were not good men, but selfish and hard-hearted; and so when they saw the crowds of beggars entering their compound, they at once gave orders that they should be turned out and told not to come again, but to go to the eldest son's quarters, as he was more interested in their cases than they were. Therefore they went to the house of the eldest son, who, following the example of his father, did what he could for the relief of their necessities.

Now it happened that one day some holy men visited this eldest son and asked for alms. They came at a bad time, when he had only two loaves within the vessel. However, he told them to wait, while he took these two loaves and sold them in the bázár. The few paisás, which he received for them, he gave to the holy men. When he gave the money to them, they knowing that it was the price of the two loaves, enquired why he, the son of such a wealthy and good man, was in such reduced circumstances. He told them that his brothers had appropriated all the money, and that he did not care sufficiently for it to go to law concerning his portion. The holy men were very pleased, and much desired to compensate this unearthly-minded son. Accordingly they told him to prepare one of the rooms in his house and sleep in it; and it would come to pass that one night a woman, Daulat by name, would enter his house; and when he heard the sound of her footsteps ascending the stairs he was to open the door of his room, let her come in, and then chain the door; and on her asking to be let out again, he was to say to her: "*Daulat jama karuni chhai zallat. Hár hún sár nah káńsih hanz*," which means, "I have not got any money. I think it a sin to amass wealth; and so you will not be faithful to me." "But," continued the holy men, "she will promise never to go away; and then you can open the door." Saying this, they blessed him and left.

According to the instructions of his saintly visitors, the eldest son thoroughly cleaned one of his rooms and arranged it as if for a wedding-chamber, and at night laid down in it to rest. He had not been asleep for more than two hours, when he was awakened by a creaking on the stairs. It was the woman coming up. So he opened the door to let her enter. No sooner had he opened the door then a little flame came floating along in the air until it settled upon his forehead, but he did not feel the heat of the flame, nor did it leave any mark behind. In a minute or two he returned to the room, but not seeing the woman who talked with him (for she had been turned into the little flame) he laid down again upon his bed and slept.

On rising in the morning he heard that the king had ordered his troops to march to a distant country against another king who had unlawfully seized some certain lands and villages; and the king paid the soldiers their wages beforehand in gold mohurs. The soldiers, however, did not like this arrangement, they were afraid that they would lose them either through thieves, or in some other manner; and so they returned them to the king with the request that he would send them to the late rich merchant's sons and get them exchanged for paper money, which they might cash at the merchants in the country whither they were going. The king complied with their request and sent the gold mohurs to the late merchant's sons, but they replied that they were not able to fulfil the king's wishes, as they had no transactions with the merchants of that country; and, moreover, they were not known by them, and so their letters would not be respected.

In the midst of this difficulty the eldest son of the late merchant came to the king, and said that he would arrange for the payment of the troops if his Majesty would trust him. The king said, "Yes, you are a good man; I will send you the money."

When the eldest son got the money he put it into a big earthen vessel, and in the midst of the gold he put a letter for one of the merchants of that country whither the soldiers were going, asking him please to distribute the money amongst them according to the orders of the king. He then closed up the mouth of the vessel with a piece of ordinary oil-skin, and gave it to one of the soldiers, telling him to give it to a certain merchant on arrival at the journey's end; "I should be so thankful," he said, "if you would please take this *jar of pickles*. My friend will be so glad to get them." The soldier readily promised to take the greatest care of the jar, indeed many offered to take it, so grateful were they one and all for this man's convenient arrangement concerning the money. On arriving in that country the pot was handed over to the merchant named, who at once opened it and read the letter. The next day the gold mohurs were paid to the troops, who were astonished at the shrewdness of the late merchant's eldest son. Readily they each one set apart some of the money as a present for their benefactor, while the king made him his private secretary and banker. Eventually he became as wealthy and as great as his late father; and in the time of his greatness he did not forget the sick and the poor.

Dayih sund páwur, yĕmi yĕtih áwur.
Wheresoever, whosoever has taken possession, that is the place of the Deity.
A man's house and lands are sacred; no person can take them from him.
Da,í the Deity, destiny (Sanskrit).

Dawádáras korah záyih; muddaádáras báguni áyih.
An only daughter was born to the plaintiff; she came in marriage to the defendant.
Quoted when an unlikely event happens.

Dazah-wunih nárah gajih ai dizĕn dárit tatih tih yijih nah put phírit.
If he is cast into the burning fire-place, he will not return thence (before fulfilling his work).
A good, sharp servant.

Dazanas dod.
There is pain from a burn.
To lose anything is not pleasant.

Dazihmatshih wálinjih zulahbuk.
Clawing the burnt liver.
Unguis in ulcere.

Dĕdi kawah ditsthas nádánas?
Tawah khutah diziham wázah-gánas.
Aniham ḍagah ḍagah khĕmahah pánas;
Ḍulagani dimahah manz maidánas.
O mother, why did you marry me to a foolish man?
Better that you had given me to a prostitute's cook.
He would have brought me scraps of dinner in his wrap and I would have eaten them;
And I would have lolled the whole day upon the grass.

Ḍeḍi talai charas dazán.
At the king's porch charas burns.
Cheeky without shame, and before his master!
Charas is the exudation of the flowers of hemp collected with the dew and prepared for use as an intoxicating drug.

Deg chhĕh teg.
The pot is a sword (*i.e.*, makes ravage with one's income).

Dĕhli ká bánká múṅh chakhná peṭ khálí.

The Delhi swell has got a jolly face, but his stomach is empty.

A Delhi Paṇḍit determined to pay Kashmír a visit. When he reached Vernág he engaged a man as cook, with whom he had the following conversation:—

Paṇḍit.—"Cook."

Cook.—"Yes."

Paṇḍit.—"Bring about three-quarters of a pound of flour from the market, and make thirty-three loaves. Ten guests will be present at dinner this evening. So that there will then be two loaves for each guest, and something for each to take home with him, if he should wish to do so."

Cook.—"I do not understand you."

Paṇḍit.—"Never mind. Do as I tell you. The first day, when we entertain strangers, we do so."

The cook brought a vessel full of a water and placed it in front of the Paṇḍit.

Paṇḍit.—"Where is the food?"

Cook.—"It is the custom in this country not to give any food to the stranger on the first day—only a vessel-full of water."

Paṇḍit.—"No! I am sure you must be mistaken.

Cook.—"I also think that it cannot be the custom in your country to feed ten men with three-quarters of a pound of flour."

(The Paṇḍit in a rage. *Exit.* Cook.)

Dĕminen koṅg.

Saffron with sheep's paunch.

Not worth the candle.

Saffron is used as a condiment, and is eaten only with the best meat.

Dewas tah ḍraṭháyıkas dizih tîl tah tahar, ádmí sanzih bad-nazarih nah kĕṅh.

Oil and rice can be given to (appease the anger of) the ghosts and demons, but nothing can save us from the evil-eye of man.

Cf. "Mĕh chham," &c.

Dıgámih diwai Nádigámih pĕnjih lĕwai.

The great melá is at Digám, but the washing of the mound is at Nadigám.

Digám is a village near to Shupiyon. There is a great melá there in the month of July; and people, whose little children have died during the year, go to the place and offer clothes and food in the names of their deceased children.

On the same day there are festivals also at Mańgám and Trigám, which are a great distance from one another, and both of them very far from Digám. It is written that "He who visits each of these places in one day, shall ascend to eternal bliss." One man did so, riding upon a swift horse, and afterwards man, horse, and everything went up into the clouds out of sight. Another man by the name of Krishna Saráf also succeeded in visiting these three villages in one day; but for some reason or other he was not taken up.

Digih púńtshuv tah dugih hár.
A small paisá for a peck and a cowrie for a blow.
The over-liberal person.

Dih thap tah nih dastár.
Seize him and take his pagrí.
A respectable vagrant, who lives by "sponging" on others.

Dik ná tah manaṭi dab khĕt?
You will not give? (of course you will); but it will be after much wrangling and quarrelling.
Threatening "distress for rent."
Manaṭi dab, lit., a strike of a stone, but here it means going to law, or giving a man a good thrashing.

Dik ná tah paizár khĕt?
You will give I know, but you will eat your shoes (first).
"Putting on the screw" to get a debt.
"Eating shoes" is an expression for being beaten with a shoe.

Dil ba dil gav áinah; yut wuchham, tyut wuchhai.
Your heart and mine are like a looking-glass; as you see me, so I shall appear to you.
Be friendly and I will be friendly, and *vice versá*.

Dilah nah tah kilah dí dí.
Not willingly but with a little shoving and pushing.

Dilas phulai gatshih ásuni, gulich phulai kyah yiyih bakár?
There must be blossoming of the heart, and then the flower-blossom will not be needed. *Cf.* "*Ásas gatsi,*" *&c.*

Dihkis bágas dúr kar gásil.
Adah dĕwah phulí yĕmburzal bág
Marit manganaî umrih hanz hásil.
Maut chhuí patah patah tahsíl-dár.

Keep away dirt from the garden of your heart.
Then perhaps the Narcissus garden will blossom.
After death you will be asked for the results of your life.
Death is after you like a tahsíldár.

A saying of Lal Dĕd's.

Diluk khur-khurah mĕh, Múlih, kústam, manake kotar mare,
Narih losam lukah hanzai larih ladán.
Yĕlih pánah myánuv kadit ninanai panane gare.
Patah patah nerí lukah sásá narih álawán.
Trávit yinanai manz maidánas sáwit dachhane lare.

Make far from me proudness of heart, O Father,—from the pigeon-hole of my heart.
My arm is wearied from making people's houses (*i.e.*, from helping others, giving alms, &c).
When, O my body, you are turned out from your house.
Afterwards, afterwards, a thousand people will come waving their hands.
They will come and set you in a field, laying you to sleep on your right side.

A verse of Lal Dĕd's constantly quoted in part, or *in toto*, in time of trouble.

Hindús burn the bodies laying them upon the right side, with their head towards the south, because the gods and good spirits live in that direction, and Yama, the angel of death, also resides there.

Dinawálui diyih ; dinal kyah diyih ?

The generous person will give (whether he can spare or not) ; the prostitute (although "flush with coin") will not give.

Dísh dínas tah Shádi Ganai nah.

All the people except Shádi Ganai (her husband) will live with her.

A faithless wife, or a fruit tree, of which others pluck the fruit, while the real owner gets nothing.

Shádi Ganai was a butcher's wife, and a very wicked woman.

Ditut ná, zih zangah phutrit ?

Has it not been given to me? Yes, but after breaking my legs.

Once upon a time there was a man who was carried away by the thought that God was "The Giver," and that somehow or other He would give food to those who sat all day in the house meditating upon Him. This man sat in his house for three days without food. He became so thin that he could scarcely walk. He then went up to the roof of his house and sat there, thinking that, probably, God meant him to live upon air. In a short time he became faint and senseless, and rolled off the roof on to the ground, and broke his legs.

The people heard of this and brought him sherbet and cooked meat. The man soon revived, and said the above words, which have passed into a proverb.

Cited when a man has obtained his living or any position with great difficulty.

Dizih berih yĕtih pherih.
Dizá yárih yĕtih gatshih tárih?

One should plant the tree at the edge of the field, where it will spring up.

Shall it be planted in the place where the fir-tree grows, where it would be checked and die?

To lend money without interest.

Dobi sund garah nanih íz doh.

The washerman's house will be known on the great feast-day.

The washerman's family wear the clothes which are sent to them to be washed; but on the day of the feast everybody takes all their clothes, and so the poor washerman and his family are left almost naked. (This is not true of every washerman).

Persian.—*Khána i gázur ba roz i 'íd ma'lum shawad.*

Dobi sund hún, nah garuk tah nah gáthuk.

The washerman's dog is not of the house or of the ghát.

Expectations unfulfilled.

The washerman's dog fares very badly as a rule. He is always following his master to and fro from the house to the ghát in hope of getting some scraps, but it is very seldom that anything is thrown to the poor animal.

Hindustání.—*Dhobí ká kuttá na ghar ká na ghát ká.*

Ḍoḍ gátul.

A philosopher and a half.

A wiseacre.

Dod nah tah dag nai kawah yiyam ushye?

I have neither pain nor smart, why should I cry?

Let every man bear his own burden.

Dog dit tih bárav; dog hat tih bárav.

Strike a man and he complains (before the magistrate), and strike him a hundred times and he complains (and no greater punishment ensues to the striker).

A variant of this both in words and meaning is:—

Dog dit tih bárav ; dog hĕt tih bárav.

Whether he strikes another, or whether he himself is struck, it's all the same—he grumbles.

Doh chhuh diwán tshoh ; doh chhuh khyáwán goh.

(One) day gives rest, (another) day causes to eat manure.

It is not always sunshine.

Doholih khotsán tah rátalih mandachhán.

Fearing by day and being ashamed at night.

An altogether wretched and bad character.

Don bátsan hunz har gayih wahráts hund rúd.

Strife between husband and wife is like the monsoon rains.

Although Kashmír is out of the tropics it is visited by periodical rains, which finish about the last week in July.

Don kulai batah wáwah.

The wife of two persons, because of food.

"The bitter cry." Anything for bread.

Don saláh tran wáhwelá.

Agreement with two people, lamentation with three.

Two are company, three are not.

A Pír once sent his horse to a certain village, that it might graze upon the beautiful grass there. He particularly told the servant to lead the animal and not to ride it. When the servant had gone some distance the Pír sent another servant to look after the first servant, and, especially, to see that he was not riding it. He went and found the man leading the horse, but being both of them tired, and the horse also tired, they rested awhile, and then set forth again, both of them riding the horse.

The Pír was still suspicious about the horse, thinking that the two servants would perhaps agree together, and both of them mount him at the same time. So he sent a third servant to look after them. The third servant came and found them both astride the horse. "I will tell the Pír," he said, "I will explain the whole matter to him." "Don't, don't," they replied, "but you come also and ride, and we shall have a jolly time." The man consented. They all rode the horse at one time, and arrived at their destination. But the next morning the animal died, and great was the distress of the three servants ! !

Don ungajan chhuh nerán tás.

One snaps with two fingers (not with one).

It takes two to make a quarrel.

Ḍoni kulis kújih-waṭ.

A pestle to the walnut-tree.

A sharp fellow in their midst, of whom they are afraid.

Dostí khutah chhĕh rástí ján.

Truth is better than friendship.

Dostas sĕzmani tah dushmanas wukarmani.

A straight open countenance to your friend ; a downcast look to your enemy.

Most frequently cited by the mother, when her son wishes her "good-bye" before going to his day's work.

Doyih athah chĕh tsar wazán.

Clapping is with both hands.

It takes two to make a quarrel.
Hindustání.—*Ek háth se tálí nahín bajtí.*

Drág tsalih tah dág tsalih nah.

The famine will disappear, but the stains will not disappear.

During one of the terrible famines that have now and again visited Kashmír, a brother was nearly dead from want of food, when he suddenly remembered a long-forgotten sister, and determined to go to her and see whether she could help him. On his arrival his sister happened to be making bread ; but she was too sharp for him. She had seen his coming, and guessing the reason of his long-deferred visit, took up the burning hot bread and hid it under her arm. Her bosom was very much scorched by this, and she retained the marks of the burn up to the time of her death.

Kashmír has suffered very much in morals from famines. Driven to extremities the people seem to have lost all sense of self-respect. A little knowledge of the people and their language quickly convinces one too forcibly of the truth of the above words.

Drágas zí chhai goyá kih Mágas nárah phúh.

Employment in time of famine is like the warmth of a fire in the month of January.

Drálah hunar chhai byákhuí.

An agent's profession is another matter.

There's nothing that he is not up to.

Merchants keep such men by them. At the time of bargaining they come in as if unawares and try to make a bargain for the sáhib, or intending buyer, out of pure good-heartedness. The Drál gets a commission on the sale. He is a good-for-nothing, unprincipled fellow. There are two or three kind of Drál lúk. Those who lend out money at interest, those who hire out their daughters for evil, and the merchants' agents.

Dráti náṭah.
Like a sickle to cut meat with.
A stupid workman.

Dú-zang khasán tsú-zangis.
A two-legged mounting a four-legged.
A man of inferior rank promoted, and "lording it" over others.

Dudas kanḍi tsúrani.
Picking thorns or bones out of the milk.
An overscrupulous Bráhman.

Ḍul chhuí dazán.
The end of (your) garment is burning (with envy).
Extreme envy and jealousy.

Ḍum-ḍumah tah Jumah Baṭ.
Jumah Baṭ and his drum.
A very poor man.
Jumah Baṭ was a town-crier for some time. He was a man of good family, and had seen better days.—*Vide "Goḍah dráv," &c.*

Ḍumaṭas ruṅz.
(Like) a marble against a ḍumaṭ.
Advice to a fool.
These *ḍumaṭs* are very big conical stones (lingáms), and according to the Pandits as old as the Pándavas. They are supposed to be the petrified bodies of wicked men, whom some good people in olden times cursed, because they were troubled by them, and so they became stones.
Gulistán of Sa'dí.—*Tarbiyat ná ahl rá chuṅ girdgán bar gumbad ast.*

Dumb tah tsap kúṅsih mah dap.
"Stomach and bowels. Don't tell anyone."
When a father forbears to beat his child, and another person blames him for his leniency, he thus replies.

"*Dúmbá, Jajír*" "*Taiyár, Sábo.*"
"O dúmb, Hukka." "Ready, Sáhib"
A sharp, willing servant.

Dúmbah shurinai khukarbáṭi háwán.
Showing a thing (mask, &c.,) to frighten the Dúmb's children.
"Don't suppose that you're frightening me."
The *Dúmbs* are a plucky lot of fellows. They carry the letters at night through the jungle and over desolate hill and plain.

Dunyá chhuh nah akí danjih rozán, pántsh doh sokh tah pántsh doh dokh.

The world does not continue in the same state ; but there are five days of happiness and five days of sorrow.

Dunyá tah dyár.

The world and wealth (go together).

Duragi hanz Duragi lúr ; yits máj tits kúr.

Durag's stick (according to her height) ; and as mother, so daughter.

Dúrih, dúrih chhuh manats meṭhán ; nakhah, nakhah chhuh kand ṭeṭhan.

From a distance black pepper is sweet ; near at hand sugar is bitter.

Distance lends enchantment to the view. Familiarity breeds contempt.

Dushmanah sandih lagih nah kanih tsanjih ; dostah sandih lagih poshih tsanjih.

The slap of the hand from an enemy will not hurt, but the angry touch, even with a flower, from a friend, will wound.

A king sentenced a man to death by stoning. The order was that every man in the city should throw a stone at the prisoner. A friend of the man heard of the stern order, and said within himself, "What shall I do? How can I throw a stone upon my friend? I must not, and can not, hurt my dear and kind friend." Accordingly he plucked a flower, and determined to throw that when the time came, and to throw it so skilfully that the people would think that he had thrown a stone. He went to the place of execution and flung the flower at his friend, who then spoke the above proverb.

Dyarahwol chhuh nah boḍ ; batahwol chhuh boḍ

Not the rich man, but the man who gives dinners, is great.

Dyutmut khairát hyutnam phírit, shukrani májih tsul tup nírit !

What was given to me was taken away again, Shukr's mother lost a hair or two (that is all) !

G

Gabar chhiá lubar zih gai guris nishih tah ani ?

Are children like manure, which people go and buy from the milkman ?

Children are not so easily obtained, that they can be so easily spared.

Gabih buthih rúmah-hún.

A sheep in appearance, but a wolf at heart.

A wolf in sheep's clothing.

Gabih tih wutsh lat.

A sheep also can lift his tail.

The smallest worm will turn being trodden upon.

Gád chhĕh daryávas andar treshih búpat marán.

The fish dies from thirst in the river.

Every opportunity, yet he did not succeed.

Gád yĕlih chhĕh khĕwún handrer, tah adah chhĕh lagán buth.

When the fish feels the icy-cold it leaps upon the bank.

Affliction is a hard, but a good, teacher.

Gádah tasbih tah thukah tahárat.

(To carry) rosary (in one's hand) for loaves (and fishes) is as if to (perform) tahárat (with one's) spittle.

Tahárat is the Muhammedan's ablutions before prayers.

Gádah tolit pársang.

Seeing whether the scales were correct, after the fish had been weighed.

Without premeditation.

Gádav hĕchhih wutah tah hánzuv hĕchhih zál.

The fishes learnt to jump and the boatmen learnt to use the net.

An asylum for the maniac—a prison for the blackguard—a net for the fish.

Gagar-mírani gang.

The hole of Sir Rat.

"He has well feathered his nest for some time."

The rat is always laying up stores. A Pandit dug out the hole of a rat the other day and found pieces of cloth, iron, little piles of rice, apples, &c., enough for several months' provisions.

Gagarih hanz khĕtsarih lĕj.

The mouse's khĕtsarih lĕj.

Khĕtsarih lĕj is a saucepan in which spiced rice is cooked. The mouse is very fond of this rice, and as it does not remain very long when the mice are by, so money does not continue long in the hands of a man in debt.

Gagur chhuh karán bráris mát.

The rat nonplusses the cat.

Cited when anyone or anything small has escaped the oppression of a greater, and also caused him a little trouble.

Gagur tsáv hakirih banih. Hĕt kyah tsáv zih khĕt dráv?

A rat entered a stock of wood. What did he take with him going in, and what did he eat coming out? Nothing.

In státu quo.

Gagur wĕtsih nah pananih wáj, patah hĕt máj!

The rat himself cannot get into his nest properly, and yet he takes his mother after him!

Hardly enough for one, and yet two or three people are to share in it!

Gajih súr kuḍum, pajih súr lodum tah trowum gayim treh kámih.

Lálah wuzanowum, dudahan chowum tah sowum, gayim sheh kámih.

I took out the ashes from the fire-place, I put them into a basket ,and then threw them away. I have done three works.

I woke up the baby and gave him a little milk, and then I put him to sleep again. I have done six works.

As busy as a hen with one chicken.

Gám chhuh khám; shahr chhuh mánindi bahar.

The village is kachcha (*i.e.*, not the place to get anything); the city is like a river (there everything goes on swimmingly).

Gámas garah karyá wád?

Shall one house give answer to the whole village?

"What can I say? You are all against me."

Gámuk suh tah shahruk hún chhuh barábar.

A village tiger and a city dog are equal.

A stupid man from the city is equal to the great man of the village.

Gáni budán tah yindar katán.
When the prostitute becomes old she spins the wheel.

Gánṭh kawah zánih páz sund shikár ?
How can the kite know the prey of the hawk ?

Gánṭh kyah zánih bachah dod tah hánṭh kyah zánih putrah dod ?
Does the kite know anything of the pain of his prey ? Does the barren woman consider the child's pain ?

Cited by the beggar as he turns away unhelped from the rich man's door.

Gánṭh nah kunih tah gánṭah aul ?
No kite anywhere, but the kite's nest ready.

Building a stable before the horse is purchased.

Ganz tsul gámah tah ganz phakah nishih mukale.
The tanner has run away from the village and the people are relieved of the tanner's smell.

Rid of the offending party.

Gar gunḍah.
The fat man of the house.

A lazy master of a house.

Gar manz Gangá.
Ganges in the house.

Hindustání.—*Ahl i kismat apne ghar baithe hí daulat páenge*
Yár ghar á jáegá to dhundhne kyun jáenge.
Gurú Nának to Angad.

Gar na báshad bĕbih andar nárah pháh, ján i shírín míbaráyad khwáh ma khwáh.
If there is not the warmth of fire in one's bosom, the precious life will certainly come out.

"Warmth of fire in one's bosom" refers to the kángar.

Gar pĕṭh zámuthur bar pĕṭh hún.
A son-in-law who lives always in his father-in-law's house, is like a dog at the door.

Hindús are so very fond of their children, male or female, that they cannot bear the idea of a separation, and so the sons-in-law are invited to come and dwell under the same roof. Nearly every wealthy family has its *quantum* of sons-in-law, who generally spend their time in eating, drinking, smoking and sleeping at the expense of their fathers-in-law. In this way they contract the most demoralizing habits, and are a scorn and reproach to all right-minded people. Such are called Gar Zámuthur. In Bengal they are called Ghar Jamá'í.—*Vide* "Hindus as they are," p. 73, f. n.

Garah gav tsakah-náv, dakah dakah pakanáv.

The house is like a manure-boat, (only) by constant shoving and pushing (does) it makes progress.

Tsakah-náv is a large barge generally stuffed full of vegetable manure gathered from the Ḍal lake. These boats are so loaded that only an inch or so appears above water; consequently a little stoppage might cause it to sink. They are towed and pushed along to their destination, and are at once unloaded on their arrival.

Garah kur anih tah kánih, garah rov múnmúnih.

A blind woman and a one-eyed woman tried to keep house together, but they disagreed and brought the place to ruin.

Disagreement means ruination.

Garah wandai garah sásá garah ñerahah nah zah.

O home, I offer you a thousand houses, and I will never go out from you.

No place like home.

Garazmand chhuh dewánah.

A selfish man is mad (so grasping is he, and so incessant in his solicitations).

Garí nun tíl.

Salt and oil in the house.

Cited against a man, who makes money on purchases for his father, but does not take up any special work for himself.

Gári gojih.

(Like) the kernel of a water-chestnut (singhárah).

A Kashmírí curse, meaning "May your eyes start out of your head through trouble and sorrow." Also when a person is not sharp at finding any thing, another person will sometimes say, "You, gári gojíh, can't you see it?"

Garí warih dagán.

Pounding spices in the house.

A coward.

"Pounding spices in the house" here means living indoors and afraid to stir out.

Garíbas tsáye tsúr tah mandinĕn tám kurhas jashnah.

A thief entered the house of a poor man, and they feasted themselves until mid-day.

It is of no use for a poor man to complain. The police only vex him more, until he is obliged to bribe them to keep quiet.

Again these words are often quoted when more than the invited people are present at the wedding-feast. Hearing the sound of music passers-by go in, are lost in the company, and eat, drink, and steal to their hearts' content till mid-day.

Garih chhukah, kih nah yazmanah handih?

Are you in your own house, or in your disciple's house?

Bráhmans and other holy men do not eat much in their own houses, but save the money. When they visit their disciples' houses, they eat their fill.

Cited to a child who is going beyond bounds at the dinner.

Garih diyin tah zámin mah atsin.

Better to give something from the house than to become surety for anyone.

"He that is surety for a stranger shall smart for it."—Prov. xi. 15.

Garih gaṭah tah mashídih tsong.

Darkness in the home, but a light in the mosque.

Miserable and miserly at home, but pleasant enough and liberal abroad. A frequent answer to the Mullahs, when they become importunate in their demands for contributions towards the support of the mosques.

Garih manz chhuh garyál; dam ganímat ast.

The bell-striker at the hour; breath is as spoil.

A man, Ázún Khán by name, became mad from much reading, and went about the city shouting these words. He was of very good family, but turned a fakír. All his money, excepting a small portion which was given to his wife and children, was distributed amongst the poor. The wife married again, and the children were taught a trade, and are now earning a respectable livelihood.

Garih nah bazin tah naubat wazin!

No oil in the house and the band plays!

A man who is obliged to stint his stomach in order to cover his back or feed his horse, or pay his extra servants. A hard struggle to keep up appearances.

Garih tih hák parih tih hák ná-hakkah zúah garí drák.

Vegetables in my own house and vegetables in another's house.

O life, you should not have come forth from your house.

Vegetables here means trouble. Cited when one has trouble in the house and goes to another person's house and there gets more trouble.

Garih yĕlih tsalih, tai Sháh sapanih rází; adah há málih chhuí Tázi Baṭ kún.

When a man escapes from the house, and the king is happy, then, O Father, is Tazi Baṭ's arrow.

After adversity comes prosperity.

A man overtaken by misfortune ran away from his house. To support himself he hunted with his bow and arrow. The king of the country had promised that the man who could shoot an arrow through his ring at a given distance should receive a robe of honour and other rewards. The ring was hanged up in a certain place and a man always stationed by it to see fair play and report to the king. The poor man was shooting birds one day near to the place where this ring was suspended, when by the will of God the arrow was whirled by the wind straight through the ring. The man in charge immediately sent word to the Court, and the poor hunter was rewarded, and able henceforth to lay down his bow and arrow and live in ease.

Gúṭah hún tah shúṭah hún tah puji hún, yim trĕh húni chhih hihí.

The landing-place dog, the river-bed dog, and the butcher's dog, these three dogs are alike (a wretched lot).

Gatsh Prunts tatih chhai zúlah.

Go to Púnch and there get ague.

I wish you were at Jericho.

Púnch is about five marches from Srínagar in a north-west direction. It is a compact town and has a good bázár. Rájá Motí Singh resides there, and holds a considerable tract of country in fief under his cousin, the present Mahárájah of Kashmír and Jammún.

Gáv diyih nah tah wutsh chĕyih nah.

The cow will not give (milk) and the calf will not drink it.

Step-mother and step-children, who generally hate one another.

Also cited concerning an old servant and his master. Both have got to dislike one another, but each does not like to give the other "notice to leave."

Gáwih chhuh wonamut haṭih kini ditam tah laṭih kini dimai.

The cow said, "Give to me by the throat (*i.e.*, feed me) and I will give to you by the tail" (*i.e.*, I will supply you with milk, ghí, and butter).

Feed a servant or an animal well and they will serve you well.

Gĕr chhuí ámut.

You have got very earnest (about this work).

There was a lazy woman, who never cared to spin or to do any work. Her husband spoke to her about her laziness. She replied, "Ah! let me alone now. The time is coming, when I shall be so fond of work, that I shall get through any quantity in no time."

One day they were going to Tulamula, and as they were starting, the wife said to her husband, "I should like to do some work. Get me a spinning wheel." The husband said the above words, but he could not at that time obtain a wheel.

Gĕwahah tah gyav khyom brárih.

I would sing but the cat has eaten my ghí.

Circumstances are so that a person is afraid to speak or to act for himself.

Hindustání.—*Kahun, má mar jáe;*
Na kahun, báp billí kháe.

Gil tih chhĕh dánye káṅchhán.

Gil also wants some rice.

Envy.

Gil is a Muhammedan woman's name.

Gov már bozan sárí tah dándah már nah bozán kaṅh.

Strike a cow and everyone will exclaim, ("what a shame to strike the cow which supplies you with milk!"); but strike an ox and nobody will say a word.

The cow here represents the great man and the ox the poor man.

Gov záv wutsh suí mĕh gutsh.

The cow bore a calf, which I should have (and *will* have).

Where there's a will there's a way.

Gríst sund hakhur hyuh.

Like a farmer's young untrained ox.

A useless fellow.

Grustu agar auliyá báshad láik-i-búriyá nest.

If the ploughman becomes a "lord," yet he is not then even fit to sit upon the matting.

A Persian proverb with only the first word altered. Persians say *Dihkán agar, &c.*

Grustú zih hustú.

The husbandman is like an elephant (*i.e.*, a strong, big clumsy fellow).

Guḍah dráv Jum Baṭ ḍum ḍumah hĕt ; patah dráyas Roshan bĕnih poshih málah hĕt.

First came out Jum Baṭ, bringing a drum; afterwards came out Roshan, his sister, bearing a garland of flowers.

From horses to asses.

Jum Baṭ was formerly a well-to-do officer in H. H. the Maháràjah's Court. He became very poor and was obliged to do the mean work of a town-crier. His sister, too, equally humbled herself by going about the city selling garlands of flowers.

Guḍah lorih-han tah patah korih-han.

First (he asks for) your walking-stick and then (he wants) your pet daughter.

Hindustání.—*Unglí pakaṛte pahunchá pakaṛná. Boṭí deke bakrá lená.*

Guḍanich kulai chhai híi tai zíi ;
Duyim kulai chhai garih garih dríi ;
Trĕyim kulai tsatán sumah tah kadal ;
Tsúrimih badal lagih nah kaṅh.

A first wife is as jasmine and income ;
The second wife swears hourly by your name ;
The third wife cuts bridges, great and small ;
The fourth wife—there is no one like her for all manner of wickedness ; she is a hopeless character.

"Swears hourly by your name" means she makes great profession of love for you. Kashmírís frequently swear by the person or thing they most love.

"Cuts bridges" is said of mischievous and extravagant wives, who altogether hinder their husbands from crossing over to the other side, where prosperity and peace are to be had. The reader will please remember that Kashmír is a valley full of rivers and streams.

Guḍanich kulai chhai rani matsuí ;
Duyim kulai chhai totih keṅtshah ;
Trĕyim kulai chhai tálih makatsuí ;

The first wife goes mad over her husband ;
The second wife—there's something good in her ;
The third wife is as an axe to the head.

Guḍanuk sodá gatshih nah ráwarun.

One must not lose the first offer (lit., trade).

Kashmírí traders, like those of some European countries, are very superstitious about refusing the offer of the day's first customer. They will frequently rather lose than allow him to depart without purchasing something.

Guh graṭṭah-bal.
Manure by the mill-house.
Cited against a man who after promotion is reduced to his former rank.

Guh zánih tah bílchih.
The dung will know and the spade (but I am not the person to have to do with, or to know anything about, such a mean affair as that).

Guhali gupan nún khĕwán, garih gupan mún lĕwán.
Jungle cattle eat salt while the home cattle lick the wall.
Charity should begin at home.

Gur baḍih son, dánah khĕyih chon.
Our horse will grow big and will eat your grain.
Cited when a wife's relations keep her rather a long time; also when a friend borrows a horse or anything, and is not particular as to when he returns it.

Gur chhuh nah khĕwán pĕts; yĕlih chhas buchih lagán, tĕlih chhuh khĕwán mits.
The horse does not eat the bulrush, but at the time of hunger he will eat earth.

Gúr dapiyá, kih myon dud chhuh tsok?
Will the milkman say that his milk is sour?
Hindustání.—*Apní chháchh ko khaṭṭá koí nahin kahtá.*

Gur garih tah nakhásas mul paritsán.
Leaving the horse in the house and going to ask the nakhás its price.
Wishing to sell the goods without first showing them.
Nakhás is the officer appointed over the sale of all horses in the valley. No person can sell a horse without first arranging the price with this officer and paying him one áná in the rupee.

Gur ján sum ján, yál ján, chál ján, kadam nai.
The horse is a good one; the hoofs are strong, the mane is nice, the whole appearance is beautiful; *but* the step is bad.
A man with one glaring fault.

Gúr kawah zánih kur haharit?
How will the milkman know how to marry his daughter? (*i.e.*, outside his own class of people).
"Like blood, like goods, and like ages,
Make the happiest marriages."

Gur kyah pakihĕh sirá chhuh pakán.

The horse does not walk, but the secret walks.

People generaly take a man for what he seems to be, and not for what he is. It is not the real man they see walking but his disguise, his secret.

> "For man is practised in disguise,
> He cheats the most discerning eyes."
> Gay's Fables.

Gur zanánah, tah shamsher, yim trĕnawai chhih be-wafá.

A horse, a wife, and a sword, these three are unfaithful.

Persian.—*Asp o zam o shamsher wafádar na báshad.*

Gúras gáv bali toshán baṭas gáv khĕt roshán.

The cow-herd's cow, whether she gets a good meal or not, is a comfort to him ; but the Paṇḍit's cow eats and is angry.

What is the good of keeping a beast for mere show ?

Guri chhuh dupamut "Khasawunis khárat, wasawunis wáltam."

The horse said "I will help you to mount the ascent, but you lead me down the hill."

Gúri garih chhuá wuts̱h ráwán ?

Does any harm happen to the calf in the milkman's house ?

A servant of a good master; a son of a good and clever father.

Gúri garih wats̱hi kur báhih wahari dán.

The calf lowed after twelve years in the milkman's house.

A little child sometimes speaks after a long silence. After many years of barrenness sometimes a woman gives birth to a child.

Gúri wohawah chhuá wuts̱h marán ?

Does the calf die by reason of the milkman's curse ?

A child's reply to a parent's hard threats and words.

Gurih khasit tih bĕṭhchod tah gurih wasit tih bĕṭhchod.

Whether on horseback or on foot he is a scamp.

Do what you will somebody will speak evil of you. You cannot please everyone.

The Kashmírís have a story similar to our school-book story of the "Old man and his donkey."

A very wicked Kashmírí owned a pony. One day he was riding upon the animal, while his daughter was walking on in front. The passers-by on seeing this cried out, "What a shame ! What a lazy, cruel man !" The man felt a little ashamed of his thoughtlessness, and calling his daughter took her up with him on the pony. Thus they proceeded for some distance, when other people met them and exclaimed, "Rather a big load for a small pony"; whereupon the man and his daughter both got off and led the pony along by a string for the rest of the journey.

Gurih sawári tah khárachih atah-gat.

To the mare riding, to the foal trouble.

Going to work a man calls after his mate to come along as well. The latter replies as above, "What is the good? I should only be like the foal running after its mother."

Atah-gat corresponds to the Hindustání ána-jána. Here it means trouble, because people run about hither and thither in time of distress.

Atah-gat is also the name of that money which the Hindú father places in the hand of his married daughter when she goes on a visit to her husband's family. The "going and coming" pay.

Gurin lágik náe tah khar gaí padar dárit.

The horses got shod, and the donkeys put out their hoofs (for shoeing).

Seek not what is beyond your position.

Gurin nah poshán, lĕz phalin chob.

He can't manage the horses, and so he beats their manure.

Too weak to trouble the "big guns," and therefore he oppresses the poor.

Gurmut pánsah tah runmut myunḍ.

Money made up (into gold, silver, and copper ornaments) is like a cooked mouthful (*i.e.*, they are ready for sale in case of need, and until then they are useful ornaments).

Gursas mál tah tsuḍ hĕt patah kani.

Wishing to drink the butter-milk, but hiding the vessel behind him.

To eat little when dining out, and to refuse more, yet all the while longing to eat a big dinner.

Gyav khĕwán tah gardanih kun athah lágán.

Eating ghí and then feeling his neck (to see if he was getting fat, the fool,—as if results would happen so quickly as that)!

H

Há málih, Há máji!

O father, O mother!

Among other occasions used on the following:—A man wants a loan, and the person whom he asks for this loan, replies: "I would lend it you willingly, but '*Há malih, Há máji,*' when shall I get it again!

Habbah sháh toṅi tĕlih nah tah wuni.

O Habbah Sháh, tumour *wálá*, then, not now, was the time (for removing it)!

Opportunity passed.

Habbah Sháh had a big ugly tumour on his forehead which might easily have been removed at one time, but he allowed the opportunity to go by.

Hachivis guris zachuv zín.
Tas kus khasih? Mahí-Dín.

A saddle of rags for a wooden horse. Who will mount him? Mahidín.

Let a fool have to do with foolish things.

Mahidín was a great student. Report says that he was well-up in all languages and religions; at all events, he became mad and his name a proverb. His son now wanders about the city in a mad condition, and everybody does him honour.

Hájih Bábah machámah, khĕnah tsariyá?

O Hájí Bába, give me some dinner? Is it any trouble for you to eat?

This is replied sometimes, when any person wants a special favour from another person; or when a servant applies for increased wages, &c.

Machámah is a company dish consisting of rice, vegetables, raisins, colouring matter, and sugar.

Hákah tsúras galih chapát.

A cabbage to a thief is as a slap on the cheek.

Little punishment for a small theft.

Hakímas tah hákimas nishih rachhtam Khudáyo.

O God, deliver me from the doctor and the ruler.

Both Muhammedans and Hindús are frequently heard praying this prayer as they squat by the ghát in the morning, washing themselves.

Hakk nah páthih tah inám !

I've not got my rights, and yet he gives me a reward !

When Kashmírí people give a little more than they intended, or think right, for any article, they are apt to tell the shopkeeper that the overplus is largesse. The seller would then reply as above.

Hál gatshuni chhĕh pál gatshuni.

To form habits is to make pain (*e.g.*, a habit of drinking, smoking, gambling, and extravagant dining, &c.)

Halálas hisáb tah harámas azáb.

A reward for things legal and punishment for things illegal.

Hálav galan ná tah dánĕs dáh karit ?

The locusts will certainly decrease, but (meanwhile) they are destroying the rice.

Man dies but his influence remains.

Small numbers of locusts visit Kashmír almost every year. Sometimes a great army of them invades the valley and does terrible injury to the crops.

Muhammedans eat the locust. They dry them in the sun, then grind them into powder, and afterwards make cakes of them. They are regarded as a great delicacy.

Bústán of Sá'dí.—*Na dar koh sabzí na dar bágh shakh ;*
Malakh bústán khurd o mardum malakh.

Halĕn búnan wukari thán ; hihĕn hihí samakhán.

Dented covers for dented saucepans ; and like men for like men.

Hammám karih rúzah tah táwis garib ;
Bukhári karih garib tah táwis rúzah.

A wealthy man can build a bath-room and a poor man can make it hot ;
A poor man can build a fire-place and a rich man can burn it.

The whole world is one great family, each member of which, be he ever so lowly, is indispensable for the help and comfort of the other.

Hamsáyah wandiyav, garo.

O house, I will make an offering to you of my neighbour.

To try and pass one's misfortune on to the head of another.

In time of sickness and trouble people are accustomed to make offerings unto the house. Sometimes a ram is slain, and the priests are assembled and fed, and special worship is paid to the gods. Instead of offering anything at his own expense the man in the proverb wished to offer something belonging to his neighbour.

Haná truk maná ranih, kachal truk karih nah kĕnh.

A person with a little tact will cook a maund (*i.e.*, will do something), but a dull, ignorant person will do nothing.

Hangah nah tah rangah nah zangah zíchh hashye.
Dod nah tah dag nah. Kawah yiyĕm aushye?
I am independent of you, O long-legged mother-in-law.
There is no pain or agony to me. Why should I weep?

No love is lost between mothers-in-law and their children-in-law.

Hánṭh gayih baras gánṭ dit.

The barren woman fastened her door and went.

No heir to look after the property.

Hánṭih záyáv gubar shituli pajih dáryáv ás.

A barren woman bore a son, and the small-pox swallowed him up.

A man who suffers much pain rather than give up a work, but after all dies in the midst of carrying it out.

Hánzas gubeyih lulih, ditshan dárit kulih.

It became a weight upon the boatman's bosom, and so he threw it into the river.

Cited when a man of some family marries his son to a daughter of lower birth, or does anything else equally ignoble, because he cannot afford to do the right thing.

Hánzas yĕlih chhuh daryávas andar wáv yiwán, puth namah chhuh bronṭh namah karán tah bronṭh namah chhuh puth namah karán.

When a storm arises on the river the boatman rushes from the fore-part to the hinder-part of the boat, and from the hinder-part to the fore-part.

A man in trouble knows not what to do.

Hapi-háyun.

Scarcity (lit., an outcry is raised).

While these words are being written there is *Hapi háyun* in the city of Srínagar concerning rice. For some reason or other rice is scarce and dear.

Hápat ashud hyuh gomut suh chíz náyáb.

Like the bear's ashud that thing has become scarce.

It is said that when the bear gets this grass, he devours it most greedily, and becomes unconscious for six months afterwards.

Hápat yáraz.

A bear's friendship.

A stupid friend.

A bear formed friendship with a man who was passing through his jungle. For some time he brought his friend large quantities of honey. One day the man fell asleep after eating the honey. While asleep a bee attracted by the sweetness alighted upon his mouth. The friendly bear seeing this thought that he would save the man from the pain of a sting, and so he went and fetched a great piece of rock and aimed it with all his might at the place where the bee was. The stone frightened away the bee, but killed the man! Cf. "Folk-tales from the Upper Punjáb," by the Rev. C. Swynnerton, *Journal Asiatic Society*, Bengal, Vol. LII., Part I., 1883; also the story of the calf who got its head into the pot in "Notes on some Sinhalese Proverbs and stories in the Atíta-Vákya-Dípaniya," by A. M. Senánáyaka; also the story given in "Dasent's Norwegian Folklore," where a goody is discovered by a friend beating her husband's head with a mallet in order to make a hole for the head in a shirt, which had been previously thrown over it; also the Makasa Jataka, where a son broke his father's bald head to kill a mosquito, which had settled upon it.

Hápatas ai aut ásiheh tah suh kariheh ná tsuchih?

If the bear had flour would he not make bread?

Cited against a poor man with extravagant ideas.

The bear may be sometimes seen smacking his paws together as natives do when they are making chapátís.

Har kar, har kar, har wizih sur kar.

Fight by all means, but at the time of fighting be careful.

Hár khĕwán gus tah kár mári mári.

The starling eats dung and then shakes his head in a pleased sort of way.

A shameless man.

Har rangah musíbat chhuí ak diwánagí.

Every kind of misfortune is a madness.

Hárah tsúr.

A cowrie thief.

A mean fellow, a stint.

Harámuk mál harámachih watih; nah khĕyih pánas tah nah nĕyih athih.

Ill-gotten wealth goes in the way of wickedness; the getter neither eats it himself, nor takes it with him.

Persian.—*Mál i harám bud bajá e harám raft.*

Hardah gurus mĕtras, sontah gurus shĕtras.

Autumn butter-milk for the friend, and spring butter-milk for the enemy.

The autumn grass is much better than the spring grass; consequently the milk is better in the autumn.

Harafas gawáh tah mĕndis sharík.

A witness against (my) words but a sharer in (my) mouthful.

The man who is always "loafing" about like the mahalladár or spies, appointed over every village and district in Kashmír.

Hárih ai wunṭh kunun ásih tah hár nái ásih tah kĕrizis kyah?

If an elephant is to be sold for a cowrie, and there is not a cowrie, what can be done?

Nothing can be done without money.

Hárih aní bázarah kanit tsĕh chhuí syud bozanah yiwán.

You think him a righteous man, but he would sell you for a cowrie in the market.

Hárih gov náv kyah?

What is the name to a Hár? Hár, of course.

"What's a table? A table, you stupid!"

Hár is a black and white cow. People give a special name to every cow except this one.

Harih, harih samih koh.

Gradually from chippings a mountain is made.

Many a little makes a muckle.

Hárih nah jái; nábad phalis shái!

No place for a cowrie, but place for sweetmeats!

"The doctor orders this and that, but how can I afford it?"

Hárih sodá tah bázaras khalbali.

He has only a cowrie to spend, but he rushes about and makes a stir all over the bázár.

Hárih tah totas wanun.

(May as well) speak to a starling (or a parrot).

An inattentive person.

Hári ṭang tah zulahnai; muhuri tsont tah zulit.

If the pear cost only a cowrie it should not be peeled; but if the apple cost a muhur it should be peeled.

Natives of Kashmír, from H. H. the Maharájah down to the humblest subject, seldom ever skin a pear, but always skin an apple. Apple-skin, they say, is not easily digested.

Harkat kar tah barkat karí.

Be up and doing and God will bless you.

Persian.—*Himmat i mardán madad i Khudá.*

Haramukhuk Gosáni.

The jogí of Haramukh.

Haramukh is a mountain 16,905 feet high, to the north of Kashmír.

A person with a bad memory.

There was a Jogí who tried to mount Haramukh. Every day for twelve years he climbed to a certain height, and every night for the same space of time he descended as far as he had ascended. How it came to pass he could not tell. Perhaps he was a sonnambulist. At any rate every morning he found himself reposing quietly in the very spot, whence he had started on the previous morning.

One day, the last day of these twelve years, a shepherd was seen by this Jogí coming down from the mountain. The Jogí asked him whether he had reached the summit and what he had seen there. The shepherd replied that he had reached the top of the mountain, and had seen a sweeper with his wife, and they were milking a bitch with a human head, and they had asked him to drink that milk, which he had refused to do, because he thought that it was unholy; and then they threw some ṭiká upon his face, which, perhaps, was there now The Jogí knew that that the supposed sweeper and his wife were none other than the god and goddess Shiva and Párvati, and so he went close up to the shepherd's face and licked off the ṭiká. He was then caught up into the clouds much to the astonishment of the poor shepherd.

The reason the shepherd was able to climb the mountain and the Jogí unable, was, that the shepherd went up heedlessly and totally ignorant of the great deities who resided on the summit. ("An ignorant man fears nothing.")

A boy with a dull memory works hard all the evening, and the next morning, when he comes to appear before the schoolmaster, he finds that he knows nothing, and is like the Jogí, as he was, and where he was, before.

Háruch gugaj tah Láruch gunas chhih barábar.

A June turnip and a Lár serpent are equal.

A native would not eat a turnip in the month of June on any account.

Gunas (or *af'a*) is a short, thick, round-headed serpent, whose bite is generally fatal. Some say it has a black back and yellow belly; others that it is ash colour. It is met with principally in the district of Lár. The native method of treating snake bites is amusing. "When a person is stung on the arm or leg, a ligature is applied between the heart and the wound, which is besmeared with foam. The patient has 'arak and conserve of roses given him to eat, while music is played to cheer him up."

Lár is a parganah of the Kamráz district.

Hasah Matin wasamat.
Hasah the madman's wealth.
A spendthrift's money.

Hash tih baḍ tah nosh tih baḍ lĕj duz tah wálih kus ?
The mother-in-law is great, the daughter-in-law is also great ; the pot is burnt, who will take it off the fire ?
Somebody must do the work.

Hash gayih tah noshih kur árám.
Grandmother (on husband's side) died and the daughter-in-law got peace.
These old dames have great authority over the entire household.—*Vide* " Hindús as they are," Chap I., pp. 3, 4.

Hasti dareyi nah wávah tah bujih kaḍ kapas.
The elephants couldn't stand because of the wind, but the old woman went out and gathered the cotton from the plant.
A poor, insignificant man can often accomplish what kings and others in authority have utterly failed to do.

Hasti yaḍ gásah gyaḍ.
A handful of grass for an elephant's stomach.
A mere drop in a bucket.

Hastis yaḍ phaṭ tah bangih dĕlih wáṭh !
The elephant's stomach burst open and they mended it with hemp-skin !
Imperfect repairs.

Hatah dedi ruhana man ḍái, tah kheni sum nah ak kuj !
"O, mother, two and half maunds of onions will be given to you ;" and she has not got a plant to eat !
Promise of help, but no means of fulfilling it.

Hatah juwah puṅtshú mĕh tih hĕtah manz.
Hie, sir, here's a puṅtshú. Take me into your company.
A man who forces himself upon people who do not particularly care for him.
Puṅtshú is the twentieth part of an áná, a small coin, not in use now, but to be obtained in the bázár.

Hatah múr hakím.
The doctor killed a hundred men.
A doctor of some experience.

Haṭih gav zih maṭih gav.

A promise is a charge to keep.

Workmen who have promised to do some work, and on that promise have received some rupees in advance, often repeat these words as they walk away from the person's house.

Haṭis khash tah hangani míthi.

Kisses for the chin and an axe for the throat.

A traitor.

Háziras bog náziras chob.

A share of the dinner to each of those present, but a beating for the cook.

Sic vos non vobis.

Hĕh pañtsh, dih pañtsh barábar.

To take five or give five—all the same to him.

Poco curante.

Hĕllah karo, Hájo, pallah, chhuí dúr.

Be encouraged, O pilgrim, though your destination is far off.

Encouraging a man in a difficult work.

Hĕmáyat ásin tah háwuni mah pĕyin káñsih.

Patronize and be patronized, but do not tell any one, lest there should be harm (to the person patronized).

Keep your own counsel.

Hĕmí kĕmi.

Like an insect to the pod (so is sin to a man).

Sin brings its own punishment with it.

Hĕnah ás tah mĕh nah rúh.

Involved in difficulty, or taken prisoner, but for no fault of mine.

The guiltless punished for the guilty.

Heng ás nah tah watsharuí chhĕh!

She has not got horns yet, she is only a calf!

Cited concerning a woman who bears her first child late in life. A beardless man. An elderly person without a grey hair.

Herat áyih wanduní kah nah tah nah kañh.

When Herat came eleven days of winter, or nothing, remained.

Herat (*Shiva-rátri*) is a Hindú festival held on the fourteenth of the dark fortnight in the month Phágun (Feb.—March).

Herih wutshas anigaṭih, but chhulum baritih naṭih yĕt garas yíi waṭih.

I came down stairs in the dark and washed my face in a waterpot filled with water. This must be done in this house.

If you go to Rome you must do as Rome does.

Hisáb hárih tah bakhshish kharwárih.

To take account of every cowrie, but to give away money by the maund (80 lbs).

Careful but generous.

Honav ratshuí íd.

A festival without dogs.

Pleasure without difficulty.

Hond marán kih nah kaṭ, Lalih nalawaṭ tsalih nah zah.

Whether they killed a big sheep or a small one, it was all the same, Lal always had the nalawaṭ in her plate.

Hardly treated.

Lal Dĕd was very badly treated by her mother-in-law. One of the ways in which this woman delighted to tease her was by sending a stone called nalawaṭ in her dinner. Cf. "Panjab Notes and Queries," No 20. Note 743.

Honih chon buth nah-tah chúnis kháwandah sund tih ná?

You have not a face like a bitch? Then your husband has (*i.e.*, all the lot of you are bad).

Honih khĕyih jĕts sán, búni khĕyih panah sán.

He will eat a bitch, fur and all; and he will eat a chinár tree with the leaves.

Quærenda pecunia primum, virtus post nummos.

Honin nĕtán tah monin tachán.

Fleecing dogs and scratching walls.

Ploughing the seashore.

Hor káv.

A black and white crow.

A marked man.

Hud gav kunuí myund.

Just a morsel without vegetables left.

Natives are accustomed to eat their dinner in the following manner. First they take a mouthful of rice, and then a little vegetable, and so on regularly, until the meal is over. Should there happen to be a little rice left, but no vegetable, &c., left to eat with it, that little rice is not eaten.

Hud is dry and poor food; without vegetables, &c.

Cited concerning one who is experiencing a little trouble in his old age. All the previous time he has been very prosperous.

Hukm-i-hákim o hakím chhuh marg-i-mafúját.

The ruler's and the doctor's orders are (like) sudden death (*i.e.*, they both must be obeyed quickly).

Hul gaṇḍit batich natsán.

Tightening her girdle the duck dances.

Cited against a woman, who wishing to quarrel, goes and unites in a "row" going on close by. Kashmírí women have terrible tongues and most shrill voices. At the time of quarrelling they screech, shout, and dance to any extent.

Hul gaṇḍit har karán.

To tighten one's girdle and fight.

He means business.

Hul kyah karih sĕdis?

What shall a crooked man do to a straight man?

The strength of a good character.

Hún ásin tah kúns mah ásin.

May you be a dog, but not a younger son.

Younger sons are generally the father's butt, the mother's scorn, and the brother's fag.

Persian.—*Sag básh khúrd ma básh.*

Hún kus nĕtih tah kúr kus mangit nĕyih?

Who will fleece a dog and who will take and marry a girl?

A good marriage is not such an easy matter.

Hún nah tah kutsurui.

Not a dog but a pup only.

A childish-looking or childish-mannered person.

Húni húni har karán tah shálah sinzih ṭungih wizih kuní.

Dogs fight among themselves, but at the time of the jackal's cry they are united.

Enemies are united against one common foe.

Húni luṭ ai thawizĕn kandílas andar, tatih tih nerih húni luṭui

If a dog's tail be set in a kandíl, there even it will remain a dog's tail.

Place does not alter race.

Kandíl (Kandíl, Arabic,) is the painted wooden or silver box about $1\frac{1}{2}$ ft. long and $\frac{3}{4}$ ft. in circumference in which the heron's feathers are fixed, and from which they depend. As many as three hundred feathers are sometimes worn, and as much as one rupee has been given for a feather. Rich people keep them hanging from the ceilings of their rooms from fear of the cat. Poor people can only afford to hire them for weddings, &c.? There are three or four heronries in Kashmír.

Húni mázas wátal wázah.

The sweeper is the cook for dog's flesh.

A wicked, dirty man for bad, dirty deeds.

The *Wátul* has been called the gipsy of Kashmír, and indeed these people have all the manner and appearance of gipsies. They live separate from others, and by reason of their indiscriminate use of food are despised by all others, both Muhammedans and Hindús. It is a moot point whether the gipsies are not the descendants of Kashmírís, who were obliged to leave the valley at one time and another on account of persecutions and famines.

Húni neyih bastah khalari.

The dog took away the piece of leather (while the men were quarrelling over it).

The dog represents the lawyer.

Húni sund hyuh sabúr, achh púr, balái dúr, buthis núr.

May you have patience like a dog, and may your eye keep undimmed. Let misfortune remain at a distance from you, and let cheerfulness be always upon your face.

A Kashmírí's blessing.

One may often see both Hindú and Muhammedan women spreading forth their hands in a supplicating manner and offering this prayer as they squat by the river-side in the early morning.

Húni worán tah kúrawánah pakán.

The dogs bark but the caravan goes on.

A dog may as well bark at the moon.

Húni-wushkah yúr nah wawán túr bowán.

Tares spring up where we do not sow them.

Húni-wushkah literally is dog-barley.

Hunih mashídih hund jinn.

The ogre of the deserted mosque.

A wretched, selfish fellow.

Húnis athih auṭ mánḍanáwun.
To knead flour by a dog's paw.
Ne sutor ultra crepidam.
Shírín o Khusrau.—*Ki az búzína najjárí na ayad.*

Húnis chob dinah nerih gasuí yot.
You only get manure from hitting a dog.
What is the good of a policeman beating a poor man? He will not get a bribe.

Húnis mukhtahár.
A string of pearls to a dog.
Casting pearls before swine.

Húnis pyav "Sábirah" náv, suí, há málih, zánih yas wuthit áv.
The name "Patient" has been given to the dog, but he knows, O father, whom he has come to bite.
A generally good man, who now and again breaks out into a fit of passion, &c.

Hurih hĕn wurih kyah tah dánas?
What! will he throw a handful of grass into the fire-place?
Like a handful of grass in a fireplace is a little money in a big concern—soon swallowed up.

Hurdus tah burdus!
A beating and smiting!
Such a hullabaloo!

Husih wun tah musih áyih patsh.
A woman said something and she believed it.
Credulity.

Hyut kami tah dyut kami.
Who took and who gave? (God).
"The Lord gave and the Lord hath taken away."—Job i. 21.

I. J.

Jahámúk tamok.

Tobacco from Jahám (*i.e.*, splendid tobacco).

Jahám tobacco is said to be the finest in the valley.

Jahán chhuh ashkun mazhar.

The world is a theatre of love.

Jamáat gayih karámat.

A company of men is as good as a miracle (*i.e.*, difficult matters are easily accomplished by their mutual and united help).

Ján kus chhuh ? Panun pán.

Who is good ? I myself.

Suum cuique pulcrum.

Jánah, ditah dastár pánah roz tah wuḍah nun.

Beloved, give me your turban and you remain bareheaded.

Cited when a man asks for something which is indispensable to you.

Jandanui chhĕh zuwah ásán.

Lice is in the beggar's ragged cloak.

A quick reply given to the importunate mendicant.

Lice here stands for money. Hence "You've got as much money as there are lice and dirt sticking to your garment."

Jandas pári, yath karizih wandas ráhat.

Blessed be the ragged garment, which keeps me warm during the winter.

The poor man's retort when twitted concerning the antiquity of his garment.

Jangas manz chhai ṭhíl tih tah gúli tih.

You get purse and bullet, too, from fighting ; (therefore think over the matter before you enter the lists against an adversary.)

A man had an ass which he used for carrying loads by day, and was leaving out in the field at night to pick up what grass the poor animal could find there. The ass rebelled against such treatment, and one night ran away to the king's stable, and was there fed most liberally along with the royal horses. He became very fat and strong and was very happy ; but, alas ! a war commenced, and when the enemy had arrived near to the king's capital, all the royal horses, and the solitary ass, were turned out and sent forward to the fight. There the ass saw one horse after another shot down, and becoming afraid he escaped back again to his former master. "Here is the gûli as well as the ṭhil," said he, as he galloped back. "Better to have little and sure."

"Jaṭ paṭ" zih Khudái raṭ.

"Quickly" you must lay hold upon God.

There is but a step between you and death, or some terrible misfortune, or some great event. You must act at once. Then throw yourself upon God to prosper you.

Nec Deus intersit, nisi dignus vindice nodus.

Jáyih chhuko zih sháyih chhuko.

You are safe in your own place.

Landed and house property are sure investments.

Jawánas nah rozgár; lukuṭis máj marani; tah buḍis áshani marani. Yim trĕnawai kathah chhĕh sakht musíbat.

A young man without work; a mother dying and leaving a baby; the wife of on old man dying. These three are terrible misfortunes.

'Id gáh wasit sun kyah ranav? Watih karav maslahat katih karav dán?

Yĕndaras bihit gúṭah panun háwai, thusih pan khárai ajih dusih tán.

Daharih pántsh gaz paṭ páwah náwai; háwai garah karuṇ kĕhŏ gav.

Sulih wulih gov pántsh zah tih nov cháwai; umrih tháwai gursah tamanná.

Katih pĕṭh watih pĕṭh búnah phuṭaráwi; háwai garah karun kĕho gav.

Sĕmit khĕt chĕt pingah thoh tháwai; háwai garah karun keho gav.

Lĕj pashpáwai máj mashráwai; háwai garah karun kĕho gav.

Going to 'Id gah what shall we cook? Let us take counsel on the road, where we shall make the fire-place.

Sitting at my wheel I will show you my wisdom. I will stretch the bad cotton to half the height of the wall.

I will get a five-yard thán for you out of six pounds of wool; I'll show you the manner of my house.

I will never get the milk at early morning from five cows; but I will keep you all your life waiting for milk.

At a word upon the road I will break the pot; I'll show you the manner of my house.
I will eat and drink with my friends, but keep the millet-seed and straw for you. I'll show you the manner of my house.
I will give you the strainings of the pot; and you will forget your mother. I'll show you the manner of my house.

A lazy, ill-tempered woman.

The author of these words is unknown, but everybody knows them and quotes them, in whole or in part, and sometimes in song, against that woman, through whose bad temper, indiscretion, or extravagance, the husband has been brought to ruin.

'Id gáh, 'Id., Arab., (the place of sacrifice), is a beautiful park-like plain lying just outside the right of Srínagar. At its northern end there is a fine old wooden mosque overshadowed by some lofty chinár trees. The mosque is called the 'Alí Masjid, and was built in the time of Sultán Husain Bádsháh by Khwája Hasti, Sonar, about 1471 A. D. No Muhammedan observes the fast of the Ramazán with greater strictness than the Kashmírí.

Thán is a piece of cloth. A five-yard thán would be an extremely small one; and six pounds of wool, if properly spun, &c., should make a full thán of ten yards or more.

Illat galih tah ádat galih nah.

The ill may go, but the habit will stick.

Ilm be-amal goyá kih an sindis athas mashal.

Knowledge unused is like a torch in the hand of a blind man.

Persian—*'Ilm i be 'amal zambúr i be-'asal.*

Ilmas gatshih amal ásuni.

Knowledge should be brought into use.

Insán chhuh póshih khutah áwel tah kanih khutah dur.

Man is more fragile than a flower, and yet harder than a stone.

A man's own pain or trouble affects him, but not he tears and pain of another.

Insánah sund kímat chhuí satowuh-shat rupayih.

The price of a man is Rs. 2,700.

Two men get angry with one another and fight. The above saying is generally quoted by the man who is getting the worst of the scrimmage, and wishes to end it.

Two reasons have been told me why this sum especially has been set as the price of a man. One reason is, that in the days of the Mughals Rupees 2,700 was the fine imposed upon every murderer in lieu of his life. Another reason is, that Akbar, like other equally great and envied monarchs, was accustomed to sleep in secret places. Sometimes he would disguise himself as a faqír, or as a shopkeeper and sleep by the roadside or in a shop. One night he wandered a little farther than usual and found himself in a foreign and uncultivated country. Strange to say, his favorite minister, Bír Bal, had also strayed to the same place. They met, and while they were engaged in conversation, an one-eyed man came up to them, and said to the king, "You have taken out my eye, which I think to be worth the sum of Rupees 1,200. Give me this money, or restore to me my other eye." Akbar was nonplussed by the man's sudden appearance and audacious request; but Bír Bal was equal to the occasion, and replied, "Yes, it is quite true. We have your eye; and if you will come to-morrow morning, we will return it to you." The man agreed and left. Bír Bal immediately sent off to the butchers for some sheep's eyes. After some time they arrived, and he had them put each one separately into a little wooden box by itself. In the morning the man came again; and when he arrived he was informed that the king had several eyes by him, and that it was impossible to tell which particular one belonged to this man. Would he kindly allow his other eye to be taken out, so that it might be weighed and measured; in that way they would be able to tell which of the number of eyes belonged to him.

The man was blinded for life, and henceforth gave no more trouble to the king. (So much did the poor man value his sight, that he estimated each eye at Rupees 1,200, and the whole rest of the body at Rupees 300 only.)

Insánas gatshih ásuni khoe.
Poshas gatshih ásuni boe.
Politeness is required in man.
Scent is required in a flower.

"As charity covers a multitude of sins before God, so does politeness before men."—Greville.

Insánas tah insánas chhĕh títs tafáwat,
Yíts khudáyas tah bandas chhĕh.
Between man and man there is as great difference as there is between God and a slave.

There are no two persons alike.

Jumah Mashídih handin nimáz athah.
The Juma Masjid people have given up praying.

While people from the country come in crowds to the great mosque of the city, the people living close to the mosque sit in their shops all through the Friday hoping for trade; and they are not disappointed.

Nimáz athah, lit., prayers from the hand—out of hand—gone.

Izzat chhuh pananis ásas andar.
Honour is inside your mouth.
Take heed to your words.

Izzatich hár tah be-izzatich kháár chhĕh barábar.
A cowrie obtained honourably and a kharwár obtained dishonourably are equal in value.

K

Kahah rĕt sanz búsh.

Like an eleven month's man.

A man who stints himself now, that he may be rich hereafter.

A man hearing that rice was cheap and good, bought as much as he thought would be sufficient for the next year, and stored it away in his house. Kashmírís are constantly storing something or other, so that their houses generally resemble a small godown. Well, it happened, that this man had not correctly reckoned, and that there was only enough for eleven months in store. What was he to do? He had spent all his money, and to borrow he was ashamed. Accordingly he determined to fast for one month, and stupid man like he was, he thought that it would be much better to have the fast now instead of having to look forward to it all through the eleven months. He had not faith in God to supply his wants hereafter. The consequence was that the man and wife and all the family died just before the fast was over, and left eleven months' rice in the house!

Kahan garan kuní táv ; himmat ráv tah wanav kas?

Only one frying-pan for eleven houses ; courage gone ; and to whom shall we speak?

Time of great distress.

Kahan gáv rávmuts̱.

Eleven men have lost a cow between them.

A great loss, but many to share it.

Kahan gayih kuní wani, tim gayih rani anúní.

Eleven men came to the same unfortunate state ; they each went and fetched a wife for themselves.

Cited when several male members in a household are unfortunate.

Kahan kah watah.

Eleven roads to eleven men.

Tot homines, tot sententiæ.

Kahan kunuí shaitán.

One wicked fellow for eleven men.

Hindustání.—*Ek machhlí sáre táláb ko ganda kartí hai.*

Kahan máli puturan kunuí śránah-paṭ.

One loin cloth to eleven fathers and sons.

Climax of distress.

Kahan thawán sái akis nah tshanán wái.

He promises eleven people but does not throw food to one.

Great promises but little deeds.

Kajih hanzah korih sat.

Kaj and her seven daughters.

There was a poor deaf woman who had seven daughters, whom shesupported with the greatest difficulty. At last God seeing her struggle gave her seven handfuls of food secretly every day. After a time the mother thought that if she left one daughter to go her own way, she might save one handful of food, or, at all evens, have a little more to give to the others. But God only gave her six handfuls then. After a while she sent another daughter away and then another, but still God continued giving one handful less for each girl dismissed, until at last not one daughter and not a scrap of food were left to the woman.

Kákun háput.

Father's bear.

Nothing really to be afraid of.

Kashmírí parents are accustomed to frighten their children into good behaviour by saying "There is a bear coming. Quiet, quiet," &c.

Kal ai karak tah kají marak; kal nai karak tah marak nah zah.

If you worry, it will bring you to the grave; but if you do not worry, you will never die.

'Tis not from work, but from worry, that half the people die.

Kalam-zan, shamsher-zan, kuste-zan chhih be-aklas nish barábar.

A quill-driver, swordsman, and brothel-keeper, are (each one) no more than an ignorant man.

Kalas pěṭh gári phuṭarit khěni.

Breaking a water-nut upon one's head and eating it.

Earning with difficulty.

There was a very godly Hindú, a Rishi, living in Kashmír. Upon a certain day one of his disciples came crying unto him and saying, that his mother had died. The Rishi enquired the age of the woman, and finding that she was very old, he told the man not to weep; because it was time that his mother should die. The disciple, however, did not agree with this, and begged the Rishi to allow her to live a few years more. The Rishi told him to crush some water-nuts (*Traba bispinosa*) upon his mother's head; and it should come to pass that she would revive, and live as many years as there were broken water-nuts.

Now the bereaved son did not like the idea of breaking hard nuts upon his deceased mother's head; still it was the order of the Rishi, and so he did so. Eleven nuts were broken and for eleven years longer the mother lived.

Kali sanz bol-básh zánih kali sund mol máj.

Only a dumb man's parents understand a dumb person's speech.

A little child's prattle is comprehensible only to the parents; and a man's speech is understood by his countrymen only.

Kalas tih raz, nalas tih raz.

A rope for the head and a rope for the legs.

A strict watch over any body or anything.

Kaláyih bisini ṭhulas karán treh sini.

A tin finger-ring turns an egg into three dishes of meat and vegetables.

A great show, but little under it.

Kalis munḍis Khudáí rázi.

God is pleased with the dumb, simple man.

"*Kali nun zih nunuí?*" "*Kali, syun zih syunui?*"

"O dumb man, salted?" "Yes, salted." "O dumb man, unsalted?" "Yes, unsalted."

A story of a nervous young Englishman comes just now to mind, which exactly illustrates this saying. He was breakfasting out; and at the breakfast-table the hostess remarked, "I'm afraid your roll is not nice, Mr——." "Oh, yes, thank you," he replied, "it is splendid." In a little while eggs were placed upon the table, and Mr.—— took one, which turned out to be bad. The host, who was sitting close by Mr.——, noticed this, and begged him to let the servant take it away and give him another; whereupon Mr. —— said "Oh! please don't, I like bad eggs."

Kam gatshih khyun tah gam gatshih nah khyun.

Better to eat a little than to eat grief.

"Any price rather than you should be angry," says the shopkeeper to the customer.

Kámadewan chhus athah ḍolamut.

Kámadev has smoothed that man's face with his hands.

Cited on seeing any beautiful man or woman.

Kámadev is the Hindú Cupid or Eros, the god of Love, thought to be one of the most pleasing creations of Hindú fiction.

Kamas chhuh kamál tah tsaris chhuh zawál.

Perfection is to the less and destruction to the more.

A man somewhat spare in speech, expenses, &c., will become great; but a man extravagant in words and expenses, &c., will come to ruin.

Kamínas khidmat chhĕh zamínas chob.

To serve a mean man is like beating the earth (*i.e.*, it is a profitless work).

Kanah-ḍol chhui Boṭani sodáhas barábar.

A man who turns away his ear (from scandal, &c.), is like the Botan or Ladák trade (*i.e.*, receives great profit).

A brisk trade is carried on between Kashmír and Ladák. I have heard that about lbs. 128,000 of kil-phamb (pashm) or shawl-wool are imported annually into the valley by the buṭahwáni or Ladák merchants. For the preparation, &c., of this wool, cf. Drew's Book on Kashmír and Jammú.

Kanah kapas kaḍuni.

To bring cotton from the ear.

Impossible. Some people attempt to do things in an impossible way.

Cited also against that servant who hears everything *pro* or *con* about his master, and then goes and retails his information to his master.

Kanas chhas nah batah ladán.

I do not load my ear with food (*i.e.*, I am not such a fool as to try to put the food into my ear instead of into my mouth. I know what I'm about).

Kashmírís say that a drunkard, who was very much under the influence of drink at the time, tried to feed himself by stuffing rice into his ears; hence the saying.

Kandas tah mujih kunui sád.

The same taste to sugar-candy and a radish.

Good or evil, noble or mean, all the same to him.

Kaṅh nah kom Kulah-gom.

(Going to) Kulagom without work.

A man going an errand calls a friend, whom he meets on the way, to come along with him. If that friend does not wish to accompany him, he will probably reply as above.

The workmen of Kulagom are said to be the cleverest in the valley.

Kani lagiyá nár zih zanis yiyih ár ?

Will the stone burn, that the acquaintance should have mercy ?

"Save me from my friends."

Kani tah nunah phul gav daryávas. Kanih dup "Buh gujis." Nunun dupus "Yusuí gul suí gul."

A stone and a piece of salt fell into the river. The stone said "I melted." The salt said "That which melted, melted."

We should never complain as long as there are others worse off than ourselves.

Kánih achh surmah tah lanjih zangih paijámah.

Antimony for the blind eye and trousers for the lame leg.

"Madame Rachel will rectify it."

Kánih achh wuzih kyah nindarih ?

What will rouse the blind eye from sleep ?

What cannot be cured must be endured.

Kánih, fialá, tah athas kĕt.

"O, one-eyed man, work." "It is at hand."

A one-eyed man is always ready for mischief.

Panjábí.—*Káná, terha, badfialá.*

(Also) *Káná, kachrá' hoch—gardaná : zeh tinoṅ kamzát !*
Jablag bas apná chale, to koí na puchhe bát.

Kanih garah barun ján tah wánguj garah nah.

Better to fill your house with stones than to have a stranger in it.

Kánih gurih kah mírah-khur.

Eleven grooms for a one-eyed mare.

A very strict watch over a very wicked person.

Cited also sometimes when there are a large number of people appointed to a small work, which one man could easily perform.

"One-eyed" is an expression generally introduced to show the wicked disposition of the person or beast. *Vide supra.*

Kánih korih karyok rún tah shangun kyut gos kuṭ kámuni.

The one-eyed girl was married ; but she had not a room for sleeping in.

An imperfect arrangement.

Kanih nakhah kani tah mĕh nakhah nah kaṅh.

One stone lies close to another, but there is nobody near to me.

Sikandar-náma.—*Birahna man o gurba rá postín.*

Kanih patah chháṅpun.

Sling after the stone.

To send another messenger to get news of the first, &c.

Kánis chhuá buṭhis pĕṭh "Kániá" dapán?

Is it wise to say "O one-eyed man" in his presence?

Kanjar kuttah.

The brothel-keeper's dog.

Quoted against the person who bears much humbug and pain at the hands of another, because he eventually hopes to get some profit out of him.

There was once a dog, who day-by-day visited a certain house of ill-fame in the city. Every time the dog went, the harlots used to beat it, but nothing discouraged the dog went again and again. One day his brother dogs got to hear of this, and enquired why he thus went time after time to a place, where he generally got beaten. "I do not go there for what I get to eat," replied the dog, "but because sometimes, when the chief harlot is angry with the other harlots, she says, turning to me, 'This dog shall be your husband. That is the reason of my enduring all this abuse."

Kanjar kuttah.—Kanjar is Hindustání; the Kashmírí ordinary word is gán. Kuttah of course has been Kashmírised from the Hindustání kuttá.

Kár-i-Khudá zánih Khudá.

God knows his own work.

Kár gaí karit tah phishal gaṅ zĕt.

The work is all over, and an unlucky child is born.

The deed is done. No alternative now.

Several times are mentioned in the Nechih-puter as unlucky moments for a child to be born in. One time, Mul, is especially unpropitious. A child born at that time is sometimes separated from its parents, that it may not bring harm upon their house; at all events, it is an object of much care and expense to its father and mother, until its fate, perhaps, changes.

Karím nanahwor.

Barefooted Karím.

Give a dog a bad name and you may as well hang him.

Karím one day was seen walking without shoes on. The people called him "Barefooted Karím," and although always afterwards he wore nice shoes, yet the people continued calling him so up to the time of his death.

Kashírih kahai garah.

Only eleven houses in Kashmír.

Dark days.

The reader may have noticed the frequent occurrence of the number eleven, and especially in the last few pages. "Like an eleven months' man"; "Only one frying-pan for eleven houses"; "Eleven men have lost a cow between them"; "Eleven men arrived at the same unfortunate state"; "One wicked fellow for eleven men"; "One loin-cloth for eleven fathers and sons"; "Eleven grooms for a one-eyed mare"; and "Only eleven houses in Kashmír," &c., &c. As far as one can ascertain from the limited means of information at hand, this number is quite peculiar to the country. Captain Temple, in his most valuable and interesting "Survey of the Incidents in Modern Indian Folktales" (one of the appendices of "Wide-awake Stories") does not mention this number. The numbers 1, 2, 3, 4, 5, 6, 7, 8, 9, 12, 13, 14, 18, 24, and larger numbers are quoted as occurring in several tales, but never the number eleven. This is somewhat remarkable, and the only reasons suggested for the frequency of this number in "Happy Valley" folklore are the following stories:—Nearly 800 years ago a faqír named Bulbul Sháh came *viâ* Tibet to Kashmír. When he had been here a little while he succeeded in turning Rentan Sháh, the son of Rakí, then king of the Valley, from Hinduism to the faith of Islám, and then Rentan Sháh killed all the Hindús except eleven families.

A variant of this story, leading to the same result, is that Zainu'l-ábadín had a most hot-headed son called Sultán Hájí, or Sultán Hyder. One day as this youth was going down the river Jhelum, when the boat reached 'Alí Kadal (the fifth bridge), he shot an arrow at a water-pot, which a little Panḍitání girl was carrying on her head on the bank close by. The pot was broken to pieces, but the water was not spilt owing to its having been instantly turned into ice, which remained perfectly still upon the girl's head. The little Panḍitání went home crying to her father, a Rishi, who was so much enraged with the young prince's conduct, that then and there he cursed him, saying, "May his hand be paralysed." It happened according to the Rishi's word. From that moment the prince was unable to move his right hand.

When Zainu'lábadín heard what had come to pass he was much grieved, and at once went to his son's house to enquire further of the matter. Said the prince, "I fired an arrow and broke a little Panḍitání's water-pot, and soon afterwards I felt that my right arm was utterly powerless." The king then summoned his ministers and bade them enquire where the little girl's parents lived, and when after some time they had discovered the abode, he himself went to beg the Rishi's pardon, and to beseech him to invoke the gods that they might restore the hand of the prince. The Rishi heard the king's request and prayed, and then turning to Zainu'l-ábadín said, "The prayer will be answered, if you will take one of my daughter's grass shoes and burn it, and then rub the ashes thereof over the prince's hand." The king thanked the Rishi for his kindness, went away with a glad heart, and did as he had been directed; and no sooner was the prince's hand rubbed with the ashes of the burnt shoe, then its former use and strength returned. There was great joy in the court that day.

When the king saw this, he perceived that these Hindús were a very holy people; for none but the good and righteous could thus afflict and recover again by their curses and prayers. Accordingly, he at once began to think of a plan for rendering them unholy. Persian teachers were introduced into the valley, and the Hindús were ordered to learn that language; and they were also commanded to eat yesterday's food and pickles under penalty of the king's great displeasure. A band of officers called Tsráli were appointed to see that this latter order was carried out. Tsrál is the ancient name for the functionary called Mahalladár, for which see note to "*Khauf kahund chhui, &c.*; cf. also note to "*Mol gav tsrol,*" *&c.*

At length through threatenings and bribes all but *eleven families* complied with the king's order. Another story says that all but *eleven families* refused to obey, and so were killed or obliged to flee the country.) In consequence of this the Hindús became unholy; therefore their prayers and curses were of no avail, and they remain so to this day, eating yesterday's food and studying Persian.

However, the gods could not lightly pass over this matter, and therefore a Jogí went to the king and predicted that he would soon be ill, which prediction was fulfilled.

On a certain day the king became very sick and the next day he was worse, and so he continued until all hope of his recovery had quite gone. While in this state the Jogí with his disciple was walking about outside the palace, and telling every one that he could divine; and that by virtue of his art he was quite certain that there was no other remedy for the king but the following:—

"The Jogí must take out his own soul from his body and place it within the lifeless body of the king." Presently Zainu'lábadín died, and the Jogí with his attendant was admitted within the palace and conducted to the corpse. In a minute or two the Jogí and his disciple were left alone in the death chamber. Turning to the latter the Jogí said "I am about to take out my spirit, and put it within this corpse. Take care of my body after death, and put it in some secret place." It was so done; and when the king's wazírs and servants came into the room afterwards they beheld Zainu'lábadín sitting up in his bed well and strong. Great were the rejoicings of the people and great the gratitude of the king, who lived for many, many, years after this.

These accounts are most perplexing. Rentan Sháh, the son of Rakí, has perhaps been mistaken for Ratan Sháh, the successor of Rájá Ven or Vená of Ventipúr, concerning whom the people say that a famous faqír named Bulbul Sháh flew over from Baghdád in a night and converted him and all his subjects to the Muhammedan faith on the following morning. But again this Rentan may have been Runjun, son of the king of Tibet, who invaded Kashmír in the time of Sana Deva, 1315 A. D., assumed the rule of the country, and became a Muhammedan under the name of Shams-ud-dín (the sun of the faith).

A story just crops up, in which Rájá Ven is called Ratan Sháh!

Then in the second story Zainu'lábadín has certainly been credited with the evil deeds of his father, Sikandar Butshikan, of whom it is related, that he did put to death all Hindús who refused to embrace Islám. (Cf. latter part of story attached to "*Maṭṭanuk baṭah,*" &c) Zainu'lábadín is generally represented as a good and merciful king. "Tawáríkh-i Bírbal" says; "He was good and kind to every one, whether Musalmán or Hindú, and he brought back again to the Valley the Bráhmans, who had been compelled to leave it during the oppressive reign of Sikandar."

A few notes from a Persian work by the late Díwán Kirpá Rám, and entitled "Gulzár-i-Kashmír," are still more confusing. Runjun, son of the king of Tibet, is now Sultán Rattanjeo, an imbecile prince of Tibet, who as a mere child was brought into this country and so knew nothing of his father's religion, and was therefore easily converted to Islám by Bulbul Sháh. Sulṭán Shams-ud-dín was the third ruler of Kashmír after Sultán Rattanjeo. It was during Sikandar's successor's, Sultán 'Ali Sháh's, reign (1418—1424 A.D.) that those Hindús who refused to embrace Islám were obliged to leave the country, and while on their way out of the country many of them were seized and burnt alive.

Whatever the truth may be, it will be seen that the Kashmírí Hindús, especially, have reason to remember the number eleven. (Cf. also Drew, "Jammu and Kashmír," p. 69.)

Kathih khutsh watih pakawani.

A bribe for a word and bakhshish for just going (to call a friend, &c.)

A man keen upon bribes and gifts.

Kathih suĕt chhuh wálán hánthi dud.

By a word to cause milk to flow from the breasts of a barren woman.

The power of a word in season.

Kathih suĕt wasih wĕh tah kathih suĕt wasih srĕh.

A word stirs up anger or love.

Katih, Bá, ák? Kut, Bá, gatshak? Kyah chhuí náv? Sirinih ás. Sirahom gatshah. Sas chhum bastih. Salih chhum náv.

Whence have you come, Brother? Whither are you going, Brother? What is your name?

I have come from Sirin. I shall go to Sirahom. I have some pulse in my wallet. My name is Salih.

A take-off upon the conventionalities of the day. Notice play upon the letter س sín.

Ḳáts̲ur dapán báts̲an guts̲ nah dánah dyu n.
Kon dapán son guts̲ nah kaṅh tih yun.
Khosah dapán gosah guts̲ nah kúnsih gats̲hun.

The brown-haired man (or woman) says, "Why should I give food to my family?"

The one-eyed person says, "We do not want to see any one."

The khosah says, "Why should any person be angry?"

Kashmírís say an ordinary brown-haired person is invariably stingy and selfish; a one-eyed person is generally disrespected, cf. "*Kánih fialá*," &c.; and the khosah is a man with the little goat-like beard who has got a name for affability,—*cf.* "*Khosah khĕn.*"

Ḳáwah, káwah, káwah, hat.

A crow, (another) crow, (a third) crow, a hundred crows.

A lie increases as it goes.

Cf. "The Three Black Crows—Byron.

Káwah yanihwol.

A crow's wedding company.

A bad wedding arrangement; everything upside down.

These words are the first line of a little verse sung, or rather shrieked forth, by little children, who gather together in different parts of the city at evening time to play, and watch the crows come home to roost. I have seen thousands upon thousands of crows, a procession, at least, half-a-mile in length, returning past my house; and a tremendous noise they make during the five minutes or so they are passing. This is the song the little children shout:—

Káwah yanihwol.
Murádun mol.
Diham nai ras han.
Kaḍai mulah aul.

Of which the translation is:—

O company of crows.
Keen after your own interest.
If you don't give me a little wine.
I will pull out your nest by the roots.

The crow, on account of its bold and selfish character, is called in Kashmír "The father of Matlab.

Káwan gojih tshar.

A big basket of kernels for crows (soon gone).

Cited to a man who gobbles up his food quickly.

Káwan hichháv kakkú sund pakun. Pananuí pakun muṭus.

A crow learnt to walk like a cuckoo, and forgot his own walk.

Sikandar-náma—*Kulághe tage kabak rá gosh kard.*
Tage khweshtan rá farámosh kard.

Káwas nish náṭih-han.

A small piece of meat in a crow's claws.

A bad debt.

Káwi kur káv zih tshĕṭiwoni tráv.

The crow has cawed; throw away the tsheṭiwon (*i.e.*, the water in which Hindús wash their hands after a meal); and be off to your work.

One of the divisions of the city of Srínagar is so far removed from the Sher Garí (or Sher Gaḍí,) where all the state apartments and government offices are situated, that the government servants, who reside there have to rise and eat their breakfasts early, so as to arrive at their posts in the Sher Garí at the right time.

Káwuj yután kilih kilih khĕyam, tután mashinam nah sitam chháni.

As long as the burner of the dead will not poke me (*i.e.*, to arrange my body so that it may burn quickly and properly), so long shall I not forget your tyranny.

Káyur nár tah parud yár, yim donowai chhái nah wafádár.

A pine-wood fire and a strange-countryman friend, these two are not lasting.

Kázis tah lántshas myuluí kyah?

What has the kází to do with an eunuch?

The judge is not for the good but for the evil.

There are many eunuchs in the valley and they are all Muhammedans. Nearly all of them live in Táshawán, Srínagar; and are employed in marriages to make amusement, or at funèrals to join in the lamentations.

Kĕhkih chhuh dán kánin pĕṭh, trĕh man ranán tah sheh man thĕkán.

Kĕhkih's fire-place is in the top storey; she cooks three maunds and boasts six maunds.

A lying braggart.

Kĕnh mah tah ditam tah kani tali nitam.
Don't give me anything but let me have your ear.
A patronising look from those in authority is worth a large sum.

Kenkahlachih chhuh pĕwún, ḍáyih garih yád.
A lizard remembers a matter one hour afterwards.
Natives believe that this animal treasures up enmity against a man and bites him afterwards, when he can do so safely.

Kentsah chon tah kentsah myon, suí gav wisah-pon.
A little for you and a little for me, this is friendship.
A friend is one not merely in word, but also in deed.

Kentsan dítham gulálah yĕtsuí ;
Kentsan zontham nah dinas wár ;
Kentsan tshunitham náli brahma-hatsuí.
Bagawúnah chánih gats namaskár.
To some you gave many poppies (*i.e.*, sons) ;
And some you haltered (with a daughter) for murdering a Bráhman (in some former existence).
O Bhagawant, (the Deity, the Most High,) I adore your greatness.

Kentsan dyuttham aurai álav, kentsav racheyih nálah Wĕth.
Kentsan achh lajih mas chĕt túlav, kĕnh gaí wúnan phálav dit.
Some Thou (O God) called from Thy heaven ; some held the Jhelum in their bosom.
Some have drunk wine and lift their eyes upwards ; some have gone and closed their shops.
Whom God will, God blesses.

Kentsan dyuttham yut kiho tut, kentsan yut nah tah tut kyah ?
God has given to some (blessing) here and there (*i. e.*, in both worlds), and He has given to some nothing either here or there.

Kentsan rani chhai shihij búní, nerav nĕbar shuhul karav.
Kentsan rani chhai bar pĕṭh húní, nĕrav nĕbar tah zang khĕyiwo.
Kentsan rani chhai adal tah wadal ; kentsan rani chhai zadal tshai.

Some have wives like a shady chinár, let us go under it and cool ourselves.
Some have wives like the bitch at the door, let us go and get our legs bitten.
Some have wives always in confusion, and some have wives like bad thatch upon the roof.
Lal Dĕd's sayings.

Kĕṭah kaḍáí tah búzar josh.
False coin and bázár noise.
The consequence of going into the bázár. It is better to have things made at home. Then one may be sure of no deception.

Khairah nah bog tah sharah.
No share in the good, but in the evil.
A real friend.

Khairas tújíl tah nyáyas tátíl.
Quick to do good, but slow to quarrel.
Good advice.

Khairuk gom tasallí chánih sharah nishih rachnam Khudái.
I have got the comfort of having done good ; God will bless me from your wickedness.

Khaish-i-zan pĕṭh kani, khaish-i-mard sar-gardán.
A woman's relations are honoured, but a man's relations are despised.

Khám tama huchhimatsih kolih.
An avaricious man goes to a dried-up stream (*i. e.*, gets no profit).
Avarice is always poor, but poor by his own fault.

Khám tama tah apazyor.
An avaricious man is a liar.

Khán baḍá khán baḍá, manzbág chhĕs kum tsuṭ aḍá !
A big tray, a big tray, and in the middle of it half a loaf of chaff !
Ostentation.

Khanabalah Khádani Yár.
From Khanbal to Khádan Yár (*i.e.*, as far as one can go in a boat in Kashmír).
Dan to Beersheba. Land's End to John O'Groat's.

Khánamálăn nah koj tah parzanan mimuz.

No breakfast for the son, but a luncheon for the meaner domestics.

Khandawáv bor.

A shawl-weaver's load, (*i.e.*, a little light load).

Shawl-weavers are in general a sickly class. If they get five traks instead of six traks of paddy, the proper measure now-a-days for one rupee, they will not notice they have short weight; on the contrary, they will think that they have seven traks. (A trak is 4¾ sers.)

Khandawáv hĕmáyat.

Defending a shawl-weaver.

Rájá Kák, who died about eighteen years ago, was over the shawl trade in Kashmír. If any person in those days took upon himself to order or harm a shawl-weaver, he was immediately summoned before Rájá Kák and severely punished. Consequently these weakly, ill-paid people then enjoyed such immunity from petty tyranny, as they do not experience now.

My servant (I am sorry to say) is constantly striking and commanding others "as good as himself." He thinks that being the servant of the sáhib he is infinitely superior to ordinary folk, and has a licence to do so. Frequently he receives the above reply, "Who are you, a shawl-weaver, to do such an act?"

Khar bud tsalinai tah vĕd bud laginai

May bad knowledge (lit. an ass's understanding) flee from you and good knowledge (lit. that derived from a study of the Vedas) stick to you.

A Kashmírí Pandit's prayer before teaching his child, or before sending him to the Bráhman to be taught.

Khar khĕnai khar-kháv.

(Called an) ass-eater before he has eaten the ass.

Undeserved blame; a false charge.

"*Khar kiráyih. Âshnái kyah?*"

"Worked like an ass. What is friendship?"

Work is work, whether done for a relation or friend, or not; and the labourer is worthy of his hire. Don't be afraid to ask for the money.

Khar pútis guri pút lonahwani.

Asking a colt as a gift after buying a young ass.

It is the custom in Kashmír to give "a trifle in" with the purchase. This is called dastúrí.

Kharas gor yáj
A big sugar-biscuit for the donkey.
Instruction is wasted upon the stupid man.

Kharas kharkharah.
A comb for the donkey.
Honour given to one not worthy of it.

Kharas khasit tah buth path kun karit.
Mounting the ass with his face towards the tail.
A brazen-faced fellow.

The whole saying is—

Kharas khasit tah buth path kun karit ;
Kálahchan manjanak kharahan phírit !
He mounted the ass with his face towards the tail ;
And at night he asked the ass from them !

During the rule of the Pathấns, debtors were sometimes punished by being made to sit upon an ass in this way and driven through the bázár. A certain Pandit was once thus treated, and was such a shameless man as to ask the government for the ass, when his ride was over.

Kharis ráj dáyanuí garin.
A wicked man's reign is of one hour's duration.

Khatt dit tah chhĕh dapán, zih sánĕn chhih bar wathí.
Giving a bill of divorcement, and the woman saying, "The door is open to me."
Some hope of re-instalment.

Khauf kahund chhuí ? zih pananis mahalladárah sund.
Whom do you fear ? My Mahalladár.

A *mahalladár* is an officer in charge of a division of the city. His principle duty seems to be to spy over the people in his district. He is always fee'd by the people, and generally hated by them, which is no very great matter for surprise.

Khĕ, khĕ, gomut ghás mautich chhas nah khabar.
Eating, eating, he has become lustful, and there is no care of death to him.

Khĕh gávi gásah dharmakih pásah.
O cow, eat some grass for the sake of dharma.
Come let us be friends again.

Dharma is a Sanskrit word, and means the duties of the masses of the Hindú people. Sometimes these are called Abhi-dharma.

Should the family cow be sick, the owner will often stroke her neck and face, saying the above words. Great is the love of all Hindús, and especially of the Kashmírí Hindú, for the cow. It is gratitude that prompts this affection, and has lead the Hindús to regard the cow as sacred—gratitude to the beast for sustaining them during their wandering southwards over barren mountains and through treeless deserts. If it had not been for the cow's milk then, probably hundreds upon hundreds of them would have perished; and so in gratitude to the cow, which furnished them with sustenance and carried their burdens, the Hindús magnified her into a god, and worship and honour her accordingly.

Khĕmas khár tah horas nah hár.

I will eat his kharwár and not pay him a cowrie.

A bad debtor.

Khĕnah khĕwán tah máshihwit.

Eating dinner, but as if he did not want it.

A very nice, prim, proud fellow.

Khĕnah khĕwán tah wĕnah tsári tsári.

Eating his dinner, as though he were picking the wĕnah plant.

Wĕnah is a plant like mint in shape of leaf and flavour. It is a favourite of Shiva's, in whose worship it is much used.

Khĕnah khush hál tah kámih dilgír.

Happy enough at your dinner, but sorrowful when at work.

"If any would not work neither should he eat."—II. Thess. iii. 10.

Khĕnah manzah wukus.

Separate from eating.

A quarrel in the house; father and son will not eat together.

Khĕnah myúṭh tah horanah ṭyuṭh.

Sweet to the taste but bitter to pay for.

Fly the pleasure that bites to-morrow.

Khĕtah, mallah, kentsháh. 'A'úzu bi'llah.

Ditah, mallah, kentsháh. Na'uzu bi'llah.

O mullah, eat something. (Ans.) Let me fly to God.

O mullah, give something. (Ans.) God defend us.

Khĕomut pánsah wápas dyun chhuh ḍanḍas barábar.

To give back a paisá that has been eaten, is equal to losing it.

An "eaten paisá" means a spent paisá.

Persian.—*Zar dádan barábar ján dádan.*

Khetí málik suětí.
The field must be always under the eye of the master (*i.e.*, needs constant looking after.)
Mind your shop and your shop will mind you.

Khěwán pánas tah thekán jahánas.
He eats to himself, and then makes a boast (of his grand dinner) to the world.
A selfish braggart.

Khěyiheh Tsrális horiheh nah mális.
He would eat a Tsrol's money, but would not pay (even) his father.
A man who will make money any way, but will not pay any one, even, his own father.
For *Tsrol*, *cf.* note "*Kashiri kahai garah.*"

Khidmat karizih nah Baṭah gúnas hati wahari dapŏs ner pánas.
Never serve a vile Pandit, for after a hundred years (service) he will tell you to go away.

Khizmat chhěh azamat.
Service is greatness.

Khojah byuṭh wán tah děgilav sán.
The Khojah sat in his shop among the pots.
Carpenter with tools, but no work, &c.
Shopkeepers make a great display of pots, although sometimes there is nothing in them. A very poor Khojah is here supposed, all of whose pots are empty.

Khojah chhuh khushí karán kih něchuv chhum gáṭul ; něchuv chhus pámah diwán kih moluí chhum be-akl.
The Khojah is happy in the thought that his son is wise ; the son is reproaching his father for his foolishness.
Gulistán, chap. VI.—*Khwája shádt kunáǹ ki farzandam 'áqil ast o pisar ta'na zanáǹ ki padaram fartút ast.*

Khojah chhuh pathuí tah ṭáv wot broṅṭh.
The Khojah is behind, but news of him has come on before.
News beforehand.

Khojah Háji Bánḍiyas suět mujih bájwat.
To go shares in a radish with Khojah Háji Bándi.
Little people cannot afford to speculate, though there may be every chance of making a lot of money quickly.

Khojah Háji Bándi was a great man in Srínagar. One day he saw his son playing with the greengrocer's son, and noticing that the other boy had a nice shawl on, he went off straight to the greengrocer and said, "Look here. I see that your business is thriving, and so would like to do something in 'your line' for myself. Will you go partners with me? Will you give me rupees 1,000, and allow me to spend the money in radishes? I also will give rupees 1,000, and we will share the profits half and half alike.—You know how these vegetables pay for growing." The greengrocer agreed and paid the money. Radishes were purchased to the extent of rupees 2,000 and planted. When the month of February came round, the two partners determined to take up their radishes, but, alas! they were every one a failure. The poor greengrocer was ruined, whilst the wealthy Khojah simply lost a little money.

Khojah Momuni ṭhul, kah heni tah bah kanani.

Khojah Mom's egg; buy at the rate of eleven and sell at the rate of twelve.

A non-paying concern.

Khojah Mom once brought up eleven melons with him from Báramula direction, to sell in Srínagar. On reaching the custom-house he was obliged to give twelve melons as a tax for his eleven melons. He gave the eleven melons and then went and sold his blanket to purchase another melon to give the toll-taker. Things were carried on in a very loose way in Kashmír in those days. Khojah Mom then went and sat down by a cemetery and would not allow the people to bury their dead without first giving him some money. In the course of a few days the king's son died and a great company, including the king, went to bury him. When the crowd reached the burial-ground, the Khojah went forward and said, "I cannot allow you to bury the body." The king enquired, "Who are you to speak thus?" The Khojah answered, "I am the queen's brother-in-law," "*Buh chhus Rání hund hahar.*" When the king heard that, he begged the Khojah to permit the burial of the body, and gave him a large present in money. On the king's return to his palace he told his wife about the relation whom he had met in the cemetery, and she replied, "O king, how stupid you are! Did you not know that men only have hahars—not women?"

A wealthy man, the Khojah now began trading again, and used to buy eggs at the rate of eleven and sell them at the rate of twelve. *Cf.* "story of the villager who, going to sell his eight brinjals in a village where there were nine headmen, returns *minus* vegetables and basket, because he had to conciliate the headmen with a brinjal apiece, and the ninth with the basket," given in "Notes on some Sinhalese Proverbs and Stories in the Atíta-Vákya-Dípaniya," by A. M. Senánáyaka.

Hahar is Kashmírí for the Hindustání sálá.

Khojah, nun tíl kahı?
Khojah, what's your salt and oil?
Cited by people when asked to do something beyond their power.
A Khojah through change in the prices of things lost all that he possessed. For some time, however, until his case was thoroughly known, the people came as usual to enquire the prices of his goods. The poor old man would sit at the back of his shop and cry, "Humph! What's your salt and oil?"

"*Khojah sá gúmah han niyihawah.*" "*Asi trov pánai.*"
"O Khojah, you were turned out of your little village." "(Oh, no,) I left it of my own accord."
Salvá dignitate.

Khojah tih mod tah tsás tih baleyih.
The Khojah died and got relief from his cough.
Death puts an end to all troubles.

Khojah, tsah tih yik nah, tah buh tih samakhai nah zah.
O Khojah, you will not come to me, and I shall never see you again.
Lamentation over a corpse.

Khojah wagavi hĕyih mukimánah, tah Khojah wagavi kanih tah mukimánah.
If the Khojah buys a mat, it is a fee, and if the Khojah sells a mat, it is a fee.
Khojahs are very sharp in striking a bargain.

Khojah, wuthá tshun tah sudah kamih.
O Khojah, take a leap. What's the good?
Look before you leap.

"*Khojah, wulash.*" "*Suh tulán pánah pathrah.*"
O Khojah, (give me) the remains of your dinner. (Another man replies, What is the good of asking him?) He himself even picks up (a piece, if it falls upon) the ground.
A stingy person.

Khokhar Mírun bror.
Khokhar Mír's cat.
Too lazy to do it himself.
It is said concerning this cat that it would scratch the ground immediately on seeing a mouse, as if to inform its master that there was a mouse about, if he liked to try and catch it.

Khoran nah kúnsh tah Púshi náv.

No shoes for her feet, and yet her name is Púsh.

Kúnsh—a kind of shoe having high iron heels, and the uppers lessening towards the heels, worn only by the very respectable class. *Púsh* is a grand name.

Khoran nah khráv tah Padmáni náv.

Not a patten even for her foot, yet called Padmán.

Padmán is a Hindú female name of great honour. The Padmani or Padmini (Sanskrit) are the most excellent of the four grades into which womankind is divided by the Hindús. Abu'l Fazl thus describes her:—"Padmini, an incomparable beauty, with a good disposition; she is tall and well proportioned, has a melodious tone of voice, talks little, her breath resembles a rose, she is chaste and obedient to her husband," &c. The name Pámpúr (chief town of the Wíhú parganah, Kashmír,) is supposed to be derived from padma, a lotus, and púr, city, hence, "the city of the lotus" or "the place of beauty," from the beauty of its inhabitants; which must have very much degenerated of late years.

Khosah khĕn.

Khosah's dinner.

When a lot of men are hired for one work, so that the work may be quickly accomplished, people say "*Khosah khĕn*" style.

A certain king made a great feast for all his subjects, and commanded them all to appear on a certain day, except the one-eyed people and those who had not beards (*i.e.*, big beards, the Khosah folk). Everybody obeyed, and each had placed before him a great tray of food of about six sers in weight. The order was that each man was to finish his trayful on pain of punishment. This was a difficult matter. A Khosah, however, who had made up for his deficiency by an addition of a little goat's hair, was equal to the occasion. He suggested that they should all gather in small companies around the trays and eat their contents one after another. In this way the royal order was fulfilled.

A variant of this story is as follows:—

A great man had married his daughter, and as is customary on such an occasion, he made an immense feast. He invited one hundred people, but ordered that only men who had beards should attend. However, a Khosah, sticking goat's hair upon his chin and face, determined to go.

Now the bride's father, being very anxious that his wish should be carried out, himself stood at the entrance door and tried the beards of the guests as they passed in. The Khosah feared the examination; so when the time came for him to have his beard pulled, he begged that that appendage might be left alone, as nearly one hundred people had passed in and were found to be thorough bearded men. The host, supposing him to be some great man

—perhaps the father of the bridegroom—allowed him to go by without a trial.

Twenty large dishes of food were provided for the guests, and as a good dinner such as this, was not to be obtained every day, the Khosah suggested that they should finish the dishes; and the only way to finish them, was for them all to stick at one dish until they had got through it, and then go on to the next, and so forth, until the whole twenty dishes were completed. The plan succeeded.

The Rev. A. W. Burman, in a most interesting article contributed to the "Church Missionary Intelligencer" for October, 1883, and entitled "Notes on the Sioux Indians," thus writes:—

"During their sacred feasts a curious law is enforced. *Each person is compelled to eat whatever may be set before him, no matter how great a portion he may receive, or else pay some one of the company to do so for him. Not a scrap of food must remain uneaten when the company breaks up.* As no invitation to such a meeting can be refused, and there may be occasionally, two or three in a night, at each of which a bountiful help will be served, this must prove a somewhat formidable rule."

Khotan wáts pulan tah konshih baḍai chhēs ati.

Khotan had arrived to grass shoes, but a little shoe was in her walk and manner.

A person considerably reduced pecuniarily, but who still continues the same high manner and extravagant way of living.

Khudá chhuh ṭhulas zú diwán.

God makes the egg to live.

Have faith in God.

Khudái chhuh diwán tshali yá bali, nah tah zaminih tali.

God gives without our knowing or working, or else from out of the ground.

Khudáyih sund páwur, yami yĕtih áwur.

God dwells, where he has taken possession.

Khudáyih sunz khar tah náwidah sund phash.

God's scab, and the barber's rubbing.

To trouble a man, whom God has terribly afflicted.

Kashmírís suffer very much from a disease called scald-head (favus).

Khuntis pĕṭh khunt.

Misfortune after misfortune.

Khur ai ásih bilkull sáf totih ásanas hat phĕpharah.

If a scabby head be perfectly clean, still there remains a hundred pimples upon it.

A great man who bears traces of his previous mean estate.

Khuri tih zágun tah wálah-wáshih tih.

A fishing-net, a lying-in-wait, and a net spread for the bird.

Per fas et nefas.

Khrú, Shár, tah Manḍak Pal ; manzbúg chhus Ludawis nár.

Khrú, Shár, and Manḍak Pal ; in the middle of them Ludu is burnt by fire.

Shekh Núr-ud-dín cursed the village of Ludu, because the inhabitants were once rather uncivil to him. In consequence of his curse, every year some houses in this village are destroyed by fire.

The natives, both Muhammedans and Hindús, are terribly afraid of the curses of their saints and religious leaders. Only a few months since I witnessed the burning-down of a house at Pámpúr, which had been cursed the previous evening by a Jogí, because the owner would not give him some wood for a fire. The Jogí was present at the time, and from his manner and a few hints which I picked up on the occasion, I am almost convinced that the Jogí was the incendiary.

Khyun dyun puláv tah athah chhalun grumit.

Giving puláv to eat and cow's urine to wash the hands in.

To nullify the good done by abuse of word or look.

Khyun gatshih teuthuí yuth bĕyis khush yiyih.

Dinner must be eaten in a manner pleasing to the other.

Kibras chhuh násh.

Destruction to pride.

Pride goes before destruction.

Kijih pĕṭh kájiwaṭ ; welinjih pĕṭh wukhul.

A pestle upon a peg, and a mortar upon a clothes-line (will not hold, but will tumble).

A man appointed to a work for which he is in every way unfitted. A weak man thrust into temptation. *Prendre la lune avec les dents.*

"*Kisar láriáyí dalis dul den.*"

"The barley stained the hem of the garment. Clean it."

Shiva Kák was a Pandit of very high family and great learning. In course of time he was appointed overseer of the village of Wutrus in the Koṭahár district. His duty was to collect H. H. the Mahárájah's share of the grain in that village. Once when the harvest was over and the grain all gathered in he invited the villagers to come to him to the granary, where he would give them each one his share of the produce of the season. When the distribution was over, and while he was returning to his house, somebody noticed that his clothes had been stained by the dirty grain and told him to shake it off ("*Kisar láriáyi dalis dul den*"). On this remark the thought struck the Paṇḍit, what an unprofitable business this was, and thence his mind took flight into loftier regions. "Behold," said he, as though to himself, "Behold, O heart, the state of affairs. Here am I, who all this day have been giving away, returning, as I came, empty-handed, nay, worse than empty-handed, for my garments have become stained. Listen, O heart, thus will it be with you. When you die you cannot take any thing with you. Empty-handed you arrived and empty-handed you will return; moreover, you will repent your birth, because in this life there is naught but sorrow and pain." Therewith he tore his clothes from off his back, and went to live in the jungle near his village, there to give himself up entirely to a religious life. Attracted by his devotions the goddess Umá (Párvatí) appeared unto him in a dream, and said how pleased she was with him, and promised that he should know more and more of things divine; and as a guarantee for these words three springs arose in that place, by the which if any person in sickness or trouble offered the sacrifice of Homa (a kind of burnt-offering, the casting of ghí, &c., into the sacred fire as an offering to the gods), he, or she, would be immediately rid of these things.

On awaking from his sleep, Shiva Kák saw the three springs, and while engaged in worship close by them, behold! several apsarás (beautiful female dancers from the Court of Indra), came and sang to him and played some heavenly music.

It was some time after this that a famine arose in the country; and great was the distress of the people. There was no rain; and harvest-time came, but there was no grain to gather in. Thousands upon thousands of the poorer classes perished, and the corpses of horses and cows and sheep and goats were to be seen stretched out in every direction. The ruler of the country was very much grieved, and thought of several plans for the relief of the people, but what could he do against the great monster "Famine!" One night, however, he sent for his minister, and asked him with much expectation what he would advise, and whether there was not a religious mendicant, to whom they could apply. "Yes," replied the minister, "there is one called Shiva Kák, who resides in the jungle, a good and holy man, and in favour with the gods." On hearing this the ruler went to Shiva Kák and worshipped before him. "Wherefore came ye hither?" said the faqír. "For this reason," answered the ruler, "that my country is dying from lack of rain. O pray ye that rain may descend and water the ground." Whereupon the faqír bade him to make a burnt-offering (Homa) unto the gods, and promised him that then it would rain. The ruler did so, and the rains came and replenished the parched lands, so that they yielded food again, and the people lived.

There are other tales concerning this man—one especially good, wherein the king is said to have sent to seize this Shivá Kák, because he was so very holy, and got his prayers answered so quickly; but as soon as the king's messengers drew near, lions and bears came forth from the hills to devour them, &c., &c.

Koh koṭwal tah yár subadár.
Mountain the police-officer, and pine-tree the district-officer.
No government. Everybody does as he likes.

Kolih kújiwaṭ khasih nah hukh.
The pestle will not come forth dry from the river.
A poor fellow, who has a case in the Court.

Kolih khutah kol tarani.
One river is colder than the other.
Out of the frying-pan into the fire.

Kolih tshunun chhuh ásán tah khárun mushkil.
It is easy to throw anything into the river, but difficult to take it out again.
Easier to fight than to conciliate; easier to give than to take.

Kom gayih húni, "durah" kurus zih gayih.
Work has become a dog, and "durah" has frightened it away.
A workman afraid to undertake a certain work.
Durah is a word spoken sharply to frighten dogs away.

Korĕn hande tálie gorĕn grumit kúmani gav.
The daughters' stars were so unlucky that the milkmen got only a little, even, of the cow's urine.
A daughter, born under an unlucky star, so hard to get married.
Hindús have a custom of washing their daughters' hair with milk and cow's urine two days before the marriage.

Korih hund batah gav dorih hund gĕs.
The daughter's dinner is as dirt in the streets.
It is thought most despicable to depend upon one's daughter's husband for a living.

Korih lĕkh gayih torih dab.
To have one's daughter abused is like receiving a blow from an adze.

Králasuí chhuh khunḍ bánah ásán.
To the potter a broken vessel.
The washerman with a dirty shirt on; the cobbler, &c.

Krám chhiá pám zih tsak yiyih?

Is krám a reproach that one should become angry, when another calls him by it.

Krám, a nickname. A name which has been added to the original name by reason of the man's special calling, or because of some peculiar circumstance which has occurred to him. For instance:—There was a very respectable citizen of Srínagar, by name Jáfar Mír, who had a beautiful pear tree growing in his court-yard. One day during a heavy wind this tree fell down, and in its fall wounded Jáfar Mír's grandfather, who unfortunately happened to be sitting under it at the time. Henceforth ṭang, which is the Kashmírí for a pear, was added to his ordinary name by the common folk; and even to the present day the third generation are thus named.

Totá Rám, who now has the supervision of H. H. the Mahárájah's mules, is never called Totá Ram, but Totá Khachchar.

Búni Wátul is thus invariably called, because he happens to be the clerk of accounts to the wátul or sweeper class.

Sahaz Chhán, *i.e.*, Sahaz the carpenter is so called from the reason that one of his predecessors for a short time helped a carpenter in his book-keeping.

Darím Kándur is the name of the Pandit, who accompanies the baker's coolie on his rounds with the bread-basket every morning. Kándur is the Kashmírí for baker.

Tálib Kalah is a well-known character in Srínagar. Kalah means a head, and this word was added to the family name by the common folk, when Tálib's father, who was a Naqqásh, or painter, tumbled from off the ladder, upon which he was standing and decorating the roof of the Shálimár Bágh pleasure-house, and very severely bruised his head.

Hájí Muhammad Sádiq came to this country from Bombay six years ago, or more. He brought a parrot with him; that was sufficient. From the moment that this was known everybody called him Totá Hájí.

Nearly every person I have met with has a krám, with which the majority are not at all pleased. I can only account for the extreme frequency of these nicknames from the fact, that there are so many people of one and the same name, and a difference sometimes must be made.

Kranjilih, kranjilih, poni sárun.

To take up water in a basket.

To draw water in a sieve.

Krayih khutah chhuh insáf.

Justice is better than worship.

Kruhun baṭah tah chhut Ḍum tah wazul Musalmán.
A black Paṇḍit, a white Ḍum, and a red Musulmán (are wicked, deceitful, characters).

Kruhun ubur gar gar kare ; chhut ubur dare nah zah.
Susmár már kare ; wád kare nah zah.
The black cloud will only thunder, the white cloud will never stop raining.
The malicious man will fight, but without giving an answer (*i. e.*, he will not smite openly, not just at once, he will not retaliate at the time, but will wait until he gets a quiet opportunity).

Persian.—*Az abr i safed bitars o az ádam i narm.*
Az abr-i-siyáh matars o az ádam i garm.

Kub-kul kus ? Muṭih hund tulah kul.
Which is the crooked tree ? Muṭ's mulberry-tree.

Who is the fag ? The badly-paid, hard-worked junior servant. *Gopál Muṭ* had a garden, in which was a stumpy and crooked mulberry tree. All the boys and girls of the neighbourhood were wont to come and annoy Gopál very much by climbing his tree. It would sometimes be filled with children, singing and shouting, and making a great noise. In short this tree was a source of nuisance to Gopál and everybody around. The regular reply to the question, " Where shall we play to-day ?" was at " Gopál Muṭ's mulberry-tree." Every little boy or girl could climb it, it was so small ; and nearly every child in the neighbourhood did.

The above saying is frequently cited by the under-servant in any establishment, who is constantly imposed upon by the other servants. They are so small in years and inferior in position, that everybody feels a perfect right to send them there, or command them here, or to tell them to do this, that, or the other thing.

Kubis lat dawáh.
A kick is as medicine to the crooked old man.

'Tis false mercy to try and patch up an old, decrepid man.

Kuchĕh-hánz kanz hyuh.
Like a kuchĕh—boatman's mortar.

A fat man.

Kuchĕh-hánz, a class of boatmen who pound rice at so much the kharwár for the great folk in the city. They keep boats to carry about the rice in.

"Kuḍaris nishih doh kĕthah kuḍut?" "Yíi dupnam tih tíi kurum."

"How do you manage to spend your days with this passionate man?" "Whatever he says to me I do."

Anything for peace and quietness.

Kukaran mukhtah chhakun.

To scatter pearls for the fowls.

Casting pearls before swine.

Kukaras kunuí zang.

But one leg to the fowl.

A certain master-in-trade gave a fowl to one of his apprentices to kill for him. The young fellow killed it and cooked it; but being exceedingly hungry he was tempted to break off one of its legs and eat it. When the fowl was placed before the master, he enquired the reason of there being only one leg. The apprentice replied that the bird must have been born so. The master became very angry and went about the room beating the young man and saying, "Where is the leg? Where is the leg?"

One day, when there was a great storm and the wind blew fierce and cold, a cock belonging to the master was observed to be standing on one leg only. The apprentice was delighted to see this, and went at once and called his master: "Sir, sir, there's another fowl of yours with only one leg." The master went outside, picked up a little stone, threw it at the cock, and cried "hish-h-h-h," and the cock at once put down the other leg. "There, you fool," said he to the apprentice. "Ah," replied the young man, "you didn't throw a stone at that other fowl."

The Kashmírí Pandit who told me this tale does not know a word of English and extremely little Hindustání. I particularly asked him where he had heard it. He said that he didn't know, but that he had heard it when he was a little boy, about thirty years ago.

Kukĕr dapán "Mĕh kyah ráh!
Batak ṭhulan dyuttum pháh."

The hen says what a wrong I have done!
I have given heat to ducks' eggs.

An ungrateful protégé.

Kukĕr kariheh ná mán tah pútĕn kyah karih?

Of course the hen would have self-respect (if she could); but what would the chickens do?

A good and respectable man overwhelmed with a large family, or rather degraded by it, *i.e.*, he has to seek some inferior situation for the boys, because he cannot afford to teach them a profession, &c., or else he has to steal, and lie, and take bribes.

Kukĕr tachhán tah púti hĕchhán.
The hen scratches and the chickens learn.
As the old cock crows the young ones learn.

Kukĕrih hinzih latih chhih nah púti marán.
Chickens do not die from the hen's kick.
Spare the rod and spoil the child.

Kukĕrih hinde batak ṭhulo tsah kawah zának "tití tí?"
O duck's egg, hatched by a fowl, when will you know "tití tí?"
Don't interfere in matters unknown to you.
Tití tí is the call to fowls at feeding-time.

Kukur ai khĕyi khár, totih sapadih nah khár.
If a fowl eats a kharwár, it does not appear (in the bird becoming bigger).
If a man of low birth becomes rich, he does not become great.

Kukur ai thawizĕn muktah ḍeras manz tatih tih hĕyih tachhun.
If the fowl should deposit a pearl in a heap, there even will it be scratching.
The man who, for his purse, or his stomach, will do any meanness.

Kukur gatsihah bah trak?
Could a fowl become 12 traks in weight?
Can such a man ever become great? No.

Kukur yak kas haif du kas.
A fowl is enough for one man, but for two it is nothing.

Kulah pĕṭhai zulm dafá.
From the very beginning oppression is overcome.
God is the beginning of the world; the king is the beginning of the kingdom; the husband is the beginning of the house—if anything goes wrong, these and nobody else can right it.

Kulis khasit guḍah rab.
To climb a tree and spread mud over the trunk.
To promote a man and afterwards degrade him.
It is a favourite amusement among the villagers to climb a tree and then get the trunk plastered with mud. This causes them to come down with a run, and not unfrequently they are hurt by the sudden shock.

Kuni haṭ chhĕh nah gajih tih dazán.
A single stick upon the hearth does not burn.
A man is no good alone.

Kunih gabih muṭhi lĕj.
A vessel of muṭh for the one ewe.
A spoilt only child.
Muṭh is a species of leguminous plant.

Kunih gabih shál.
The jackal (attacks) a single ewe.
An only child will die.

Kunuí láṭ phentane ; akuí phash tah rentane !
Just enough to go round once and yet he fastens it like a grand pagrí ; only just one stroke (in the water would clean it), but he wants soap-nut for it !
A poor man with great ideas and expensive wishes.

Kunuí ṭang pup ján, phut bharit khám nai ; garah andarich sun ján, gámah andarich zám nai ; wuparah sunz lĕk ján, piturih sunz páminai.
A single ripe pear is better than a whole basketful of unripe pears ; a second wife in the house is better than a zám in the village ; a stranger's abuse is better than a cousin's curse.
Zám is a daughter's husband's sister.

Kúr baḍanas tah tser papanas chhuh nah kiṇh tih lagán.
In a girl's growing and in an apricot's ripening there is no delay.
Kashmírís say that girls grow faster than boys. The growth of the latter is hindered very much by anxieties, &c.

Kúr chhĕh ásanas chhenráwán tah nah ásanas manda-chháwán.
A daughter lessens the wealth of the rich man, and is a cause of shame to the poor man (*i.e.*, it costs a lot of money to get her married into a suitable family).

Kúr chhĕh khúr.
A daughter is as a heel (*i.e.*, a great hindrance).

Kúr dizih nah Ishíbare.
Tatih kúr buchhih mare.
Siriyih khasĕs nawih gare.

Do not give your daughter to a man from Ishíbarí;
Because there she will die from hunger.
There the sun rises after nine garis.

Gari is a space of time equal to our twenty-four minutes. The mountains hide the sun from the village until a late hour.

There is a very famous spring in Ishíbar, called Gupta Gangá, after Guptanatsarí, a rikhi, a very holy Hindû. He was so holy that he frequently visited Gangá, and Gangá was so pleased with the trouble which he underwent to see her frequently, that she one day said to him, "You suffer much to see me; now I will go and visit your village." Guptanatsarí asked when she would come and where he should meet her. She replied, "Throw your cup into me and get to your house. Wherever you see this cup again I shall be there." The man threw his cup into the water and went his way. On reaching his village the following day he saw his cup floating about in a little spring, wherein he at once bathed.

There is a great festival in honour of this spring every April. H. H. the Mahárájah has just issued an order for six temples to be built in Ishíbarí for the priests, &c., in connection with this spring.

Kúr gayih lorih rus piyádah.

A daughter is like a runner without his stick.

These piyádahs or chobdárs give their orders showing their sticks, and then the demands, &c., are paid. The chobdár is of little authority without his stick.

Kur, kur, karán pananih garih tah ṭhul tráwán lúkah handih garih.

Crying "kur kur" in your own house, but laying eggs in the house of another.

Kur kur is the chuckling of a hen.

Kurí, ditsmak gúrí gáman, tári khanjih losai kanjih tsápán.

O girl, I gave you to singhárá villages, but your jaws are tired with chewing the shells.

Apparently a good marriage, but it turned out to be a most unfortunate one.

Singhárá villages.—Villages wherein those people live who gather this water-chestnut. The Singhárá is found in the lakes of Kashmír. It ripens in the month of October, when it is gathered by the people in enormous quantities. (Cf. "The Abode of Snow," p. 377.) These people are called gári-hánz. The nuts are sometimes fried with butter, and eaten with salt and pepper; but generally they are crushed into a flour or meal, of which cakes are made. These cakes are eaten with ghí and salt, &c. To the gárí-hánz these water-chestnuts serve as a substitute for rice.

Kuṭi kukur.
The room fowl.
An eaves-dropper.

Kutsamut hún hyuh rud daryávas manz buḍ pánah khut buṭh tah barin lúk.
Like a wet dog if he remained in the middle of the river he got drowned; and if he climbed the bank he wetted the people.
A man who is doing no good for himself or for others.

Kutsuri kkyos buḍah húni sandih hasah.
The pup bit the man at the old dog's incitation.
A great, respectable, man never beats a refractory servant, but always gets another servant to do it for him.
Has, an exclamation for stirring up a dog to fight.

"*Kutuí gatshak, giliye?*" "*Berih, berih, khuáh.*"
"*Kihai karinih, giliye?*" "*Thulan dinih pháh.*"
"*Kátiyáh chhíi, giliye?*" "*Kah kih nah bah.*"
"*Akháh ditai, giliye?*" "*Putrah máz kaṅh.*"
"*Kihai gok, giliye?*" "*Khudái luduk ráh.*"
"Where are you going, O water-fowl?"
"Along the path to the field."
"What are you going for, O water-fowl?"
"(Going for)—to sit on my eggs."
"How many are they, O water-fowl?"
"Eleven, or twelve (they may be)."
"Give one to me, O water-fowl."
"By my son's life, I have none."
"What's become of them, water-fowl?"
"God has destroyed them."
Distress.
A woman bereft of her children—any person at all miserable—is often heard chanting these lines in a most melancholy tone.

Kyah gav Harih Tsandar Rázanih rane!
Lutásh thawun pěṭh kane;
Topih múdus bozagune.
Šonah ṭúṅk chhih hěwán zálahwune.

What has happened to Hari Chandar, the Rájá's wife!
She has placed Lutásh (her son) upon a stone;
And he has died from the bite of a snake.
And the "káwij lúk" are taking golden paisás for the burning.

Chanted in a most melancholy tone by the Hindús in time of great trouble.

Most Bráhmans can tell folio upon folios of stories concerning this Harischandra, who was once ruler over the whole world; and then by way of alms parted with his wife and child and kingdom. It was after his separation from his wife, that the poor woman, now obliged to go into the jungle and cut her own wood, once laid her child upon a big stone, while she clomb a tree to cut off some of its branches, that a snake came forth from the grass and bit the boy, so that he died. Shevya was the wife's name, and the child's name was Lutásh or Rohitáswa. Great was the grief of the woman, who somehow got back to her first husband Harischandra and told him what had occurred. Harischandra became overwhelmed with sorrow, and caring no longer to live, he at once went and sold himself for "sonah ṭúṅk, *i. e.*, the golden paisás wherewith to pay the "káwij lúk (or burners of the dead) to burn his son's body.

L

Labah kolanih kanadarih.

The tassel on the roof of Labah Kol's house.

This man built a house so high, that a man on the roof of it could not hear any one in the court below, let that man shout as loudly as he was able. It is a Kashmírí custom to affix wooden tassels to each corner of the roof by way of ornamentation.

Cited when a man does not hear or accept.

Lál shinásuí zánih lálach kadr.

A ruby-dealer will know the worth of a ruby.

A bon chat, bon rat.

Lálan mulah mul.

Price upon price (*i.e.*, a great price) for rubies (but not for this article).

It is to the interest of the buyer to depreciate the goods in question.

Lántsh buḍán tah pulahari phirán.

The eunuch gets old and weaves grass shoes.

Hard times for the old people who have not been able to save for their old age.

Grass shoes, or rather sandals, are worn by the poorer classes in Kashmír.

Lánt̲shah garih sutuk.

Sutuk in the house of an eunuch.

An extreme improbability.

The sixth day after a Hindú child's birth birch-wood is burnt in the house, and a lighted piece of it is passed around the head of the child and of all the persons present. This is the work of the midwife, and the custom is called *sutuk* in Kashmírí. After this purificatory act the mother is allowed to leave the room for a short time, &c. Cf. Sanskrit word "sútak."

Lant̲shas mál haṭih tah nál.

An eunuch's property consists in his (jewelled) throat and (embroidered) garment.

These eunuchs, who are all Muhammedans, are hired to sing at weddings or weep at funerals. They get a lot of money sometimes, but generally spend it all in jewels and embroidery work. They are very particular about the work around the "nál," literally, the border of the garment, called the "kurtah," round the neck and down the breast. Most extravagant work is lavished upon this part of their apparel.

Láph gatsinam máph!

God forgive my boasting!

Often cited by the Kashmírí, when he has promised to do any work. He is afraid lest God should become angry at his pride and check him.

Lár khĕwán pánas tah ḍákar tráwán bĕyis.

He himself eats the cucumber, and belches in the face of the other man.

An extremely selfish man.

Lar lorit tah kuṭ.

To pull down a house for a room.

Cited when a thing costs more than it is worth.

Lári kini Láhur.

To go to Láhor by way of Lár.

A roundabout way, on journey, or in work.

Lár is on the Ladák road.

There is a tale in Kashmír about a man who was once asked where his nose was. He did not reply by at once putting his finger on that organ and saying "Here it is;" but he pulled up the right sleeve of his long cloak, and passing his right hand around his head, eventually and with great difficutly, touched his nose with it.

Laren báts tah bátsan batah.

A family is needed for the house and food is needed for the family.

An empty, desolate house, or a poverty-stricken family, or a man without knowledge, &c.

Latah liwan.

(Like a) spade for the feet to kick (and shove).

A butt for the master's anger, &c.

Laṭih kanih latshul.

A besom instead of a tail.

Turning good into bad.

Latiye wĕthranih matiye ái.

O woman, you have come in a poor wretched state.

Natives are great swells when they visit their relatives. This is quoted when any person does not attend to this custom.

Láv bud gayih sáv.

A young intellect is rich.

Láv—a boy between the age of twelve years,—free from care, and able to devote himself entirely to study.

Lazan mazákh pazan.

Unworthy people deserve to be played jokes upon.

Lĕj tah ṭĕkur chhĕh kuní ; manzbág zálán pĕtsih tul pán.

A lĕj and tĕkur are the same (*i.e.*, both are made from earth, both are employed in the same work, both are heated in the same furnace, &c.), and the grass burns itself in the midst.

Be careful not to separate friends, lest in so doing thou destroy thyself.

Lĕj and *Ṭĕkur* are two earthenware vessels used in cooking ; one is a little bigger than the other.

Lĕj tih tsúr, gag tih tsúr.

The pot a thief, the fireplace, also, a thief.

All of them thieves together.

Lĕjih milawan.

A sharer in the pot.

Close friendship.

Lĕkh chhĕh nah rĕk zih dalis lárih.

Abuse is not bird-lime that it will stain the hem of the garment.

Lĕlis pharun chhuh phak.

To steal a pot is like a smell (certain to be detected).

Lochih hanih bud han.

A great matter from a little matter.

An angry word sometimes causes murder.

Log nah tah jog áv put phírit.

Couldn't do the work—the lazy stupid fellow ; and so he returned.

A man begins a work and is not able to finish it.

Lokachár chhuh bĕbih nár.

Childhood is without care.

Bĕbih nár, lit., fire in the bosom. Kashmírís whilst squatting on the ground in the winter time place their kángars under their long cloak next their skin. Give a Kashmírí a kángar and he is perfectly happy. Hence the words " bĕbih nár" come to mean without care.

Lokachár chhuí andahkár.
Childhood is darkness (*i.e.*, the time for sowing wild oats).

Lokachár chhuí mokahjár.
Childhood is freedom.

Lokah hund katit nĕthanun pán ;
Lokah handih rachhit nĕputrah pán.
Spinning for others, and one's own back bare ;
Nourishing other people's children, and oneself childless.

Lokah hundih khándarah mĕthar áradani.
To make one's friends happy at the people's wedding feast.
Dé aliéno corio líberális.

Lokah hunzi máje putrah dag pĕyiyai.
O, mother of the people, the pains of travail will come upon thee.
Cited to a lazy fellow, who eats the bread of another's labours.

Lokah sunz har chhĕh lokas diwai.
The wrangling of the people is the people's pleasure.
Not a few quarrels in Kashmír are excited purely and simply for the sake of a tamáshá.

Lokan kits wánti gáv, mĕh kits shánti gáv.
For the people a cow with milk, but for me a cow that does not give milk.
"Everybody seems prosperous and happy except me."

Lonchih lamun.
To pull the garment.
Asking a man to "pay up."
Shopkeepers, and. especially, hawkers, frequently lay hold of a man's "phĕran" until he pays for the goods just purchased. A mission servant brought me a "tsádar" or wrap the other day, saying that he had seized it as the owner had not paid for a book bought from our city book-shop.

Lorih kuṭanis dastár gandun.
To bind a turban on the top of a small stick.
To give work to a man who is unfitted for it.

Lorih mínit puṭ.

Measuring paṭṭú with a stick.

A suspicious arrangement, because a properly marked yard measure is the proper thing.

Paṭṭú is a course woollen cloth manufactured in Kashmír. The cloth is washed like blankets are washed in Scotland, by trampling them under feet.

Lorih piṭhi saruf pilwun.

To extend a snake towards a man by means of a stick.

Any mean false trick played by a friend.

Lotámanah sund ṭhap.

The seal of Lotáman.

A man careless of his accounts.

Lotáman was a Kashmírí banker of great fame and respectability, but most careless concerning his books. He would put his seal to any paper presented to him. The consequence was that he suddenly found himself bankrupt, and ended his days most sorrowfully

Lúk nai ásih tah buḍ katih gatshih paidah?

If there were no (young) people, whence would the old people be born?

"Young and old, this and t'other,
Cannot do without each other."

Lúsamatis láyun.

To beat a tired man.

A sick man ordered to work, or a tired man asked to go a fresh journey.

Lúṭas tah husas bájbaṭ.

A partnership with plunder and uproar.

M

Machh kyah zánih pámpuri gat ?
Will the fly understand the revolutions of the moth (around the light) ?
A place for every man and every man in his place.

Mádav Bilawani shonṭ han.
Mádav Bilav's little piece of ginger.
A sprat to catch a mackerel.
Mádav Bilav was accustomed to squat down beside any man he might see cooking his food ; and to give the man a little piece of ginger, expecting a good share of the meal in return.

Mág auwí drág wuthuí, Kángrí.
Phágun auwí zágun tsoí, Kángr í.
Tsithar auwí muthar piyoi, Kángrí.
Wahĕk auwí rahĕk katí, Kángrí.
Zeṭ auwí breṭ gayak, Kángrí.
Hár auwí lár lají, Kángrí.
Shráwun auwí yáwun súruí, Kángrí.
Bádarpĕt auwí wádar peyí, Kángrí.
Áshid auwí kásid súzmai, Kángrí.
Kártik auwí nárah-tik lazmai, Kángrí.
Manjhor auwí konjih lajai, Kángrí.
Poh auwí toh ludmai, Kángrí.
January came and there was a famine for you, O Kángrí.
February came and a plot was laid against you, O Kángrí.
March came and you were put to a mean use, O Kángrí..
April came and where will you abide now, O Kángrí.
May came and you were thought a senseless thing, O Kángrí.
June came and you were pursued, O Kángrí.
July came and your youth was numbered, O Kángrí.
August came and sickness fell to you, O Kángrí.
September came and I sent a messenger for you, O Kángrí.
October came and I placed a bit of fire in you, O Kángrí.
November came and you were a matter of anxiety, O Kángrí.
December came and I burnt, even chaff in you, O Kángrí.

The *Kángrí* or *Kángar*, as it is generally called, is the Kashmírí portable fire-place. It generally consists of two parts, the inner earthenware vessel called kundal (somewhat like the charcoal-burner of Italy), wherein the fire is placed, and its encasement of wicker work, sometimes very pretty, being tastefully ornamented with rings and brilliantly coloured; a little wooden or silver spoon (tsálan) tied to the handle (kánjih) completes this oriental brazier, which may be purchased in any Kashmírí bázár for the sum of one áná and upwards according to the make and size. Should the kángar consist merely of an earthenware vessel a little ornamented, it is then called a manan. These are principally used, I believe, in the Leh and Ladák direction.

The best kángars are said to be made in Zainager, a big village in the Kamráz district. Islámábád, Sháhábád and Sopúr are also noted for good kángars, which are very often called after the places where they are made, *e. g.*, Islámábádi Kángar or Tsrári Kángar, &c. An ordinary peasant's kángar, very rudely made, is called Grísti Kángar, from grust, which in Kashmírí means a husbandman, while a finely-worked, highly coloured kángar used by the wealthier class is called Khojah kángar from the Persian Khájah, which means a master, a gentleman, or man of some distinction.

Kángars are also to be met with in the bázárs of those cities and villages, whither oppression and famine have driven the Kashmírí. I have heard of them at Badrawáh, Kashtawár, Rám-Nagar, Bisaulí, Núrpúr, Kángrá, Amritsar, Ludiáná and other places; but the kángars manufactured outside "the Happy Valley" always seem to be of a very inferior pattern and quality, and to be used by a very limited class indeed outside the Kashmírí emigrants.

The Kashmírí is very fond of his kángar, and wherever he goes whenever you see him, whether asleep or awake, at work or at play, sitting down or walking, he has this little fire-place held in one hand underneath his loose, long, night gown-like garment called phĕran, and in immediate contact with his stomach and thighs. As will be expected this very close familiarity generally proves very dangerous; a person is tripped up by a stone in the way and tumbles upon his red-hot kángar fire, or a child rolls in her sleep and upsets the fire-place, and burns herself, the bedding, house, and everything. There are really very few of the wealthier, middle, or lower classes who some time or another have not been more or less burnt from accidents with the kángar.

However, the kángar continues more popular than ever, and not a few songs and sayings in its honour are extant in the valley. There is no doubt that this portable brazier keeps off many a disease from the poor Kashmírí, when so terribly exposed as he is sometimes to the bitter winds, freezing rains, and biting hail;—for King Winter now and again makes Kashmír the centre of his dominions and rules supreme there.

A story is told of a native doctor, who once visited the valley to see what his skill could do for the poor people there during the severe winter season. On reaching Báramula, the place where visitors change the horse, kahár and coolie for the boats, on their way into Kashmír, he noticed a boatman with only a loin-cloth on, squatting in his boat in the cold wind, and eating some cold food. The doctor thought that the man was mad and would certainly soon die. But the boatman had a kángar between his knees, and when the doctor on a closer observation saw this, he at once determined to return whence he came, saying, "The Kashmírí people have got their own antidote for their winter cold. There is no necessity for me to go there."

It has been suggested that the Kashmírís learnt the use of the kángar from the Italians in the retinue of the Mughal Emperors, who often visited the valley, but no reliable particulars have as yet been ascertained. I have enquired from high and low, rich and poor, but no one can tell me anything, fact or fiction, as to who originated, and whence originated, this popular and necessary article. (Other particulars, concerning the derivation of the word Kángar and Kángrí, &c., &c., may be found in my article published in the August number of the *Indian Antiquary*.)

Mágí shín kunun.

Selling snow in the month of January.

An unseasonable work.

Mahárinih májih patah kanih pitur boí.

Behind the bride is her cousin (on father's side).

Take care. There's an enemy present.

It is a wedding custom among Pandits, when the bride is taken to the house of the bridegroom, to place her in a lower room, while the bridegroom is in the upper room of the house. After a little time the sacred fire is kindled in the upper room before the bridegroom, and appointed portions from the holy books are repeated. Meanwhile the bride is brought to the upper room by her mother's brother. Arrived in the room he sits behind her and is her "best man," as it were; he sees that she is thoroughly concealed, gives to her the appointed meats and drinks at the stated times, and leads her around the sacred fire.

Great friendship exists between this uncle and the bride, but intense enmity between her and her father's brothers' sons. These two are constantly quarrelling concerning property and position, &c.

Mahárinih nah gukush tah wígi phirih mukush.

At the time of the wedding the bride had not a straw, but ten days afterwards, when she returned to her husband's house her face was covered with jewellery.

Mukush is a preparation of gold and silver leaves, &c., which are plastered over the bride's face (ten days after the wedding, when she returns to her husband's house) making it look much like a model in tarnished silver. This is a Muhammedan custom.

Mahárinih nah wánkahpan tah wígi phirih lánkaran.

At the time of marriage the bride had not even her hair plaited, but ten days afterwards, when she returns to her husband's house, she wears a lánkaran.

Lánkaran (Persian, *Halyat*; Sanskrit, *Alankára,*) a jewel or woman's metallic ornament.

Ten days after the wedding the bride returns to her husband's house splendidly dressed, richly jewelled, and with abundance of furniture and provisions, &c.

Mai tih ati tah mai-kh̲ánah tih ati.

Wine is here and wine-shop is also here.

Every thing at hand.

Máj karán "kúri, kúri"; kúr karán "rĕnih, rĕnih."

The mother cries, "daughter, daughter"; the daughter cries, "husband, husband."

Máj karin "shurih, shurih"; shur mah karin "máj, máj."

Let the mother say "child, child"; but let not the child say "mother, mother."

An orphan.

Máj tah kúr, ts̲akar tah lúr.

A mother and daughter are like the handle and stick of a spinning-wheel, (necessary to one another;—and work together).

"Máj, ts̲ah thawum kángar phukit, buh yimai wustas doh thukit."

"O mother, blow the kángar and set it for me; and I will come after my work with the teacher."

"Light the kángar for me, I will be back again presently," referring to the short time one is able to work during the dark winter months. Workmen come, just lay a few bricks, &c., and go again.

Wustah, a teacher, here means a master blacksmith, or bricklayer, or carpenter.

"Máj wuhawan chhum nah kanh." "Watih pěṭh běh tah dah zani wuhawanai."

"Mother, nobody curses me." Sit by the way-side (my son), and ten men will curse thee."

They who live in public must expect to "rough it."

Máji baḍeyih tháji tih baḍeyih.

When the mother becomes great, the pot, also, becomes great.

The expenses of a family.

Májih kar dandah-tuj tah shuri khyav gásah khur.

The mother used a tooth-pick only, but the child ate a bundle of grass.

A mother's utter unselfishness.

Májih khutah kurui baḍ.

The daughter is bigger than her mother.

Case greater than the original quarrel. Wages above the work.

Májih lěk, běnih lěk, korih lěk ; tah kolayih nah lěk.

Abuse my mother, my sister, my daughter ; but do not abuse my wife.

A Paṭhán saying. Paṭháns are especially particular concerning their wives.

Májih nah lachakah tah sitáras giláph.

The mother hasn't a lachakah, but the guitar has its wrapper.

Cited against the man who has hardly means sufficient to keep body and soul together, and yet buys books and other dispensable articles.

Lachakah is the piece of woollen cloth that hangs down on the neck from the back of the head of a Muhammedan woman.

Majnunas parutshuk zih kheláfat kahanz chhěh, Dupnak, "Lailih hinz."

It was asked of Majnun "Whom do you like?" He replied, "Lailí."

Anybody or anything a man is especially fond of, is called that man's "Lailí."

Lailí Majnun—a famous Persian love story translated into Kashmírí by a poet called Muhammad Gámí.

Mákir tah kákir garin tah pharin, lějih nah bazin tshurui wih !

A garrulous, sharp, unconscientious and malicious woman, no oil in the pot,—only pride !

A woman who flatters herself that she is as good as her rich neighbour.

Mokkah mĕlih magar nakhah mĕlih nah.

Mecca shall be found but not your neighbour.

Neighbours are constantly going to law about ground, &c.

Mál fitnah yā aulád fitnah.

Either trouble about one's money or trouble about one's children.

If a man has money then he has not children; and if he has children then he has not money, because the children have swallowed it all up; in either case, however, man has trouble in this world.

Mál mast tah hál mast sandih khutah chhuí nangah mast be-parwá.

A naked man has less care than a man of wealth or a man of position.

Much coin, much care; little goods, little care.

Mál-i-muft tah dil-i-be-rahm.

Property by gift and a heart without mercy.

Mál wuchhit zagát.

Seeing (your) property give alms.

Give according to your ability.

Zagát (Arabic, *Zakát,*) a portion of a Muhammedan's property given in charity according to the rules laid down in the Qurán, cf. "Hughes' Notes on Muhammedanism," pp. 125-126.

The Kashmírís have a story concerning one Lakshman Dar, an officer of the Kashmír government. He was one day eating pulák when a jester was present to whom he gave a little portion. The jester disgusted with the meagre meal, and in order to make those present laugh, stuck a grain of rice upon a needle, and laying it outside his platter said, "Húni miṭ" *i. e.*, the dog's portion. On noticing this done in such a ludicrous fashion all the people laughed, including Lakshman Dar also. "Why are you such a fool?" they asked; whereupon the jester replied, "According to Lakshman Dar's gift I have given (*Mál wuchhit zagát*).

Huni miṭ, lit., the dog's handful. Hindús before touching their food take out two or three handfuls, as the case may be, and lay it on one side for the dogs to eat. The real idea of the custom, however, is an offering to Vishnú.

Málas chhuh mol.

Price according to property.

Good article, good price.

Máli Wĕtsár-nágah tah Bahwano, yas nah peyih dánas pĕwino tas kyah chhuh pánas rĕwano!

O fathers Vĕtsár-nag and Bawan, what a sight! He who cannot afford to have a fire in his house, yet adorns himself for the festival.

Hindús address their sacred places as fathers, because through them they think they obtain all blessings. *Vĕtsár-nág* is a sacred spring about three miles from Srínagar towards the north on the Gangabal road.

Bawan also is a sacred spring—the most sacred in the whole valley. Near to the village called after this spring are the famous ruins of Mártand or Maṭṭan

Great religious fairs are held at both of these places at certain seasons of the year, and it is the custom of the Hindú people to appear at them dressed in their best and gayest clothes.

Mális ráj tah muhtáj, báyis ráj muhtáj; ranis ráj tah sher táj.

If my father has the rule then I want something, and if my brother rules I shall be in need; but if my husband rules then (I have got my heart's desire), I wear the crown.

Mallah ḍyuṭhum amalah karán, hákas dapán kachh;
Gámuch khĕwán alái balái, musáfiras dapán mashidih chhuí yachh.

I saw a mullah performing his duty, and calling a cabbage grass.
Eating the sacrifice of the village, and saying to the traveller, "There is a hyæna in the mosque."

A selfish, hypocritical mullah.

Alái balái is the sacrifice offered to ward off, or abate, any pestilence, &c., in a place.

Mallah (*Mullah*) is a Muhammedan well-instructed in the Qurán, and generally a teacher or schoolmaster.

Mallah goí palah pĕti poni ḍalit.

O mullah, (my words to you are like) water which trickles down off the rock.

In at one ear and out at the other.

Mallah har gayih palah har.

A mullah's fight is like a fight with stones (so bitter and unrelenting is it).

Mallas ṭuk chhĕh mashdih tám.

A mullah's "beat" is to the mosque.

"Matlab" carries us hither and thither.

Mám thawih izzat tah gám tih thawih izzat.

If an uncle honours (a man) the village will also honour (him).

A smile from those in authority is worth much.

Mámah-hiharah marano dár nah tah bar no.

O Mámah-hihur you are worthy of death, there is neither shutter nor door.

You exaggerated,—you deceived me.

Mámah-hihur is the husband or wife's mother's brother.

A young woman was asked by her affianced husband's mother's brother to come and see her future home, which he described as very grand and beautiful. When the girl arrived at the place she found a very humble abode without even a shutter or a door.

Mán yá mah mán buh chhusai zorah mĕzmán.

Whether you consent or not, I will be your guest.

Mananih yiyih nah panani tah hahadánas rĕh.

A manan does not get sufficient for itself, how (then can it obtain,) flame for the hahadán ?

Manan is a kángrí without the wicker work.

Hahadán is a big cone-shaped fire-place with holes in the top, through which they stir-up and blow the fire, &c.

Mandachhhahan lántsh tim khĕwán natsi, natsi.

The eunuchs ought to be ashamed of themselves, yet they dance and eat.

A shameless person.

Mandachhanas tannah-nannah.

Rejoicing in his shame.

Tannah-nannah, supposed to represent the sound of the Kashmírí citházá. "*Tom, tom, tom, tannah nádir ; tannan, tannan tannah nannah,*" the instrument is supposed to say.

Mangawun ai tahwizen ṭangah-wani andar tatih tih karih mangamang.

If a beggar be placed in the midst of a grove of pear trees, there, even, he will beg.

"Habits are soon assumed ; but when we strive
To strip them 'tis being flayed alive."

A Kashmírí friend tells me a story of a beggar, whose son became a great man. However, his father still continued to beg. At last one day his son put the old man into a room and locked the door. At the regular times the servant carried food to him; but it was too much for the old man, who had been accustomed for so many years to stint himself, so he only ate a little of the dinner, and tied up the remainder in his clothes, crying "Yá Khudá," "Thank God," as he had been accustomed to do on receipt of alms.

Mangun tah májíi pakun tah parisuí.

Asking, even, from one's mother, and walking, even, one step, are hard.

Mangun tah marun.

To ask (a favour) is to die (*i.e*, you put yourself under an obligation—you lose your independence).

Manṭinih lĕjih pánzú.

Six pounds weight of anything to a three pound pot.

A man in adequate to circumstances.

Manuṭ tah phambah ḍyoṅg tah háyuk barábar.

A three pounds weight and a ball of cotton and the scales are equal.

A sharp fellow without any principle, who will, and can, say or do anything to accomplish his object.

Manz atsun chhuh kanz atsun.

To go between (*i.e.*, to act as a surety) is to put your head into a mortar.

A certain man borrowed some money, and persuaded a friend to become surety for him. The mean man as soon as he had obtained the money spent it and ran away from the country. The poor surety was punished by having to keep a mortar upon his head for a certain time. "*Manz atsun, chhuh kanz atsun*," cried he, as the people going by laughed and jested at him.

Manz gám jĕshnah husih rún garih.

Dancing and feasting in the village, whilst Husih Run (who has paid the expenses of the tamáshá) is indoors.

Cited when the very person who ought to be present, is not present.

Manz gani manzanis; kalah sardáras; laṭ gunahgáras tah becháras.

The middle portion (of the fish) for the middle-class man; the head for the host; and the tail for the sinner and the helpless.

Mánz thav tulit dud math athan. Shekh chhuh hákim. Kathan chhěh háts.

Rub milk over the hands and take off the colour. The Shekh is ruler. There is fear of accusation from one's words.

Oppression.

Shekh Ímám-ud-dín hated the Hindús. One day, a day fixed for the celebration of a very grand Hindú wedding, he sent an order that no wedding was to take place. The people heart-sore and weary said the above words. This Ímám-ud-dín also forbad the Hindús to wear the tíká.

Mánz is the *Lawsonia inermis*, the Indian Hinná, with which the people stain the nails of their hands and feet.

Már pěthuí gilkár ; ár khěni chhíi tsuki nár ; lár khěni chhíi shajár ; záras gindun khabardár ; kúr zěni chhai tabardár ; něchuv zun chhuí syud dastár.

One should build upon the bank of Már ; eating ár is bitter like fire ; eating cucumbers is cooling ; beware of gambling ; the birth of a girl is like a wood-cutter to you ; but the birth of a son is as a straight turban.

Már is a canal which flows through the northern portion of Srínagar. It resembles the old canals in Venice. It is crossed by several ancient stone bridges and is fringed in many places with trees and festooned with vines.

Ár, Álú-i-Bokhára, Prunus domestica.

Kúr zěni chhai tabardár—Like as the woodcutter "brings down" the trees and cuts them up, so a daughter is a continual strain upon the father's purse.

Syud dastár is an expression signifying prosperity.

Marahah tah garih chhum nah kanh.

I would die, but there is nobody in the house with me.

"Whosover is delighted with solitude is either a wild beast or a god.—Bacon.

Márakan gatshan ásuni dyárah der tah yárah der tah batah der.

For quarrelling, a heap of money, plenty of friends, and abundance of food are required.

Money—to bribe and pay court fees, &c.

Friends—to swear falsely and back you up.

Food—to nourish and strengthen in these troublous times.

Maranas nah mokal tah mast kásanas nah fursat tah hárih nah zí.

No time for dying and no leisure for shaving (he is so busy), and yet he has not one cowrie's income.

Lots of work and small pay.

Máras márih, táras tárih, yáras khyáwih tsunṭ tah ṭang.

He will smite the man, who has to be smitten, will help the man who has to cross the river, and will feed the friend with apples and pears.

A man *au fait* at most things.

This is also a Kashmírí riddle, of which the answer is a stick.

Maras tsong zálun goyá kih saras pamposh phulun.

To light a lamp in the house is like the flowering of the lotus on the lake.

A son is the lamp of the family.

Hindú saying.—*Kul ko dípak putr hai; mukh ko dípak pan;*
Ghar ko dípak istri; dhar ko dípak pran.

Maratsah wángan khár ai khĕyih ṭás kaḍih nah tyut chhuh sun tah sangín!

If he eats one kharwár of red pepper he will not smack his lips; so deep and philosophical is he!

An unexcitable disposition; *semper idem.*

Maraz galih wedah-wán ádat katih galih?

The disease will go by the doctor's shop, but the habit will never go.

Habit is second nature.

Maráz-o-Kamráz; shahr chhuh Yamráz.

Maráz and Kamráz; the city is Yamráz.

Yamráz is the city, where everything finds its way.

"O, everything in London."

These are the three great divisions of the valley. Maráz is the whole S. E. end. Kamráz is the N. and W. end and the water-shed of the Jhelum as far as its junction with the Krishna Gangá. Yamráz is the city of Srínagar, &c.

Mas pyav mas bánih, yĕs pyav suí zánih.

Wine has fallen into the wine-vessel; that vessel knows (its strength, smell, &c.) into which it has fallen.

Experience is the best teacher.

Mas wunchih pĕṭh nindar.

Sleep upon a wine-cask.

A man of property. In the lap of luxury.

Maṭ phuṭarit bobus!

Breaking a maṭ for a bobus.

Spoiling a good thing in order to make an inferior article. *Maṭ* is a large earthenware vessel. *Bobus* is a small earthenware vessel about the size of a slop basin.

The saying originated many years ago in this way. One day a child was playing fireworks with bobuses. He got some gunpowder and put a little into each bobus, and then ignited them. At one time he could not find a bobus, and so he broke up a maṭ and made something like bobuses out of the shreds. His father was very much shocked and said, "What breaking up a maṭ for a bobus!"

Matanas mashk.

Practising madness.

An unseasonable or impossible study.

Mátas tah kabrí chhuh hisáb.

There is an account between the corpse and the grave.

Matĕn hund dup chhuí baláyan thup.

A madman's speech is a check to misfortune.

A madman's word, and a good man's word, are thought to be of equal value, because mad men are supposed by the common folk to be very good. Though they sin, the people say they do not sin; for they know not sin, but are like the beasts of the field.

Matis chhĕh bataní wír.

A madman is only anxious about his dinner.

Matlab chhuh t̲saṭán put-lab.

Matlab cuts the back wall of the house.

Any thing to accomplish his purpose.

Maṭṭanuk baṭah tah Paṭṭanuk Ḍumb.

The Maṭṭan Paṇdit and the Paṭṭan Ḍumb.

There was a Ḍumb from the village of Paṭṭan, who had to take a letter of the Kárdár's to the city. (Kárdár is the Hindú overseer of a village, a government official, whose business it is to see that H. H. the Mahárájah gets his proper share of the grain.) The letter was delivered to the man at evening time, and he rose early the next morning to go to the city. It was so dark when he got up that he could not see what he was about, and so he put on the first garment that came to hand, thinking it to be his own. By the time the day dawned he had proceeded far on his journey, and the more sorrow for him that he had walked so fast and had so many miles to return, for he found that he had clothed himself with his brother's wife's long cloak instead of his own. He determined to run back as quickly as possible, because, said he, "I have sinned in that I have done this thing, and I must rectify it by all means within my power." So he went back to his house, quickly, changed his cloak, and started off the second time, and when he reached Srínagar, he carried the letter to its destination, and then went to Sĕd, Lal Dĕd's teacher, and told him what sin he had unwittingly been guilty of; and asked him what he must do to atone for it. Sĕd ordered him to visit a certain Bráhman who resided at Maṭṭan, and explain matters to him.

Now this Bráhman was a very bad character, and was at that time living with his brother's wife. When he heard what the Ḍumb had related to him, he fell into a paroxysm of grief, and kept on saying, "What a sinner I am! Here is this poor fellow in such a terrible state simply because he once put on his sister-in-law's cloak, whilst I, who am living day after day with my sister-in-law, do not have the slightest qualms of conscience." The Bráhman asked the Ḍumb wherefore he had come to him, and who had sent him. The Ḍumb replied that Sĕd had told him to come. Then they both, the Bráhman and the Ḍumb, visited Sĕd and asked his counsel. The Ḍumb was quickly dismissed with the order to perform some very small penance. The Bráhman was detained alone with Sĕd for many hours. Sĕd told him that the only atonement he could make for his enormous crime was to offer himself as a burnt-offering to the god. The Bráhman accepted the advice, ordered the pile of wood to be prepared, and was burnt.

It is written that if any man gives himself up to be burnt upon the pyre he shall ask anything that his heart may wish for at the time of burning, and it shall be granted him. Accordingly this Bráhman was enquired of as to what he liked. He answered, "I want you to give me some milk and some flesh." When Sĕd heard his reply, he became exceedingly sorrowful, and said to the people who crowded around the burning man: "O people, this man will become a Muhammedan king, who will destroy all our idols and cast all our shrínes down to the ground." This prophecy was fulfilled.

Sikandar, surnamed Butshikan, or Image breaker, was the sixth Muhammedan king of Kashmír and reigned in 1396 A.D. He destroyed all the Hindú temples and broke their idols into pieces; and when there remained not another temple for this monster to destroy, he determined to go to Amaranáth and break up the sacred emblem of Shiva, which is there in a cave. On arriving at Ganesha Bal on the way, he struck a blow at Ganesha (the son of Shiva by a daughter of Himálaya). There is a fragment of a rock here, which lies in the torrent of the Lĕdur, and has been worn by the angry waters into what the imaginative mind of the Hindú discovers to bear a striking likeness to the head of an elephant, the representation of Ganesha; (—a trunk and a pair of eyes have been painted on by a native artist), and broke his knee. Blood flowed forth in such abundance from the wound that the whole stream was coloured by it. Seeing this Sikandar became very much frightened and left off his sacrilegious works, and returned home.

Maṭṭan, a celebrated spring of water in the village of Maṭṭan or Bawan, near to which are the magnificent ruins of the temple of Mártand or the sun.

Paṭṭan is a little village in the Bángil pargana.

Matyav aneyih noshá, suh tih mateyih.

The mad men brought a daughter-in-law, and she also became mad.

Evil communications corrupt good morals.

Máyárámuni nosh.

Máyárám's daughter-in-law.

A contrary person.

Máyárám's daughter was celebrated for her contrariness. She always did the opposite to what she was told. Tell her to bring water, and she would bring earth, &c. One day a friend advised her father-in-law to order the girl to do the very opposite of what he wanted. Accordingly the man one morning asked her to jump into the fire. She went and drowned herself in the river, and there was an end of her; and the father-in-law lived happily ever afterwards.

Mĕh chham gámuts graṭtas tal phusi.

My hat is under the mill-stone.

A work to be done—no alternative.

Phusi is the cap of a Yach or Yech, the classical Yakshas. Some say that this cap is made from the skin of some animal—perhaps, the jackal; while others declare that it is perfectly white—and that is all one can know about it. This cap possesses wonderful powers. It is a mist-cap (nebelkappe) by which the wearer becomes invisible (cf. Schwartz' "Der Ursprung der Mythologie dargelegt an griechischer and deutscher sage," p. 247); and the person, who should be so lucky as to obtain one, can compel the rightful owner to do his bidding—to bring gold without stint, to furnish the rarest delicacies, and to remove the greatest difficulties.

The Yach or Yech, however, remains the humble servant of the possessor of his hat only so long as that precious article is kept safely either under a mill-stone, or under a vessel containing sadurkánz (*i. e.*, rice water kept in a ghaṛá for several months until quite sour, and then cooked with salt and spices; and drunk, especially, during the hot season). From underneath these two things a Yach cannot remove his cap, though he could carry great rocks and with a brush of his hand clear away great streams, that his master might pass over without danger.

This cap has come into the possession of several people, who apparently have not failed to profit by it. These fortunate folk, if they are Hindús, have become distinguished into a separate community, and bear the title of Yach, as Kawal Yach, Gana or Ganesha Yach, Sokha Yach, Damúdar Yach, &c.

Much might be written, if needed here, concerning the ancient and modern idea of the Yach, his origin and general character, and many stories might be told concerning the seizing of this man or creature, whatever he may be. It is my idea to get these published in a separate book or pamphlet. Captain Temple has a few interesting notes on the Yach in the "Indian Antiquary," Vol. XI., Pt. cxxxvi. p. 260.

Mehar-i-árábí chhuh kahr-i Khudá.

A farmer's love is like God's anger.

Persian.—*Yár i dih tá kár i dih.*

Mĕhnatas chhĕh mazúri.

Wages for labour.

Mĕtras gabar záí, dushmanas zangih áí.

Sons are born to a friend, and they go to their (father's) enemy and bless him.

General reply of an enemy to a friend, who wishes to be reconciled.

"*Mĕtro shĕthar muduí,*" "*Mĕtras tih chhuh marun.*"

"O friend, your enemy is dead." *Ans.*—"The friend also will die."

Death is every man's debt.

Mewagari, munjigari, bĕyih bághwán.
Yim trĕshawai chhih Kaum-i-Marwán.

The fruiterer, confectioner and gardener, these three are a Qaum-i-Marwán.(*i.e.*, a dirtily clothed, wandering sort of a class.

Kaum-i-marwán.—Marwán was the ninth caliph of the house of Abbas. Some Kashmírís say "hál-i-hairán" instead of these words.

Mírí míri phats.

From horses to asses.

☞ The above is not the translation but only the meaning of the saying. *Mírí mírí phats* is a favourite game in Kashmír both amongst children and adults. Two holes are made in the ground, one about half-a-foot deep and half-a-foot in circumference called mír, and another close beside it, about two inches deep and two inches round, called phats. The players two, three, or six, as the case may be, range themselves in order at about a distance of two yards from these holes, and one after another try to fling a walnut into the big hole. If the first player succeeds he is called mír, until some other player, also, gets in, when this other player is called mír, and so on until the last mír player. If however a player fails to get his walnut in, he is called phats. When all have tried, the last mír, who is the greatest man, collects all the walnuts from the other players, and holding them in both his hands together over the mírí hole he lets them fall. As many as fall into the mírí hole is his; but those, which chance to fall outside are gathered by the second mír and dropped by him in the same manner. Should it happen that after all the mír players have tried, there are still one or two walnuts left, which have not fallen into the mírí hole, then the phats player, if there is one, takes them, and holding them in the same fashion, but above the phats hole, tries his luck. And so the game continues.

Mírzah Razáhun gáḍah árah.

Mírza Razá's necklace of fish.

A shameless man.

This man was a government debtor, and not being able to pay his debt, he was ordered by the king to parade the streets, wearing a necklace of fish. He did so, and after he had gone the round and reached his home, he took off the necklace, cooked the fish, and ate them.

Miskín Sháhun ástán, brangáh thúd tah sharafá nah kiṅh.

Miskín Sháh's zíárat has a lofty tower, but there is no honour attached to it.

A wealthy, but an ignorant, low-birth man. A well-dressed fool.

Zíárat is a place to which a pilgrimage is made.

Miskín Sháh's zíárat is a beautiful building in the Surah-ṭeng division of the Khányár district of Srínagar.

Miṫs ai tulak sun gatshunai.

If you pick up earth may it become gold to you.

A Kashmírí's blessing.

Míṭ pund tah ziṭ umr.

A pleasant sneeze and long life (to you).

A Kashmírí blessing.

By a pleasant sneeze is meant a single easy sneeze, that does not give pain to the throat, or to the nose, or eyes. If such a sneeze happens when about any of the seven special works mentioned below, and quoted from the Sanskrit work Váráhíya, then it is a really good omen; some say that good fortune will meet you, and others that people must be speaking well of you (as foolish people in England do when their ears burn in a peculiar manner). The Váráhiya says—(i.) sneezing is a good omen if it comes at the time of taking medicine,

Remember this for you will not need to take another dose ; (ii.) sneezing is a good omen if it comes at the time of setting out upon a horse; (iii.) sneezing is a good omen if it comes at the time of argument. To him who sneezes, or hears another person sneeze, it means success ; (iv.) sneezing is a good omen at the time of retiring to rest ; (v.) sneezing is a good omen at the time of eating ; (vi.) sneezing is a good omen at the time of reading ; (vii.) sneezing is a good omen at the time of seed-sowing. Great shall the harvest be.

Except on these seven occasions it would be very unwise for a Hindú to do any other work, if he himself should sneeze, or hear anybody else do so.

However, above and beyond these, at all times, even on the seven occasions quoted above, the sneeze of (*a*) an unmarried girl ; (*b*) of a widow ; (*c*) of a barren wife ; (*d*) of a shoemaker's wife ; (*e*) and of a woman sick from cholera, is an extremely bad omen. Let not a Hindú commence any work, when he hears such, but sit down and reconsider what he is about to do or say.' Cf. "Punjáb Notes and Queries," Vol. I., notes 776, 949.

Mits ai tulazih badih banih.

If you will get earth, then get it from a big mound.

If you must work then get the service of a great man.

Mol ai kráji karih suh tih gayih máji.

If the father marries a potter-woman she is the mother.

A second wife.

Mol gav tsrol tah máj gayih aul.

Father is a tsrol and mother is a nest.

Tsrol is a Muhammedan sect, who have the choice of three employments. They can become jailors, or bootmakers, or beggars. If they select the latter they visit everybody's house, and generally get something. Muhammedans outside their sect do not eat with them. They are said to be most unkind to their children. There are about two hundred families of the Tsrol sect in Kashmír. Cf. note to "*Kashirih kahai garah*" for their origin.

Mol gutshum worah, moj gatshum sak, khĕmahas trak tah kom karahas nah ak, tas lagihĕh khunt, suh dapiham ungajih karun muthur, buh láyahas mak.

O father, I want another father : O mother, I want my own mother. (In the old days) I used to eat (with them) about twelve pounds of food at one time, and did not even once work.

O may he be wounded, and say to me pour water over my toe ; and then I will slay him with an axe.

A step-parent.

Mol moj gav kázi, akis rázi tah akis bázi.

Parents are like judges, they are satisfied with one child and displeased with another.

Kází (Qází) was a Muhammedan judge in all cases of law, whether religious, moral, civil, or criminal. The office is now virtually extinct under the British Government.

Mol pánúr, nechuv Murád Beg.

Father—a water-carrier, and son—Murád Beg.

An upstart.

Murád Beg was the head of the chobdárs in Guláb Singh's time. These people carried a staff, and besides the ordinary work of a chaprásí, they executed the state punishments, such as serving a summons, flogging, &c.

Panjábí.—*Báp na máre titarí pútur gol-andáz.*

Mondih nishih rani mángai.

Asking a husband from a widow.

Drawing blood from a stone.

Moṅgah maṭ khĕt chĕt tah kakkav.

To eat a big pot of moṅg; to drink; and then to run away.

An ungrateful servant. Untimely death of a cow or horse.

Moṅg.—Phaseolus Max or *Radiatus*; a vetch or kind of kidney bean.

Kakkav is a species of partridge, but here it means to fly or run away; to disappear.

Mordah málas chhuh khord-u-bord.

A dead man's estate is eaten and taken away (*i. e.*, the deceased's descendants quarrel over it and eventually carry the matter into court).

Mordah tih chhuh pánsas ás dárán.

The dead even opens his mouth to get the paisás.

The exceeding love of money.

Hindús place some paisás within the mouth of the corpse just after death. Cf. Note to "*Áyas wate,*" &c.

Mordas chhuh marit martabah hurán.

After death the man receives greater honour.

De mortuis nil nisi bonum.

Mordas chhih wadán bihit, batas chhih wadán wudanih.

People weep for the dead sitting down, but they weep for the bread standing up.

Loss of bread is greater than the loss of one's friends.

"Morun ai tah márun kyah?" "Rat chon ai tah woṭ dini kyah?"

"If you squeeze me why do you kill me?" "If you have drunk the blood, why do you leap?"

A dialogue between a flea and a man.

To worry a man before giving the final punishment.

Múdamatis sharbat chhukas marham pyos.

Sherbet at the time of death is as ointment upon a wound.

Opportune help is sometimes spoken of "as sherbet to a dying man."

Muḍas lorih hatah tah trukis kuní katah.

A hundred stripes for a fool, but a word to a sharp man.

Persian.—*Agar ákḷí yak ishára bas ast.*

Múdis nábad súd kyah?

What is the good of giving sugar to the dead?

Panjábí.—*Jíte na púchhe, mue dhaṛ dhaṛ píṭe.*

Mudur dain tsukih nah tah tsuk dain mudarih nah.

A sweet pomegranate will not become bitter, and a bitter pomegranate will not become sweet.

A man is according to his disposition.

Mugul díshit gatshih Phársí khasuni.

On seeing a Mughal one should speak Persian.

One should be *au fait* in all society.

Mujih pĕthah muliwĕni.

From the radish radish leaves.

"Can the fig-tree bear berries or a vine figs?"

Mulan drot tah patran sag.

A sickle for the roots, but watering the leaves.

Quoted when a son is treated better than the father.

Muli hĕt kulih tshanun.

After buying a thing to throw it into the river.

Expenditure without profit.

Mulk-i begánas andar chhuh mahnyuv sag-i-díwána.

A man in a foreign country is like a mad dog.

Munanĕn húnĕn shaposh tah mĕh nah kalaposh tih.

Muna's dogs have got a big quilt, but I have not even a skull-cap.

Not a shirt to his back.

Munih, munih Phátí kunih nai kĕnh.

Pounding pounding, O Phátí, but nothing anywhere.

Working like a horse and spending like an ass—nothing for the rainy day.

Múnis nah liwun húnis nah nast chhuh thawán.

He will not let the whitewash remain on the wall or the nose upon the dog (so cantankerous is he).

Murádí, húl. Gánṭih nuá ṭhul. Wád kar. Bád peyíyí.

O Murádí, húl. The kite has taken the egg. Give an answer. Let syphilis attack you.

A Kashmírí curse.

"The kite has taken the egg," means "Death has taken your child."

Húl is the sound made for driving away kites.

Músah Khánun kastur.

Músa Khán's nightingale.

An obstinate fellow.

This was a celebrated bird, which would sing when its master did not wish it to sing, and *vice versá.*

Musalmán marih drági. Baṭah marih Mági.

Musalmán will perish from starvation, the Panḍit will perish from cold.

It is imperative upon the religious Panḍit to bathe in the month of January, and not a few die from so doing. The ordinary Musalmán is not accustomed to fast, and so in famine time is not able to bear the limited living so well as the Panḍit can.

Mág corresponds to our month of January.

Mut tsul put-dárih kulai hĕt aṭah bárih.

The madman escaped by the back window taking his wife upon his back.

A man who forsakes his fatherland, &c.

Myánih kánz pisho tah wugrah ḍulyo, tah nunah ṭulyo.

My drop of vinegar, pot of unstrained rice, and pinch of salt.

That is best which is according to one's lot and temperament.

Kánz is rice-water kept till sour, and then used with fish, &c., as vinegar.

Pish, lit., a flea, but here means little, an atom, a drop, &c.

Wugrah is unstrained rice. The poorer classes do not strain their rice, as the doing so would considerably lessen the quantity.

Ḍul is a large earthenware vessel, big enough to bathe in.

Myon ásit chon gav, mangun hyut tah ashud gav.

It was mine and became yours, and when I began to ask for it, it was (as if) collyrium to me (*i. e.,* something to be much desired).

To give away a thing and very much want it back again.

Myon kájiwaṭ panun wachh.

(Would that you would take) my pestle (and beat) your own breast with it.

A Kashmírí curse.

Myúṭh gámas tah krúṭh pananis pánas.

Sweet to the village, but rough to one's ownself.

Charity begins at home. A gentleman should show himself such in his own house.

N

Nádán ai zánih zih nádán chhus, adah chhuh nah nádán.
If the ignorant man knows that he is ignorant, then he is not ignorant.

Nádánas nasíhat karuni goyá kih panzĕn nun dyun.
Giving advice to a stupid man is like giving salt to a squirrel. (*Cui bono?*)

Nadarĕn mál tah ḍambuk ḥít.
Wish of nadur, but pretence of ḍumb.

"A little, very little more, if you please"; and all the time he wants a plateful.

Nadur is a vegetable growing in the city lake, (the stalk of the *Lotus-Nilumbium*). It is eaten by all natives during the winter, because of its heating qualities, but it is especially eaten by Hindús on the anniversary of a relative's death, when neither fish, nor flesh, nor turnips, &c., are allowed for food, and on other great days also.

Ḍumb is thin, small nadur.

Nade nám samjhog chhuí insánah sunz zindagi.
A melá by the river (all alive with excitement one minute and quiet the next) is like a man's life.

"What is your life? It is even a vapour."

Nadharani naṭ.
Nadhar's fright.

Any special fear.

Nadhar is a cormorant (?)

Ná-fahm gav suí, yas ná-fahmas suĕt kom gats̠hih.
He is an unintelligent man, whose business is with an unintelligent man.

A man is known by the company which he keeps.

Nafas chhuh san dáwán tah ts̠úrah karanáwán.
Lust causes a man to break into a house and rob.

A glutton will steal.

Nafas-parwaras nishih yiyih nah hunar parwarí ; be-hunaras nishih yiyih nah sarwarí.

From a sensualist will not come a fondness for art ; and from an unskilful man will not come leadership.

Nafsuí myon chhuí hustuí, ami hasti munganam garih garih bal ;
Lachhih manzah sásah manzah akháh lustuí nah tah hĕtinam sárí tal.

My soul is like that of an elephant and that elephant asked me every hour for food ;
Out of a lákh and out of a thousand but one is saved ; if it hadn't been so, the elephant had crushed all under his feet.

One's craving lusts.
A saying of Lal Dĕd's.

Nágah gáḍah, wuchhanih halál tah khĕnih harám.

The fish in the (sacred) spring is lawful to look at, but unlawful to eat.

Touch not ; taste not ; handle not.

Nagrah nírit Pándrĕnṭhan.

Going out from the city and living at Pándrĕnṭhan.

A merchant's country-house.
Pándrĕnṭhan is a pretty little village about three miles from Srínagar.

Nah chhas wutsani tah nah dazani, bihit chhas labih, kanih haná khĕni.

There is no scorching or burning to him ; he just sits aside and eats a little.

" What does he care ? He has not had to pay for it."

Nah gatshĕm mánchh tah nah gatshĕm ṭop.

I do not want honey, nor do I want the sting.

" Every thing that fair doth show,
When proof is made proves not so."

Nah khair tah nah barkat.

Neither well-wishes nor blessing.

A man who earns much money, but spends it in such a way as that nobody is especially benefited by it—not even his family.

Nah tran manz nah truwăhan manz.

Neither in three nor in thirteen.

A partnership by no means.

Nalah Rázun palav.

Nala Rájá's piece of cloth.

The climax of distress.

Nala Rájá began his reign well. He was just and holy, and everybody respected him. But it chanced that one day, while he was out eating the air, he saw two or three men gambling, and noticing that they each one seemed to be most excited over the game, he thought that it must be a very interesting means of amusement and determined to learn it. Accordingly, when he got back to his palace he called his wife and began to gamble with her. He grew more and more interested in gambling, until at last under one or another form it was his hourly amusement. He was wont to lay very high stakes—sometimes a palace, sometimes an army, and sometimes a lákh of rupees. Rájás and other great men came from distant countries to play with him; and as he was more often unsuccessful than successful, he soon lost all his country and his fortune, and escaped into a foreign land. He was wandering with his wife in a jungle in the strange land one day, when nothing remained to them both but one large wrap, which they cut into two pieces and made two wraps of. The Rájá told the Rání, Damyĕntí by name, to walk about the jungle in one direction and see what she could obtain; and he would go in another direction. A peasant who happened to be in the jungle met the Rání and gave her three dried fish. She took them to her husband with great delight, and he told her to go and wash them in the river. As she was washing them behold! amrit, the water of life, came forth from her thumb and touching the fish made them alive again, and they escaped in the river. She went and told her husband, who did not believe her, but thought that she had eaten the fish. The poor woman was very much hurt at her husband's want of confidence in her, and was in much fear lest he should forsake her—leave her alone in that desolate jungle. So she arranged the bedding (which consisted only of the divided wrap) in such a way as that the Rájá could not possibly arise from his bed in the night without disturbing her. He was enveloped in one side of the wrap, upon the other side of which she was lying. The Rájá however defeated her plans by cutting his piece of the wrap; and ran away. On the road a snake bit him and his whole countenance turned quite black and was so changed that nobody would have recognised in him the Nala Rájá. However he survived and went and took service in another Rájá's establishment.

The Ráni finding in the morning that her husband had abandoned her, resolved to go unto her father's house. Her parents were terribly shocked and grieved to find their daughter in such a state. They comforted her, arrayed her again in fitting garments, and promised her, that if her husband did not appear by a certain date they would arrange for another marriage. News was sent to all the Rájás to appear at a certain date, because one of them would be chosen as the future husband of the beautiful girl.

Among the many other Rájás which were present on the appointed day was the Rájá in whose service the Nala Rájá was employed. Nala Rájá also went with him; and when he had opportunity on the way, he related to his master all that had happened to him,—his gambling propensities, his ruination, his life in the jungle and his abandonment of his wife there. When the Rájá heard this he was dumbfounded with astonishment, and fell at his feet, "My brother," said he, "why did you not tell me all this before?" And he gave unto him his own mantle and sword, and appointed unto him a full number of servants. Thus they reached the Rání's parent's palace. The other Rájá introduced Nala Rájá and recounted all that he had heard.

Great was the rejoicing in the palace that day and many days afterwards;—for the lost husband and son had been found. How glad was Nala Rájá! How happy was Rání Damyĕntí! Gifts were lavished upon them; they again lived in a grand house; had servants and horses, and every luxury; and were happy ever afterwards.

This story was told me by an ignorant Paṇḍit, and varies from the original story, for which *vide* Mahábhárata, Parab. III.

Nalam, kalam, yá halam.

Denial, the pen, or begging.

The way the Paṇḍits make a living.

Muhammedans cite this concerning their Paṇḍit brethren. The say that they lie, they write reports, petitions, &c., or they beg.

Náli gom tah nál wulnam.

He annoyed me and leaped upon me like a serpent.

A troublesome, worrying person.

Náli nah zaṭ tah máli náv.

Not a rag over the body and her name Máli.

Máli, a female name, from *mál*, meaning wealth, property.

Panjábí.—*Akhan te anhán te náon Nain Sukh.*

Nam ai wuthih tah mázas dag.
Máz ai wuthih tah namas dag.

If the nail rise there is pain to the flesh.
If the flesh rise there is pain to the nail.

Love me, love my dog.

Naman mits kaman kits?

Why is there dirt in the nails?

"You've got no family. Why do you go scraping in the dirt for money? To what purpose are you soiling your hands?"

Namedánam chhuí ráhat-i-jánam.

Ignorance is the peace of life.

Know not anything about anyone, or anything, and you shall preserve your peace.

Namrúdun hyuh dam diwán.

He boasts like Nimrod.

King Nimrod was a great oppressor, and became so proud and independent as to say there was no God ; and if there was, he dared him to do his worst. At last there came a voice from heaven bidding him to repent ; but Nimrod thought scorn concerning it. Then God sent a mosquito which entered Nimrod's nose and penetrated to the brain, causing him constant agony. Every time the pain came, the king used to send for his servant to beat him a hundred blows upon the left temple with a shoe. Eventually he was so worn by the pain that he died.

Nanawor pakun ján kuṅsh nah tang.

Better to go barefooted than to wear shoes too narrow.

Nandapúri káṅzinĕn láwah lug dyáran.
Kahan rúpĕyan kanihai ḍembah-hákah náv.
Sarmah sáz t͟sháṅḍán jumkah gráyih márán.
Búzitav dyáran kyah khuchar t͟sáv.
Ṭeṅki rúpĕyih neran halam chhih dáran.
Toshán garah zan rásh hĕt áí.
Saudá ninih wizih afsos láràn.
Búzitav dyáran kyah khuchar t͟sáv
Páṅsas nún gat͟shán ṭhulan táran.
K͟hudáyih wán n t͟shuntah ṭenḍi kháv.
Nún dit aḍhan tárat͟sih láran.
Búzitav dyáran kyah k͟huchar t͟sáv.

The money of the boatwomen of Nandapúr became rusted.
They sold one boat-load of vegetables for eleven rúpís.
They seek for collyrium to wash their eyes with, and shake their earrings (with pride).
Hear what alloy entered into their money.
When they go out to change a rúpí they hold out their skirts for the paisás ;
And on returning to their houses they rejoice as if they had brought a kingdom.
The buyer gets vexed at the time of buying.
Hear what alloy has entered in their rúpís.

* * * *

One paisá's worth of salt is only sufficient for three eggs.
O God paralyse the fingers of the baniyás.
When they give the salt they take half of it back in their scales.
Hear what alloy has entered into their rúpís.

Gafárá, a poet living in Káwaḍára, composed the above for the benefit of the vegetable-boatwomen and the baniyás; and sometimes the whole, sometimes portions of it are constantly quoted.

Nangas nindar prangas pĕṭh, sávis nindar pávis pĕṭh.

The poor man sleeps upon a bed (without a care), but the rich man sleeps upon the stairs (for fear of thieves).

Náni, bungriwáni hai auwí, achh myánih ḍíshit pachh múd wání. Kan myáni ḍíshit wan tsul wání. Náni bungriwáni hai auwí.

O grandmother, the bangle-man came, and after seeing my eyes he died in fifteen days. When he saw my ears, too, he ran away into the jungle. O grandmother, the bangle-man came.

Little children sing these words sitting upon the door-step. They are also cited when any man is filled with envy against another. He sees that man's prosperity, runs away in a rage, and dies from grief.

Nani nani karán gayih málunui gilawán torah áyih chhiṭih nuruí harám tas khoran puluhuruí.

She went in grand style to her father's house, and returned thence shaking the cuffs of her garment though she had not a grass shoe to her feet.

A stupid, trifling woman.

Nanis dub kyah chhalih?
Phákahladas kyah zalih?
What shall the washerman wash for the naked man?
What shall the fasting-man vomit?

Breeks from a Highlandman.

Nanis tar tsáyih tah dráyih;
Khanis tar walanah áyih.
Coldness to the naked man,—as it comes, so it goes
But coldness sticks to the rich well-dressed man.

Nanis wurun chhuh sudur púrun.

To "set up" a naked man with clothes is like trying to fill the ocean.

Reply to a poor debtor, or great spendthrift, to whom Rs. 100 would be a mere trifle.

Nanis wurun here means to "set a man up" in a business, to stock his shop, and marry his daughter, &c.

Nar zinih tah nadur sinih badal.

Reed in the place of firewood, and the stalk of the lotus instead of meat.

A stupid arrangement.

Nadur is the stalk of the Lotus (*Nilumbium*), which grows abundantly in the Kashmír lakes, and is eaten largely by the inhabitants of the valley. Hindús cut up the stalk into small pieces, cook it with oil and spices, and eat it along with fish, &c.

Nárah dráv sun hyuh.

Like gold come forth from the fire.

The better for his sickness, trials, &c.

Nárah wizih kyúr khanun!

Digging a well at the time of fire!

Panjábí.—*'Ag lagián khúh khatauná!*

Naras nábad tah tularih máñchh, tah halam halis ránithas dachh.

Sugar-candy from a reed; and honey from the bee; and grapes from a very crooked vine.

God brings good out of bad.

Nast tsaṭhai tah babarih ṭukhá.

Cutting your nose is like cutting the top of a babar (it only grows the stronger).

Cited to a shameless person.

Babar (Persian, *Ríhán*), the sweet basil.

Náṭah ganzarit tah ros mínit.

Counting the pieces of flesh and measuring the soup.

No chance for a thief under such a man as that.

Naṭich dimai nah tresh, haṭyuk wandai rat.

I will not give you water from the water-pot to quench your thirst therewith, but I will give you my throat's blood.

Great words but little deeds.

Natsahah tah ángun chhum tsut.
Wanahhah tah wan chhum durih.
I would dance, but the yard is small.
I would speak, but the jungle is distant.
Fear on account of circumstances.

Natsán tih pánai tah wáyán tih pánai.
He himself dances to his own playing.
A fool who laughs at his own remarks.

Nawih handi gindán pumbarih dashan; paránih handi poshán pashan tal.
The children of the new wife are playing with the fringe of their father's shawl, while the children of the old wife are crying under the roof.

Nayih andar pai.
A fence on the plateau. (Cui usui?)
An unnecessary work and expense.

Náz karizih babas tah májih máz wetsēs nah khalih;
Náz karizá kákas tah kákanih chapát láyas galih?
We should ask our parents for anything we may want; because their body will not contain them, they will be so happy to give;
We should not ask our elder brother, or his wife, for anything, as they may give us a slap upon the cheek.

Něbarah nundbon tah andarah tshutsah kon.
Outside he is beautifully and splendidly dressed, but inside he is an empty walnut.
Hypocrisy.

Něbarimis mahynivis gatshih ásun ṭiḍi tah paḍur tah yál tah chál, dár tah kár.
To the man with employment the turban (must be right), the feet (proper), the hair (behind the ear), the character (good), the beard (trimmed), and the neck (clean), (*i e.*, he must mind his P's and Q's, or else he will be turned out of his employment).

Něchivi hana wánganas sumb, yaḍ chhas ánganas sumb.
A boy about the size of an egg-plant has a stomach about the size of a courtyard.
Wangun is the *Solanum melongena*, called Brinjál in the plains.

Nekan chhuh Khudái khush.

God is pleased with good people.

Nekan lár tah badan phulun.

The good are troubled and the bad blossom.

"The ungodly, who prosper in the world; they increase in riches. Verily, I have cleansed my heart in vain."—Psalm lxxiii. 12, 13.

Neko, nek kar tah bad labih pánai.

O, good man, do good; the wicked will receive his deserts.

Neknám chhuh gatshán yĕtskáli tah badnám chhuh gatshán jald.

A good name comes after a while, but a bad name is soon obtained.

Neknám chhĕh bekh daulat.

A good name is the root of wealth.

Nĕmáz chhĕh farz tah luṭ chhuh karz.

Prayer is a duty and plunder is a debt.

A Paṭhán saying.

Nĕmázi sunz unguj.

The finger of the prayer.

"Because sentence against an evil work is not executed speedily, therefore the heart of the sons of men is fully set in them to do evil."—Eccl. viii. 11.

A Paṭhán of high family while saying his prayers in the Juma Masjid here was very much annoyed by another man poking him from behind. He gave him one rúpí to desist. The man left off annoying this worshipper, but was encouraged by the present to prosecute his wickedness upon some other worshipper. The other man, however, was not of such a quiet disposition as the Paṭhán, for he at once rose up, drew his sword and struck off the troubler's head with one stroke.

Níya'as rújub diyiñ tas Khudái.

God will give a man according to his wish.

"Delight thyself also in the Lord; and he shall give thee the desires of thine heart."—Ps. xxxvii. 4.

Nosh gayih rĕti zun ás yĕti.

The daughter-in-law went for a month (to her father's house) and it was as if she had not been away at all (time passed so quickly because they were so much happier during her absence).

Daughter-in-laws are a continual stumbling-block to the other inhabitants of the house.

Nosh layih nah hár tah khor pĕṭh máritos hund !

A daughter-in-law is not worth a cowrie ; and kill a ram for her over the feet !

Daughter-in-laws are altogether despised until they are grown up—they may develop into ugly and uncouth women, or they may die, or their affianced husband may die, &c.

A certain daughter-in-law was sick and likely to die, and therefore her mother-in-law was advised to sacrifice a sheep for her. The woman replied in the words of the above saying, the plain meaning of which is "Let her die. What does it matter? My son is not bound to her."

"*Over the feet*" refers to the custom of slaying the animal near to the closed feet of the person for whom it is sacrificed.

Nosh lúkas, kúr lúkas, ná-hakk lúkas mengah dag.

Daughter-in-law to some, a daughter to others, but as far as the unconnected man is concerned she is only a headache.

At a native marriage there is much feasting, music and dancing. A general hubbub prevails. The parents and relatives of course enjoy themselves ; but the other guests and friends, especially those who have come out of pure friendship to help and congratulate, have a hard time of it ; to them the wedding is as one continued headache.

Noshí, lajoí "málinih málinih," málin chání hai, díṭ.
Adah lajoí "áṭhih áṭhih" bastai phaṭit bíṭ.

O daughter-in-law you are always boasting of "my father's house." Look here, we have seen your father's house.

You said, too, that you would receive some flour (from your father's house) ; but the skins must have burst (and the men who are bringing it) must be sitting down (on the way).

Kashmíris carry their flour, rice, and other grain, tied up in a sheep's or goat's skin.

Noshih dup hashih kun "Wastai bun." Phírit dupnas "Zan chhaham sun !"

The daughter-in-law said to her mother-in-law "Come down." (The mother-in-law) answered, "As if you were my rival with my husband !"

Nov golih gáv pyáyih-hal khĕyá kih nah wutsh tráwih ?

The cow is about to be delivered of her first calf ; we do not know whether she will die, or give birth to a calf.

General reply to the too-inquisitive dispositions which beset a house at the time of a woman in travail.

Hal khyun, to eat the after-birth, *i.e.*, to die.

Nov natsai tah paráni diwai.

New dancing and an old fair.

When any man is seized on some charge, the kotwál comes, sipáhís come, and a crowd gathers as if to an old-established fair; and the people almost dance with excitement.

Nov nuṭ hyuh.

Like a new water-pot.

A man fresh and strong, "spick and span."

Nún nábad tah tíl phalilah tah zún tsandun tah batah mukh-tah.

Salt as rare as sugar, oil as scarce as ointment, wood as if sandal, and dinner (*i. e.*, food) like eating pearls (so expensive).

Hard times.

Nun nizĕn nah bazzázah-wán tah buchh nizĕn nah wázah-wán.

Take not the naked man to the cloth-shop, or the hungry man to the cook-shop.

Another version is :—

Buchh gatshih nah nyun wázah-wán tah nun gatshih nah nyun dubi-wán.

The hungry man must not be taken to the cook-shop, and the naked man must not be taken to the washerman's house.

Nún, tíl zyúṭ, athah myon myúṭ.

More salt and oil, and my hand is sweet.

Give me the money, and I will transact the business ; give me the tools, and I will do the work.

Núnan mún.

Wool is obtained by giving salt (to the sheep).

Money is not wasted on some people and things.

Nunih nánih hund tsinih-áshnáv.

A supposed grandmother's charcoal-relations or acquaintances.

A cousin of the fifth or sixth remove.

Charcoal-acquaintances. People from the villages often pay a visit to the city during the winter season bringing with them charcoal for sale. They sell their load, put up for a night in some person's house, and are off again the following morning.

Núrah achhĕn tsúrah ṭoli.

A heavy look about the bright eyes.

Grief.

Núrah buthis chhuh yatshán súrah buth yatímas.
The bright face becomes ash-colour, when the child is left an orphan.
God protect the fatherless.

Núrah myánih túr tsalán.
(At the look of) my bright face fever runs away.
Always carry a pleasing countenance.

Nuṭ tah hammám.
Just a water-pot and a bath.
Hardly a stick in the house.

Nyuk chhuh ásán truk.
A lean man is clever.

P

Padis tal tungul.

Fire under the sole of the foot.

"Ah! when you get a red hot coal under your foot, you will know what fire is."

Pádsháh sindis dĕwán-khánas.
Tíl o chĕrág dazán chhus.
Sári gatshán pánas, pánas;
Kunuí zaná rozán chhus.
In the palace of the monarch.
Oil and lamps are burning (burning).
All are to their own place going;
Only one (man) is remaining.

This is metaphorical language. The monarch is God, the palace is the world, and the people are the inhabitants thereof; the oil and lamps are the sun and moon, which are constantly coming and going: the people are also temporary—gradually they die off, until at last only one, and that God, will be left.

This is also a Kashmírí riddle, of which the answer is the Sun and Moon.

Pádsháhas pásbání.

To the king the work of a watchman is difficult.

A man who has come down in the world, and is not equal to his reduced circumstances.

Pahar gav, wahar gav; doh gav, koh gav;
Pachh gav, wachh gav; rĕt gav, khĕt gav;
A watch (*i.e.*, a space of three hours) gone is as if a year had passed;
One day gone is as if a mountain had become;
Fifteen days passed by is as if (the debt) had been forgotten;
And a month elapsed (without payment) is as if the money had been eaten (*i.e.*, irretrievably lost).

Pakanah páz; gandanah gosáni; khĕnah bulbul.

Like a hawk in his walk, a jogí in clothing, and a bulbul in eating.

Some people want servants manufactured to order.

Pakharporik hakhar.

The oxen of Pakharpúr.

Like a tantony pig.

Saiyid Muhammad 'Ali, a very holy man, came all the way from Baghdád to Kashmír to be Shekh Núr-ud-udín's disciple. He took up his abode in Pakharpúr, about fifteen miles from the city of Srínagar. He was one of the Shekh's favourite followers. After a time he became so enraptured with the country that he begged to be permitted to remain there altogether. Núr-ud-dín consented to this, and to save him expense and trouble, he miraculously brought all his house, ground and family, from Baghdád to Kashmír in a moment of time. There was no doubt about this in olden times; because there was the man's wife and children standing before him; and there is no hesitation in believing this in the present day, for you can examine for yourself the different style of building of the house, the different nature of the soil, the different trees and plants, &c.

This Saiyid Muhammad 'Alí, in consequence of this especial favour, became a very celebrated character. He was accustomed to speak and to act strangely, but all the people accounted him holier on account of these eccentricities. One of his orders was, that if any man was in trouble and wished to be relieved of it, he must set free an ox These oxen thus set free were to wander whither they liked, and do whatsover they wished, and nobody dared to lift up a stick against them, or to complain. In olden days several of these oxen wandered about, and were a great nuisance; but now they have been reclaimed and put to the plough. Saiyid Muhammad 'Alí was buried in Pakharpúr, and many visit his grave during the year.

Pákhuí chhuh pák.

Only the Pure One is pure (*i. e.*, God).

Panah sán khĕyih búni tah jits sán khĕyih húni.

He will eat the chinár tree—leaves and all, and he will eat the dog with the skin.

A regular cannibal, not satisfied with enough.

Panah tali ḍinj tah ḍenjih tali pan.

Below the thread the ball or knot, and below the knot the thread.

A man, who sees that he is, but will not confess that he is, in the wrong.

Panane hachih chhĕh bahah trachih.

One's own harvest (no matter how small) is as twelve traks.

The produce of one's own labour is sweet.

Trak is a grain measure containing nine and a half English pounds.

Pananĕv chhuh nah paigambar mánmut.

A prophet is not accepted by his own people.

"A prophet is not without honour save in his own country and house."—Matt. xiii. 57.

Panani kukĕr nai bad ásih tah lúkah hundih garih kyázih trávih thul?

If your hen is not a bad one, then why does she go and lay her eggs in other people's houses?

Ungrateful offspring.

Panani nam chhih pananih thar kashán.

Scratching one's back with one's own nails.

Satisfying yourself with your own money, own house, &c.

Búståán of Sa'dí.—*Ba juz nákhun o juz sarangusht-i-man,*
Na Kharad kase dar jahán pusht-i-man.

Panani pám diwán bĕyis.

Giving your reproach to another.

Some Kashmírís say pán instead of pám, and then it is:—

Giving yourself to another.

Making out everyone as bad as yourself.

Pananih athah ráwarun tah bĕyih sund ratshrun chhuh barábar.

To lose anything by one's own hand, and to receive anything at the hand of another, is equal.

To receive a benefit is to sell one's liberty.

Pananih bachhih ai animah ásih kátsah machhih gatshan paidah!

If there should be any rice-water upon your fire-place, how many flies will be born there!

Money attracts friends.

Pananih bananah tah lúkah handih wananah.

Because I am, what I am, people say this of me.

Pananih garuk hák-wák chhuí bĕyih sandis puláwas barábar.

Vegetables from my own garden are equal to puláv from another man's (house).

Puláv is a dish of meat and rice cooked together with spices.

Pananih thajih ai batah ásih kátyáh májih gabar gatshan paidah!

If there is any food in the pot how many mothers and children will be born!

Pananuí pon chhuh panis phátawán.

Breaking the log with the log's own wooden wedge.

Another version is :—

Ponuí phátawán chhuh zinis.

A (little) wedge (from the tree) splits the wood.

Set a thief to catch a thief.

A big tree in the jungle was ordered to be cut down, and already four men had gone to the blacksmith's shop to purchase an axe for the work. One man, who admired the tree, heard these men speaking together and forming their plans ; and went at once and told the tree. The tree replied, "Thanks, O friend, for the information, but do not be afraid. Four men and an axe will not do much damage to me." The next day the man came again and said, "More news, O tree ! To-morrow these men are coming to destroy you." The tree again tried to assure the man that four little men and a pound or so of iron could not do any material damage to a big tree like he was. The man went, but returned again the next day saying, "O tree, be not elated by false hopes. These men have laid a clever and certain plan for your destruction. Listen, One man will first climb you ; and cut off one of your thin top-branches. Out of this branch he will make a handle for the axe, and a wedge. Then he will prepare a hole in your trunk and insert the wedge, upon which they will strike and strike until your great wide trunk is completely severed." "Alas ! alas !" said the tree, "by this means they will bring me down ; I am certain to die."

Pananuí zágán kulphas tah táris ;
Pananuí kustám san hĕt dráv.

One's own relation lies in wait for lock and bolt ;
It is a relation who goes out with the stolen goods.

Pánas khĕtan magar dánas pevtan.

Let him eat, but let him keep his fire.

Selfish fellow, we do not want anything from him !

Pánas nishih pańsah chhuí gul tai mul,
Bĕyis nishih pánsah chhuí hil tai hech.

Your own money is flowers and wine, but another's money is but weed—nothing.

Pándah-Chhuk, nashan sukh tah korin dukh.

O Pánda-chhuk, let there be peace to your daughters-in-law, but trouble to your daughters.

Shekh Núr-ud-dín's curse upon this village, which is about three miles from Srínagar in the Islámábád direction.

Pánih rust dánih khasiyá zih nánih rust shur khasih.

Will the rice rise without water, that the child should grow without a grandmother?

A grandmother's influence in a house is very often greater in every way than that of the mother of the family.

Páṅsah ai thawizĕn murdas pĕṭh suh tih gatshih thud wuthit.

If a paisá be placed upon a dead man he will rise up.

Money will bring people back from the dead.

Hindús place a paisá inside the mouth of the corpse, wherewith it may be able to pay the ferry, &c., cf. note "*Áyas wate,*" &c.

Páṅsah gav párud tah mikráz, yat pĕṭh thawizen tat tsaṭih.

Money is as quicksilver and scissors, lay it upon what you will, it will cut it (*i.e.*, do its work).

Páṅsah nishih chhuh páṅsah phaṭán.

Paisás burst out of paisás.

Money makes money.

Panun ai márih shihilis tráwih; parud ai márih tah márithuí gatshih.

If my own (relations or friends) smite me, he will leave me in a shady place (*i.e.*, he will bury me); but if a stranger smites me he will kill me and go.

A friend's a friend for aye that.

Panun ai márih, totih kunih jáyih tárih.

If my own smite me, yet in some place he will help me.

Ad supra.

Panun khĕwán pánzú tah bĕyih sund karán dalwánzú.

Eating a good dinner in his own house, yet interfering in the matters of other people (*i.e.*, disputing for them, scandalising them, &c.)

Mind your own dinner and mind your own business.

Panun muhim chhuh háwán pánai wat.

Each misfortune will show its own way.

Panun paizár babah sunz pombar.

One's own shoe and father's shawl.

Hardly earned, dearly loved.

A boy purchased a pair of shoes with his own earnings, and one day as he was walking along in these new shoes they became very dusty. The boy was much grieved and sat down by the way side and cleaned them with his beautiful pashmína shawl, which his father had given him.

Panun wadanáwih parud asanáwih.
He made his friends to weep, but his enemies to laugh.

Panzih hund pút.
A monkey's young one *i.e.*, (a chip of the old block).

A variant of this with quite a different meaning is :—

Panzih hund pút, yusuí toṭh chhus ásún ; tas chhĕh zorah wachhas tal raṭán, sui chhuh marán.
The young of a monkey, who is dear to her ; she presses it hard against her breast, so that the young one dies.

A favourite child or servant, is often spoilt by an exaggerated affection and regard.

Natives say that monkeys love their young ones so much, that in the excitement of their affection they sometimes press them so hard against their breasts, that they get stifled and die.

Panzis dapyá punz zih mandul chhuí wazul.
Will a monkey tell a monkey that his buttocks are red ?

The crock calling the kettle black.

Parán parán par gayih k͟háli, k͟har gayih kitábah búrí hĕt.
He reads and reads until his strength is gone, and he has become like a donkey carrying a load of books.

"Much learning doth make thee mad."—Acts xxvi. 24.

Paras͟purik wázah pánai ranán tah pánai pananin athan thokah tráwán !
The cook from Paraspúr cooks the food himself, and he himself spits into his own hands (as if disgusted with it) !

Disgusted with one's own work.

Many cooks reside in Paraspúr, a village in the Lár tĕhsíl. It is a custom with the majority of cooks to first sit down and eat their own dinner (by way of tasting perhaps ?) before serving up the different dishes to the guests. Should they not like the food, they will spit into the palms of their hands and in other ways express their sorrow. Many show their grief under different circumstances in this vulgar manner.

Parini t͟sar.
Porous like a sieve.

More holy than righteous.

Parmánt͟sanah rust kur chhai burzah rust lar.
A daughter without parmánt͟san is like a house without proper roofing.

Parmántsun. At time of marriage Hindús give to their daughters a long piece of cloth called zúj, to wear upon the crown of their heads, and thence extend to the small of the back. Some for certain reasons delay giving this till some years after; but this delay means increased trouble and expense.

Burzah is the *liber* of a species of birch, used in roofing houses, and also as paper for rolling up goods in. Native writing-paper, too, is made from it.

Pashah pěṭhah shín tráwun.

To throw snow off from the roof (generally done quickly and carelessly; hence any work done hastily and carelessly.)

Pashmínasuí chhěh narmí.

Only pashmína has softness.

Only good people are gentle.

Pashmína is a fine kind of woollen cloth manufactured in Kashmír. The finest goat's wool employed in its manufacture is brought from Túrfán, in the Yárkand territory. This is called *Túrfáni phamb*; all other qualities are called *Kashmíri phamb*; though these as well as the former are found only on the animals who live on the wind-swept steppes of Central Asia.

"Patah" guftam wěsí.

O friend, I said "Afterwards."

Opportunity mis-spent.

Wěs a female friend, a flirt.

Patim gar chhěh bukuri dar.

The last hour is a hard time (*i.e.*, the last hour of a woman's travail, or of life, or of any work, &c.)

Páz panjaras andar band.

A hawk shut up in a cage.

A clever man without work.

Phágunì mujen swádui kyah?

What taste have radishes in the month of February?

What profit from an old wife or servant?

People gather the radishes in the autumn, and bury them under the ground for use in the winter. By the month of February they begin to rot and are unfit for food.

Phakír tsáyov ángan tah honih watshov dod.

A faqír came into the court-yard, and the dog was pained.

An old servant displeased with a new servant, to whom out of charity the master has given a little work.

Phal kului chhuh namit.
The fruit-tree is bending.
The more knowledge there is in a man, the humbler he becomes. Persian—*Nihad shákh i pur mewa sar bar zamín.*

Phalis hyul tah helis khár diyanai Khudá.
May God bless your every seed to a sheaf, and your every sheaf to a kharwár.
A Kashmírí blessing.

Pharih han khĕwán baḍ tah myou han karán lut.
A small dried fish ate a big fish, and (the cat) gave a gentle mew.
A man with a big appetite, but little voice.

Pharih hanz buzáyih máj lukav dupus "Gáḍai chhuh buzán."
A fisherman, roasted his mother, and the people said within themselves. "He is roasting fish."
One-half the world does not know what a struggle the other half endures to live.

"Roasting one's mother" here means selling her jewels and clothes for food. Cf. note "*Yas nah watsh nar,*" *&c.*

Pharih-hánz chhuá guri khasán?
Is the fisherman riding a horse?
Every thing will not be as we wish.

There are many kind of boatmen in Kashmír named according to their boats, or their special work. The Pharih-hánz are those who catch the little fish to be found in the Wular lake during the winter season, and cook and dry them for sale in the bázár. Cf. note "*Yas nah watsh nar,*" *&c.*

Pharih tsúras chhuh dárih kunḍ lor.
A bone stuck in the beard of the man who stole a dried fish.
A thief carries marks of detection along with him.

One day a great robbery was committed in the house of a certain person of the city, and report of the matter reached the ears of the ruler. The ruler was very much enraged, when he heard the account of such a dastard robbery. It appears that the robbers had first dined with their host and then robbed his house. Amongst other dishes provided for the dinner was a dish of broiled fish.

The ruler declared that he would have the man discovered and punished. He sent for the deputy-inspector of police, and ordered him to show the thief or die. The deputy-inspector trembled when he heard this command, but he did not despair. He was a bold and clever man. "Give me one hundred soldiers," he said, "and I will find the man."

The request was granted.

One day the deputy-inspector gave a great feast, and invited all the people of the city to come and make merry. A very large crowd was assembled. At a given moment he ordered the soldiers to silence the people and to seize the man, who should rub his beard after he, the deputy-inspector, had spoken to the company. There was perfect silence when the host, standing in a convenient position, that he might be seen by all, shouted with a loud voice, "There is a bone in the beard of that man who stole the fish." The thief happened to be present, and hearing these words, as if by instinct put up his hand to his beard and rubbed it. The movement was at once noticed by the appointed watchers, and the man was at once seized and taken before the deputy-inspector. The man's guilt was proved beyond all dispute, and he was very severely punished. Krishna, the deputy-inspector, was promoted to much honour.

Phatah Matin batah.

Mad Fatah's dinners.

This man was a great spendthrift. Quoted at an extravagant dinner, &c.

Phati Baṭ tah yaktanai.

Phati Baṭ and alone.

"Me and myself only."

Phati Pharhung.

A caricatured Englishman.

A stupid Kashmírí.

Kashmírís at their private feasts are fond of painting pictures of English people on long slips of paper and pasting these upon a long thin basket. Sometimes they put on English clothes and mimic the Sáhib's incorrect pronunciation of Hindustání words and curt salám, &c.

Phĕlas k͟hĕyih dyal.

The skin will eat the pimple.

An avaricious man.

Phiramat͟sih put͟sah prĕni kalas pĕṭh chhas zuwah aḍamam.

A slut may have a clean chádar over her head, but her head is full of dirt.

Puts.—A long piece of cotton cloth thrown over the head and allowed to hang down the back. It is the ordinary veil worn by the Kashmírí females.

Phirit phĕran.

Turning the garment.

Telling a lie; appearing different to what you really are.

Phul phuṭ tah dáwá kyah.

The joint is broken, what claim is there?

The dead wife's neglected mother.

Pilis nah tah ts̱ukí gás.

He couldn't reach the fruit, and therefore he said it was bitter.

The fox and the grapes.

Pír nah boḍ, yakín boḍ.

The pír is not great, faith is great.

One day Akbar asked Bírbal, which was the greater, the pír or faith. Bírbal replied "Faith is the greater." The emperor said, "You are wrong. The pír is the greater of the two." Bírbal was silent.

On leaving the emperor, Bírbal went and buried an ass's head in a certain place, and ordered that a mosque should be built over it.

Some years after this event, Akbar was exceedingly troubled by his enemies, and took counsel with his *wazír* as to what he should do. Bírbal advised him to go and pray for forty days in a certain mosque, and promised, that if he would there offer up prayers with a pure heart, God would certainly hear him and give him the victory over his enemies. The emperor obeyed and vanquished his enemies.

One afternoon, when Bírbal was alone with Akbar, he referred to their conversation some years ago, and asked the emperor whether he remembered it. The emperor replied "Yes"; and that he was of the same opinion still. Then Bírbal asked Akbar to accompany him to the mosque, where he had spent forty days in prayer, and see for himself what there was under its foundations. The building was razed to the ground, the foundations were dug up, and there, to the great astonishment of the one and the great amusement of the other, was discovered the skeleton of the ass's head. Akbar remarked: "You were right, Bírbal. Faith is greater than the pír."

Akbar supposed that the mosque had been erected over the bones of some Muhammedan saint, and with faith in this he prayed. Cf. "Tale of Holy Donkeys," "Leisure Hour," January, 1875.

Pír, ustád.

To call a saint a teacher (is a great insult).

Pírah khutah chhuh be-pírui ján.

A man who follows no saint (*i.e.*, who does not make any profession of religion) is better off than the man who has a saint, (but does not attend to his teaching).

"Pírah, wantam masallá," dupanas "Akí gom tasallá."

"O pír, tell me an illustration." He said to him, "From once saying there is comfort to me."

A pír visited a certain village, and was asked by the people there to give them a religious word. He said to them "Do not steal"; whereupon they smote him so that he ran away. A long time after he again went to this village, and again the villagers asked him to say something. He replied "No, no; I am quite happy from having spoken once."

Once is enough of this person or that thing.

Pírav máryov dánd, mĕh kyah rávyov zih buh wanahah kánsih.

The pírs killed an ox, what have I lost that I should tell anyone.

No business of mine.

Pish kari gunáh wagawis chob, wuchtav lúkav tamáshá!

The flea sinned, but the matting got the beating. Behold, O people, the sight!

Pitari nai ásan tah húni tih wuran ná?

If there were no cousins, would not the dogs bark? Yes.

The best of men have their enemies.

Cousins are constantly grumbling and fighting over the family property; so constant and bitter are these quarrels, that the word pitur, a cousin, has come to mean an enemy.

Pitur ai dizĕn kalah kin dánas zangav suĕt phuṭaráwih rupeyih bánah.

If a cousin be cast head-first into the fire, he will break a rupee's worth of pots with his legs (kicking about).

No love is lost between cousins.

Pitur ai dizĕn pĕni tatih tih tsaṭih yĕni.

If a cousin is asked to brush the warp with pĕni, (even then he will harm you), he will cut the warp.

Pĕn.—Natives rub the warp with a hand-brush soaked in rice water, to make the warp stronger.

Piyih nah shrapún tah ámin gogalan ás dárún.

Cannot digest rice-water, yet he opens his mouth for uncooked turnips.

A conceited, ignorant fool.

Poh áwai tshoh tshoh dĕwán. Mág chhum mol tah karĕm kyah?
Phágani pherahnam sheyih-trah pháh. Tsithar hahar kare kyah?
Wahik khasav baṭhore watsh dup watshare.

The month of December has come making gladness. January is my father—what will he do to me? In February thirty-six times heat will return to me. What will my brother-in law March do? Said the male calf to the female calf, "We will climb the hill in the month of April?"

December in "the Happy Valley" is a splendid month, if there is no snow. January, is called a father, because it is such a hard, strict month. In February the weather begins to get warmer. March is called a brother-in-law, because with its cold winds and rains it is constantly bothering the people. April is a nice month for the cattle, as the snow begins to melt off from the hills and the green grass appears. Towards the end of this month the gupan-gúr, or cow-herd, collects large herds of cattle belonging to other people, and drives them away to the mountains to graze.

Pohali nyál.

The shepherd's sign.

At the time of the crops people hand over their cattle to shepherds, who take them away in large numbers to the mountains for pasturage. Each beast has the special mark of its owner, (cf. note to *Pohol chhuh*, &c.), and should it happen that a wild beast devour it, the skin is, if possible, obtained and handed back to the owner as a proof that the animal has been slain. Cited when a man loses by lending a friend any thing, or by depositing anything in his care. Nothing but the remnants of the deposit are handed back with great sorrow.

Pohol chhuh dapán lokan, "Ak khĕv sahan byák khĕv shálan."

The shepherd says to the people (who gave him these sheep to tend upon the mountain), "One was devoured by a lion, and the other by a jackal."

At the time of the crops people hand over cattle to a shepherd, who takes them far away to pasture upon the mountains. Sometimes a thousand or more animals are in the charge of one family, and each one of these are specially marked with a cut on the leg, or a slit in the ear or tail, &c., so that they may at once be recognised by their different owners. The city people say that these hirelings generally happen to have two sons, the one called "Lion" and the other called "Jackal," who have very large appetites, and eat the sheep; so that when the shepherd says that a lion and a jackal ate them, he is not altogether (according to the popular native idea) telling a lie.

Poshah-matin aish.

The pleasure of a flower-fancier.

An easy time of it.

Many natives visit the different gardens around Srínagar, especially on Fridays, and with lute or guitar play, sing, and loll away the livelong day.

Posháken chhuh wunamut "Táh kartam sháh karat."

The garments said, "Take care of me and I will make you a king."

Táh kartam is literally "Fold me up."

Prĕnán jahánas tah wunán pánas.

He finds fault with the world and forgets that he himself is in the wrong.

Preyáguch búni nah thadán nah lokán nah badán.

The chinár of Preyág neither becomes taller, nor shorter, nor bigger.

A poor sickly child, who does not grow or become fat.

This chinár tree is in the middle of a little island just big enough to pitch your tent on, in the midst of the Jhelam river by the village of Shádipúr. The Hindús have consecrated the place, and a Bráhman is to be seen twice every day paddling himself along in a little boat to the spot, to worship and to make his offerings.

Pujis purutshuk adijih konah pachai az dupnak, "Panun ám nah kanh."

The people asked the butcher why his bones were not sold to-day. He replied, because none of my relations have been to me (to buy meat).

Puk ai ásih tah tokuí jan.

If it is cooked, then a little even is good (*i.e.*, worth having).

If he is clever, &c., then learn something from him; a little good, even, is not to be despised.

Punz ai pĕyih shethih gazah totih chhuh punzuí.

If a monkey fall sixty yards below, still he is a monkey.

Change of position does not change the man.

Purmut chhuh yurmut.

A well-read man is like a nicely cut stone.

Púshuk tih nai tsuluk tih ná?

If you have not got the victory, why do you not escape?

If you cannot stand your ground, then give it up.

Put chhukah thani.

Butter from the last turn (or last beat) of the stick.

A man fishing all day catches his first and only fish just as he is going away. A man, who has been struggling to find out, or do something all day, discovers, or does it just as he is about to give it up in despair.

Puṭ manḍit ; ṭuṭ khasit ; zanánah prasit ; kuṭ parit ; hĕndawĕnd tsaṭit ; tah insán phuṭit.

Paṭṭú must be pressed in the washing-tub ; a pony must be ridden on ; a woman must be in travail ; a son (must know the hardships of) learning ; a water-melon must be cut (before its sale) ; and a man must be broken (*i.e.*, humbled).

All things must be more or less tried by the rod of affliction, and are generally the better for having passed under it.

Hĕndawĕnd tsaṭit.—The purchaser makes the baniyá cut the water-melon before he pays for it, as it may not be red and ripe. One cannot tell what it is from the outside.

Pút, sopút, tah kopút

A son like his father; a son greater than his father; and a son less than his father.

The Kashmírís say that there are three kinds of sons.

Put put chhĕh pádsháhas gaibat.

Slander behind the king.

Abuse always follows the high and great.

Pútrah buchhih hún kochhih.

Hungering after a son she folds a dog to her bosom.

Putrah dádih muri mángai.

She holds out her skirt begging for a son.

It is quite a commonplace event for a barren woman to go to a person with a large family and beg for a son.

"*Putrah, khar tsul.*" "*Babah, pánah raṭun tah khasit is.*"

"O son, the ass has run away." O father, catch him and ride him back.

A variant is:—

Babah. Khar tsul, khar tsul.

Gobrah. Khas walah, khas walah.

Father. "The ass has got away; the ass has got away."

Son. "Go and ride him back; go and ride him back."

A rude, disobedient child.

Puz wanun chhuh achh kaḍuni.
A man may as well take out his eyes as tell the truth.

Puz wananah pan zan naṭan ; apuz wananah lagan ras.
Tell the truth and you'll tremble like a leaf ; tell a lie, and you 'll get relief and pleasure.

Pyav nah pyav ; zih Yaman khyav.
In the act of falling the angel of death ate him.
A quick death.
Yama or *Yam.*—" To great King Yama homage pay,
Who was the first of men that died,
That crossed the mighty gulf and spied
For mortals out the heavenward way."
Muir. O. S. T., v. 327.

Pyáwal zĕv.
An inventive tongue.
An imaginative, lying tongue.

R

Ráchhis dohah tah tsúras garah.

All day the watchman has to watch, but just twenty minutes is enough for the thief to steal.

Cf. Sir Kenneth's brief absence from the Mount of St. George, during which the standard of England was stolen.—"The Talisman." Ch. xiii.

Gar is really twenty-four minutes. A collection of terms used in Kashmír for indicating the different spaces and divisions of time may be interesting to some readers:—

Brunz.	=	a second, (*lit.*, just a flip of the finger).
Tsyuh	=	12 or 13 brunz.
Gar	=	60 tsyuhs.
Pahar	=	7½ gars.
Doh	=	4 pahars.
Doh-rát	=	8 pahars (*i.e.*, our full day of 24 hours).
Haftah	=	7 full days.
Pachh	=	2 haftahs.
Rĕt	=	2 pachhs (*i. e.*, our lunar month).
Warih	=	24 pachhs (*i.e.*, our year of 12 lunar months).

Aḍ rát (or nisf shab)	=	Midnight.
Patim pahar	=	3 o'clock A. M.
Kukar báng	=	Cockcrowing.
Gazal (Muhammedans) Brahma Muhúrta (Educated Hindús)	=	Just before daybreak.
Nyuk, nyuk, gásh (Uneducated Kashmírís.) Sunat (Muhammedans) Prabhát (Educated Hindús)	=	Daybreak.
Subh	=	Sunrise.
Aḍ koj	=	about 2¼ hrs. after sunrise.
Koj	=	about 4½ hrs. after sunrise.
Khanḍawáv Koj	=	about 11 o'clock A. M.
Dú pahar Manděni (especially Hindús). Sanskrit. *Madhyandena*	=	Midday.
Pĕshin (Peshí in the Panjáb)	=	about 2 o'clock P. M.
Sĕh pahar	=	about 3 o'clock P. M.
Nimuz (Muhammedans) Mimuz (Hindús)	=	about 3-30, o'clock P. M. (At this time during the long days the schoolmaster shuts his school for half-an-hour or so, that his pupils

may have time to go and eat a little food. If you asked a lad on coming from the school at such a time where he was going, he would invariably reply. To Mimuz or Nimuz, *i.e.*, to his afternoon meal.)

Digar (Dígar in the Panjáb) = about 4 o'clock P. M. (This is sometimes distinguished as boḍ digar and lukuṭ digar, referring respectively to a little time before and after the period.)

Aḍ digar = Sunset.
Shám = Evening.
K͟huphtan = Night. Bedtime, about 9-30 o'clock P. M.

Sometimes the Sanskrit word velá is added thus:—
"Aḍ rátuk velá" "Kukar bángih handih velá"; but this is more a Panjábí than a Kashmírí form of expression.—*Vide* Note 714, Vol I., "Panjáb Notes and Queries"; also Note 1011, Vol. II.

Rangari wánuk k͟hum akis khut tah bĕyis hut.

The dyer's vessel was a success to one and a failure to another.

The dyers have great earthen pots in which they prepare many gallons of dye at a time—sometimes they prepare as much as will last for six months. When the dye is ready for standing a cover is placed upon it and it is left perfectly still for twenty days. During these days should the weather be too hot or too cold the colour will not properly settle, and so much of the half-year's work will be spoilt.

Rangari wursah.

A dyer's story (therefore not to be believed).

Rangur. Dyers in the valley are generally Muhammedans. They have an ancient custom of agreeing beforehand amongst themselves that if the dye does not mix properly with the water, and after a time give forth a bad smell, (because it must corrupt before it is fit for use) they will go out and tell as many, and as great, lies as they can, until the dye-water does begin to stink. Some of the lying stories which they invent are very clever and interesting, and are believed in by not a few of the over-credulous people of Srínagar. I speak experimentally, having myself been the subject of one of these dyer's stories.

Ras laginam tah das t͟salinam.

May I get ease and be free from laziness.

A Kashmírí prayer frequently ejaculated at the commencement of any work.

Rasah rust batah gav thasah rust chhán.
Rice without soup is like a carpenter without sound.

Rástí bagair gatshih sárisuí hadd rachhun.
Besides (having) righteousness we must put a limit upon everything, (*i. e.*, have moderation).

Rat myáni kángar tah wuchh myáni ṭuk!
Take my kángar and see my paces!
A man with a proud walk.

Raṭ wandai tah puj-wánuk.
I will offer to you the blood of the butcher's shop.
Kind at the expense of another.

Rát wátán Gangahbal tah pagah nah yárahbal.
At night he arrives (in his thoughts and plans) at Gangábal, but on the morrow he does not even get to the landing place.
Always planning and never doing.
Gangabal is a stream tributary to the Sindh river; a holy lake near the top of Mount Harámuk.

Rátas waninas Lail; pagah dupnas "Suh kyah wátiheh Majnúnas"?
In the night the story of Lail was told to him, and on the morrow he said, "What relation will she be to Majnun?"
A dullard.
Lail or *Lailá* is the name of a lady frequently alluded to in the East. The loves of Lailá and Majnún are celebrated in a fine Persian poem by Nizámí.

Rátuk wádah sor nai rúd "Wulai gásah grákane."
Last night's promise was not kept, "Come, O grass-cutter."
Promises are like pie-crust, made to be broken.

Rawah zaṭ thawah katih?
A ragged rawah, where shall I spread it?
A poor braggart.
Rawah is a covering made from the fur of some animal, generally black, and imported from the Panjáb.

Raz daz tah wuṭhini chhĕs ati.
The rope is burnt (coal-black), but the twist is there (plain enough).
A man deposed or injured, but still harbouring bad thoughts.

Razí gaz tah soṭú már.

A yard of rope and a stick—strike.

Strict and swift justice.

There is a tale concerning Avantivarman, *alias* Wainadat *alias* Rájá Vĕn, one of the ancient kings of Kashmír, in which a piece of rope and a small stick are represented as fulfilling the duties of detective, police-officer, chaprásí, &c. If any man or beast or bird had done wrong, the stick and the rope would at once hasten to them, the stick would beat the offender, and the rope would bind him and bring him, her, or it, before the king for justice. Cf. "Indian Fairy Tales," the story of "The Rájá's Son and the Princess Labám," p. 156. "Here the Rájá's son found four faqírs, whose teacher and master had died, and had left four things,—a bed, which carried, whoever sat on it, whithersoever he wished to go; a bag, that gave its owner as much water as he wanted, no matter how far he might be from a tank; and a stick and a rope, to which its owner had only to say, if any one came to make war on him, 'Stick, beat as many men and soldiers as are here,' and the stick would beat them and the rope would tie them up." Cf. also "Folk-tales of Bengal," the story of "the boy whom seven mothers suckled," p. 121. "The boy took down the cage from the ceiling, as well as the club and rope. Having well secured the bird, he addressed the club and rope thus :—"O, stout club! O, strong rope! Take me at once to the other side." In the twinkling of an eye the boy was put on that side of the ocean. Similar quotations also might be made from "Wide-awake Stories," p. 294, "Old Deccan Days," pp. 174-175, "Fairy Tales from Brentano," pp. 146-154. Cf. also Wolf, Beiträge zur Deutschen Mythologie, 1., p. 12. "A lad sets out on a journey, having in his possession three wonderful things,—a buck-goat that spits gold, a hen that lays golden eggs, and a table that covers itself, without anybody's help, with the choicest food. A rascally innkeeper steals these treasures from the lad, and puts worthless trash in their place; but a stick that jumps out of a bag in which it is usually concealed, goes to work of its own accord upon the innkeeper's back, and with such effect that the lad gets his own again. The stick then returns of itself to its owner's hand."

Mr. Walter K. Kelly, in his most interesting book, "Curiosities of Indo-European Tradition and Folk-lore," commenting upon this last quotation, writes :—"The table in this story is the all-nourishing cloud. The buck-goat is another emblem of the clouds, and the gold it spits is the golden light of the sun that streams through the fleecy coverings of the sky. The hen's golden egg is the sun itself. The demon of darkness has stolen these things; the cloud gives no rain, but hangs dusky in the sky, veiling the light of the sun. Then the lightning spear of the ancient storm-god Odin leaps out from the bag that concealed it, the robber falls, the rain patters down, the sun shines once more." "This spear of Odin," the learned writer goes on to say, "is an equivalent of the asvattha rod of the Atharva-veda incantation, and both are "wish-rods" especially adapted for bringing victory to their possessor. They have also another comic counterpart in a sort of wish-rod, which serves for administering a drubbing at a distance. With such a hazel implement, cut and prepared wish the proper formalities, one has only to lay an old garment on a molehill or on a threshold, name the person intended, and whack away. That person will feel every blow as sorely as though he were actually under the stick, and if the old garment is beaten into holes so will it be with the skin of the absent sufferer." "Popular tradition is tough!"

Reh razih.

A flame to a rope.

A red flag to a bull.

Rĕtakálih gutshum potsh tah wandas gutshum lochh.

In summer I need a cotton phĕran and in winter I need a woollen phĕran.

Everything in season.

Phĕran is the chief garment of the Kashmírí, both male and female, and in shape not unlike a big nightgown with sleeves "a mile long." Sometimes the colour of these garments is red and other times blue. When made from wool they are called lochh, and when made from cotton, potsh. "Probably" the phĕran comes from the word pairáhan, the Persian for "garment."

Reyih chhuh shabnamai túfán.

The dew is like a flood to the ant.

Panjábí.—*Kírí nun tuthá dariá.*

Rish gayov pardesh dĕwah neriam Rishih náv tatih kuṭhios tamih nishih. Ná-hakkah, Rishe, gari drúk.

A Rishi went to another country, to try and get his name famous there as a Rishi, but he got less celebrated than before (in his own country). O Rishi, you left your home without a cause.

An emigre.

Rish (*Rishi* and *Rikhi*) is a Hindú sage or saint.

Rogan o záfarán az Pámpúr. Sóg az Lĕtapúr brinj az Nipúr; Barrah az Nandapúr. Puṭṭu o máhí az Sopúr; Moṅg az Králapúr. Árad az Khámpúr. Shír az Shádipúr. Angúr az Rĕpúr.

Pámpúr (the place) for ghí and saffron. Letapúr for vegetables. Nipúr for rice. Nandapúr for lamb. Sopúr for paṭṭu and fish. Králapúr for dál. K͟hámpúr for flour. Shádipúr for milk. And grapes from Rĕpúr.

Ropeyih hatas kángar band.

A kángar as a pledge for Rs. 100.

A kángar is worth a mere trifle.

Rovmut gur chhuh sheṭhah mohur.

A lost horse is valued at 60 sovereigns.

Ruchhmakho luchh tah ts͟uṭmakho kachh.

I trained you (at very great expense), a lákh of rupees ; but I turned you off at a trifle.

Losing a good servant on account of some trifle.

Rúd pĕthuí chhĕh rab wuthán.

Mud comes from a fall of rain.

Punishment follows sin.

Rúdá peyíhe, kapsá bowihe,
Wurah mújih karihak, koruh pots͟ah.

If it rains and cotton grows,
I will make for my stepmother a "bran new" phĕran.

A conditional promise, as "When my ship comes home."

A certain man was in debt and went to a friend for the loan of some money wherewith to pay it. He urged his request in the following words:—"O, my friend, please lend me the money. For God's sake help me to satisfy this impatient creditor. Deliver me from this great trouble. After a little while I shall be able to repay you with interest. The spring has come and the grass will grow over my land, and the people will send their flocks and herds to graze thereon, and then the wool of the sheep will catch itself in the brambles and thorn bushes, and I will go and collect the wool, and will spin it; and when it is ready I will give it to the weaver, and he will make a blanket out of it, which I will sell, and buy a mare with the price thereof; and when the mare has foaled, I will sell the foal for more than one hundred rupees—if a man offers me only one hundred rupees I will not accept it; and then I shall be able, and shall be glad, to pay you." The friend laughed aloud on the conclusion of this harangue. "Why do you laugh?" said the debtor, "do you not think that it will be as I say?"

Rúhan pír chhih k͟hush-hál.

The pírs are glad when people die (or over the dead).

Cited when any one speaks evil of the dead, or takes pleasure in another's misfortune. There are two ways of understanding the saying with respect to the pírs,—either that they really are pleased because of the largesse and feast which generally accompany a funeral, or that they pray for the dead as though they loved them. The one way of interpreting it is as general as the other.

Rúṭ manivzĕn nah zah kánih gatshanas káṭ pánai karih áhí páṭ.

Do not pander to a sulky angry person; and in a little while his sides will become weary, and he will come and beg for forgiveness.

Rutnun sas.

Ratun's dál.

A stupid, extravagant servant.

Gagar Wol, a collector, had a very stupid servant called Ratun. One day when the master was visiting a certain village with his servant he told the chief farmer of the village to be so kind as to give some dál, a kind of pulse, to his servant for his dinner. The farmer, anxious like all other people, to ingratiate himself in the favour of the collector, gave the servant one kharwár, or 192 pounds, of dál.

Ratun went and cooked the whole of this,—a mightly feast, some thirty or more big earthen pots full of steaming dál!

As soon as Gagar Wol returned to his quarters he was terribly surprised to find that his servant had been so stupid as to cook the whole kharwar of dál.

Ryno, ryno! kkátir chhuí, bĕnih chhai ránṭas rani chhai híi.

O husband, husband! Your idea is that a sister is a giantess and a wife is as jasmine.

S

Sabúr chhuí sunah sund ṭúr.
Patience is as a dish of gold.

Ṭúr is the dish out of which the Panḍitánís eat; a big round deep brazen dish.

Sáfah khutah sáf kyah? Ḍĕkah.
Záyulih khutah záyul kyah? Balái.
What is cleaner than the clean? The forehead.
What is finer than the fine? Misfortune.

The questions were Akbar's and the answers Bír Bal's. Undoubtedly there is reference in the first question and answer to the Hindú notion that every child's destiny is inscribed upon the forehead at the time of its birth. Some say that Brahma writes this inscription, the Kashmírí Panḍit says that Vishnu (or Hari) does. Cf. note to "*Yath núrah butihsuí.*"

Whatever is written upon the forehead "by the finger of destiny" is clean—clear—fixed; and misfortune is a hard (fine) narrow way.

Safar chhuh káfir.
The way is like an infidel.

A hard, unpleasant journey.

Sahal chízas pĕṭh jahal.
Angry over a little matter.

Sáhib chhuh bakhshanhár.
God is a giver.

Sáhib chhuh kanih talikis kĕmis tah krulas rĕzik wátanáwán.
God provides food for the worm and insect under the stone.

Jehovah-jireh.

Solomon was once sitting by the riverside when he saw an ant creeping along by the edge of the water with a grain of rice in its mouth. While the little creature was toiling along a crocodile came forth from the river and swallowed the ant, grain and all, and then took a dive into the water. In an hour's time the crocodile reappeared and vomited the ant; and the king noticed that there was not a grain of rice in the insect's mouth. "I wonder what the reason of this is," said he aloud to himself. The ant heard these words and replied, "God has planted a stone in this river, and in a hole in that stone lives a little blind worm. So God ordered me to get a grain of rice every day and take it to that worm; and gave me for a help this crocodile to carry me down to the hole of that worm, as I could not reach there by my own means.

Sáhibzádah-i-zamán hákah laṭĕn lamán.

The son of the Lord of the Age is pulling up vegetables.

A great man busying himself in little matters.

Sak͟hai diyih bár bár tah bak͟hail diyih yak bár.

The generous man will give many times, but the miser will give once only.

Samandaras manz yírah gatshit kuts mulan thapah karuni.

Floating in the sea to catch at the roots of the kuts plant.

Catching at a straw.

Kuts. Indigofera heterantha. The twigs are used in making baskets.

By the sea is here meant the Wular Lake, the largest lake in Kashmír. The natives say that Kashyápa, the drainer of the valley, brought a specimen of everything here, that could be found on the face of the earth: yea, he brought the sea also. The holy Shástras, too, declare that everything is to be met with in Kashmír, lions and all manner of beasts, all manner of birds and fruits and flowers, &c., &c., and that men must believe this though they may never see, or hear of, them!

The Wular Lake is almost oval in shape, and is at its greatest 12 miles long from north to south, 10 miles wide from east to west, and 16 feet deep; (the average depth is just 12 feet). The boatmen always approach this magnificent piece of water with fear and trembling, and once started, hasten over it as though it were a grave ready every moment to swallow them up. They have many tales, ancient and modern, true and fictitious, which they will tell with great enthusiasm if the visitor desires.

Sandijih diwán záli tah hĕndawĕnd tsalan nírit.

Taking up some mustard-seed in the hand, and a water-melon escapes.

A great loss to a careful man.

Sang-i-Pháras.

The Philosopher's stone.

The daughter of one of the principal citizens of Srínagar went to the river to drink. Instead of drinking with her hands, as is the custom, she bent down her face into the water and drank like a dog. While she was drinking a young snake, almost invisible, entered her mouth. (The people say that snakes lay eggs and that in each egg there are thousands of pieces of the finest cotton-like matter, which eventually develope into snakes.). For many years this girl nourished this snake in her stomach. She had no pain, she did not even feel any thing that ought not to be inside. In course of time she was married; and a sorry marriage for the husband it turned out to be:—for while they were both sleeping in their bed, at the dead of night, a snake came out from the mouth of the wife and bit her husband, so that he died in dreadful pain soon afterwards.

The poor woman's grief in the morning, when she discovered the cold corpse of her beloved husband, was beyond all description; she tore her hair and clothes, she beat her breasts, and shrieked aloud. The people came and enquired what was the matter, and when they heard, they all charged her with having poisoned the man. This report was carried all over the city, even to the great Mughal governor, 'Alí Mardán Khán. When he heard of it, he sent for the girl, and kept her with him. He enquired of her the truth of the matter, and the girl replied in tears that she did not know anything concerning it, and that she was asleep at the time. The governor told her to go to her room, and when she had closed her eyes in sleep, he went and sat by her to watch. He waited and waited until at last he saw a snake appear from her mouth, and put out its fangs with a most menacing look. 'Alí Mardán Khán went away as quickly as possible and informed his attendants what he had seen, and ordered them to tell this girl to make some bread on the morrow. The big oven was to be heated, and when the girl had finished making the loaf, and was putting it into the oven somebody standing by was to take her up and fling her headlong into the oven. This was done, and when they opened the oven some hours afterwards to see what had become of the girl, they found only a stone about half-a-pound in weight, which was carried to the governor and kept very carefully by him. It appeared that this was the famous alchemist's stone, and that by its means 'Alí Mardán Khán was able to transmute copper and brass and all other metals into gold. His person, his servants, his horses, his rooms glittered with gold. ('Alí Mardán Khán was the most magnificent of the Mughal governors. The expenses of each of his trips into Kashmír are said to have exceeded a lákh of rúpís.)

When 'Alí Mardán Khán was about to die he called his four sons unto him, and giving the precious stone to the eldest of them, he told him to throw it into the river (Indus).

The eldest son refused to obey this strange order; so it was handed to the second, and then to the third, but all most resolutely refused to throw away so precious a stone; at length the fourth and youngest son threw it with all his might into the water opposite Aṭak (Attock); and where the stone pitched a great blazing flame arose from the midst of the river, as of ignited gold.

'Alí Mardán Khán ordered the stone to be thrown into the river because he feared lest it should pass into the hands of another, and they become as wealthy as he.

The Kashmírís say that tho stone is there in the river to the present day. Ranjít Singh tried hard to obtain it. He had the water stopped a hundred yards above and below the place where the stone had pitched, the place was drained, and a most rigid search made, but nothing was discovered. (This is only one out of many stories extant in the valley concerning the origin of the Philosopher's stone.—Capt. Temple has a variant of the above story with some excellent notes concerning the Lamiá in 'the *Indian Antiquary,*" Vol XI., Part cxxxv., pp. 230.)

Sangal-dípuch padmán.

Sangal-Díp's beautiful woman.

Humph! you might be a grand woman!

It is related that one day Shiva and Párvatí were sitting together, when the latter rose up suddenly and ran away. Shiva followed her as fast as he could, but was not able to catch her. At last thoroughly exhausted he lay down in a certain place, Sangal-Díp by name, and went to sleep; and it happened that there in that place a madan-pit became. Shiva woke up in a great rage, and turning to the pit he said, "If you should ever see a beautiful woman like a lotus you must follow her." He then departed.

The inhabitants of Sangal-Díp are constantly going to other countries, and seizing their beautiful women, are taking them to their own country, where they teach them to ride the most beautiful and swift horses. When they are able to ride well, these beautiful women are taken close to the pit and obliged to say, "O Kámadeva, O Kámadeva, I am Padmán" (*i.e.*, a beautiful woman and like a lotus. Cf. note "*Khoran nah khráv.*") On hearing this Kámadeva comes forth and runs after her with all the swiftness with which he can run; and should it happen that he overtakes her, she will immediately be killed. After killing the woman Kámadeva returns to the pit, and it generally happens that madan (procreating principle) escapes from him into the pits, which precede his own special abode, and which have been dug for this purpose.

Díp. (Sanskrit.—Dvípa) Hindú philosophers say that the terrestrial globe contains seven díps or islands, encompassed by seven seas, the whole land and water measuring 7,957,752 yojanas. The Sangal Díp (Simhalá) is in the north direction. (Cf. *Dvípa.* Monier Williams, Dict.)

Kámadeva is generally regarded as the god of sexual love, like Eros of the Greeks and Cupid of the Latins. He is worshipped at the time of marriage; and happiness in the married state, and offspring are sought from him. (Cf. Kennedy, "Hindú Myth," &c.)

Sant gai tim, yim mutrah suĕt trámas banáwan sun.

They are faqírs, who by means of water transmute copper into gold.

Not every man is a monk who wears a cowl.

In the Chinár Bágh, Srínagar, there is a temple in memory of a deceased faqír, who was able to perform this wonder. He, also, taught a Pandit, who is now a very old man living in Srínagar, too old to do anything—even to make gold!

Muthar = Sanskrit *mútra*, and Persian *pesh-áb*.

Santoshih biyálih buwih ánanduk phal.

A harvest of peace is produced from a seed of contentment.

This proverb is credited to a holy and clever Pandit called Nand Rám, who lived at Báwan, a sacred Hindú village in Kashmír. This man wrote many rather clever verses in praise of Krishna. He seems to have been terribly dunned by the officials of Báwan, if one may judge from the following lines:—

Nand Rám aus zamindár,
Húrit diyár tas súras nah lár
Wángujwárich tsajis nah gángal.
Santoshih biyálih bowih ánanduk phal.

Nand Rám was a husbandman.
And he paid his debts; but there was always somebody after him (for money.)
He never knew what it was to live freely in his own house, but was continually obliged to lodge in the house of another.
(Never mind), from the seed of contentment a harvest of peace will be reaped.

The piece of poetry from which the above proverb is taken is the following:—

Dharmah búmikáyih wavizih karmuk phal.
Santoshih biyálih bowih ánanduk phal.
Doyih pránah dándah-júri dĕn tah rát wái;
Kumbake kurah zorah timanuí láí;
Hĕlah kar bihit yut nah rozih ak rĕl.
Santoshih biyálih bowih ánanduk phal.
Lolachih yatahpurih datah phutráv,
Wairuk srĕh yut nah rozĕs tal.
Santoshih biyálih bowih ánanduk phal.

You should sow the seeds of destiny in the soil of Dharma (*i.e.*, virtue, religion, duty, law, moral and religious truth according to the Vedas and the law).
From the seed of contentment a harvest of peace will be reaped.
Plough with the two oxen of the two breaths day and night,
Strike them hard with the whip of extreme meditation;
Endeavour so that not a spot of ground will remain unploughed.
From the seed of contentment a harvest of peace is reaped.
Break the clods with the staff of love,
That the damp of envy may not remain beneath:
From the seed of contentment a harvest of peace is reaped.

Sar chĕyih sardár, tawah patah bálah-yár, tawah patah subahdár.

First the master of the feast will drink, after that the dear friend, and then the officer of rank.

Affection goes before rank.

Cooks on tasting the dishes previous to sending them to the master are accustomed to quote these words.

Sará dúnṭhum, sará dúnṭhum, sarav khutah buḍ tel phul wátis nah auḍ.

I saw a tank, I saw a tank,—it was larger than other tanks, but it would not contain a half of the sesame flower. (*Sesamum orientale.*)

A big, fat man, but no brains.

This is also a riddle, and the answer is, a nipple, an udder.

Sarafah sunzah sat zewah.

A snake has seven tongues.

A man who speaks whichever way fancy or company-wind blows.

Hindústání.—*Sámp ke sát zubán.*

Some devtás or gods ascended to heaven to get some amrit (water of life), and when they descended to earth again they put it into an earthenware vessel, which they placed on the top of a tree. The Rákshasas, huge giants, or rather ogres, wished to possess themselves of this amrit. So one took upon himself the form of a crow, and flew, and perched upon the top of that tree and jerked off that earthenware vessel. On seeing this Vásak Nág (Vásuki or Básak Nág), a king of the snakes, with all his host came and drank up the amrit, and while they were drinking it, the rákshasa from the top of the tree cursed them. "Have I not taken all this trouble to obtain this water of life, and now you have consumed it. Henceforth let there be to you seven tongues."

Saras sarposh.

A basket-cover for a pond.

Much need but little cash.

Sari pĕṭhi sailáb.

One's head even deluged.

Head and ears in trouble.

Sarráf ganzarán diyár tah atráf ráwarán doh.

The banker counts the money and the spendthrift wastes the day.

Saruf chhuh pakán hul hul, wáj tal wátit syud.

The snake goes crookedly, yet it arrives straight within its hole.

A man who is of a different disposition out-of-doors and among strangers to what he is in his own house.

Sas chhuh nah zah síkhas khasán.
Dál never rises to the spit.

A low man will never be promoted.

Sas (or *dál*), a kind of kidney bean (*Phaseolus Max or Radiatus*).

Sas myuṭ baṭas, muṭh myuṭ kaṭas, nindar míṭ drálid kaṭas.
Dál is sweet to the Paṇḍit, muṭh is sweet to the sheep, and sleep is sweet to the son of misfortune.

Dál is the *Paspalum frumentaceum.*

Muṭh is a species of leguminous plant.

Sásas sun piṭáras bháganih tíl chirágas!
A thousand rúpís worth of gold in the piṭár, and a mite's worth of oil in the lamp!

A man with little money, but who uses it to a good purpose is of more worth to the world than the wealthy but miserly man; also the man with little knowledge, who uses it, is of more profit to the world, than the extraordinarily clever man, who reserves his knowledge for himself.

Sat buthi chhis chandas andar.
Seven faces are in his pocket.

Mr. Smooth-Tongue; every thing to every man.

Satuti sanz hĕḍar yaṭ.
The hoopoo's big basketful of mushrooms.

Slow but sure. Many a mickle makes a muckle.

Yaṭ is a big long basket which the Kashmírí coolie fastens on his back, and trots away as happily as possible over hill and dale with a maund or so of goods in it. The story is that a hoopoo once gathered as many mushrooms as would fill a yaṭ, and as he would have to gather them singly, the amassing of such a large number must have cost him much time and labour. Hence the saying.

It is also said that this hoopoo when he reached home after his labours one day asked his wife to cook some of the mushrooms. Of course the mushrooms were considerably diminished in size and weight from the cooking, but the hoopoo suspected that his wife had either eaten, or concealed, some of them; and so in the heat of passion he then and there killed her and threw the corpse out of the nest.

Sĕh kas be-pír andar mulk-i-Kashmír.
Walí Haḍ o Harí Bahádur o Sukha Pír.
Three persons are without religion in the country of Kashmír—Walí Haḍ, Harí Bahádur, and Sukhá Pír.

These three persons are now living in Kashmír, and are a great trouble to the quieter class of people. *Walí Haḍ* is a Muhammedan, the other two are Paṇḍits. Haḍ means hard, resolute, and this name has been added to Walí, because if this man is refused any thing he will sit by the house for days and make great lamentation, until he obtains his request. The title of Bahádur was given to *Harí* under amusing circumstances (according to the people's story). They say that His late Highness the Mahárájah Guláb Singh was once very ill, and the Bráhmans being consulted, they advised that a man should be found who would leap a few times upon the king's stomach and make him well. Great search was made, but nobody was found to come forward and do this strange act. At last Harí presented himself and jumped several times upon His Highness, who was immediately relieved of his pain. The title of Bahádur was accordingly given to the fakír by the common folk, and a large present of money by the Mahárájah. *Sukhá Pír* is a very big, stout and powerful man, and blessed with a monstrous appetite. Strange stories are told of the enormous quantity of food which this man now and then disposes of. Sometimes those who can afford it invite this man to their houses, and have him fed before them as a kind of tamáshá.

Sĕkih sháṭhas híi no wavizĕh ; waṭas dizih nah tsumrivi rínzi ; gyánich kath kas muḍas wanizĕh—zan rávarut kum-yájĕn tíl.

Sow not jasmine upon the sand; fire not a leathern marble against the rock ; speak not words of divine wisdom to a fool—because, if you do, it will be like wasting oil over bran-cakes.

Another version is :—

Sĕkih sháṭhas phal no wavizĕh ; rávarizih nah kum-yájĕn tíl ; Muḍas ganyánach kath no wanizĕh, kharas gor dinah ráwí doh.

Sow not seeds on the river-bed (or the sand) ; waste not oil over bran-cakes ;

Tell not matters of religion to the ignorant ; and if you give sugar to an ass, you will lose the day (*i. e.*, you will lose your labour).

Sĕkih tíl tah wĕthranih sában.

Oil to the sand and soap to the wĕthran.

Labour lost.

Wĕthran is a sack made of grass and generally used by the poor Kashmírí cultivator.

Sĕtsanih páwih atsun hasti baranih nerun.

Entering by the eye of a needle and coming out by the elephant's stable-door.

"Humble enough at first, but now so proud !"

A "risen" man.

Sĕzih ungajih chhuh nah gyav khasán.

Ghí is not to be taken up with a straight finger.

Blows bring sense.

Shábash buṭah malikah!

Well-done, simple fellow!

Praise a stupid person and you can get anything from him.

Buṭah lit. Ladákí, who in former times suffered much in bargaining with the Kashmírí on account of his ignorance of the language and dulness of intellect.

"*Shádi moj! warud kyuth?*" "*Bechanah khutah seṭhah rut.*"

"O mother Shádi! how do you like your second husband?" "It is much better than begging."

Once marry for love, twice marry for money.

Sháh byuṭh Wushkarih, yas yih khush karih suh tih karih.

The king settled in Wushkur, and whatsoever a man pleased that he did.

The king must reside in the midst of his people.

When the cat is away the mice do play.

Wushkur is a village in the Kamráz.

Shaitánah sundi kan zari.

Satan's deaf ears.

Kashmírís are very fond of sounding their own praises. Before, however, giving utterance to a word they sometimes pray that Satan's ears may be closed, in order that he may not hear them, and, becoming offended, curse them.

Shakar ai chhuí mits gatshanai;
Mits ai chhai shakar gatshanai.

If it is sugar then may it become earth to you;
If it is earth then may it become sugar to you.

Cited against the man who lies just to escape giving, or on some other trifling account.

Hindústání.—*Allah kare shakar howe.*
Allah kare miṭṭí howe.

A fakír was wandering by the riverside one afternoon, when he saw a barge approaching. He enquired, as he was wont to do, what was in the barge. The man replied "Only earth." The fakír suspecting that the man had lied unto him, prayed that God would grant this man's answer to be correct. God heard the prayer, and the whole cargo of sugar was changed into earth. Soon after this another barge came along. "What cargo have you?" said the fakír. "Earth," answered the man. This reply was true, and the fakir prayed again that if it were true, that God would turn it all into sugar. This prayer also was granted. (Cf. "Indian Fairy Tales," pp. 96, 97, 272, 273.)

Shakar mĕkráz.

Scissors of sugar (but none the less sharp and cutting for all that).

Shál gav kulih zih álam gav kulih.

A jackal got into the river, and it was as though the whole world had got in.

Panjábí.—*Ap moe jag parlo.*

Shál gub tah hákah-tsar barábar.

A jackal, ewe, and string of vegetables are equal.

Justice.

This saying dates back to the days of Noshírwán, a king of Persia in whose reign Muhammed was born (A. D. 578). Noshírwán is the Persian for just, and the king called by this name is said to have been so just that perfect peace reigned in the land both among men and beasts. Noshírwán kept a jackal, a ewe, and a string of vegetables in one and the same place; but the jackal did not harm the ewe, and the ewe did not touch the vegetables;—to such an extent did peace reign!

The jackal, ewe, and string of vegetables may also be taken figuratively as representing different grades of people, every one of whom the just king esteemed equally worthy of attention and protection.

Shál tsalit baṭhĕn chob.

The jackal escapes and the man smites the ground.

Crying over spilt milk.

Shálah sunz ṭung.

The howling of a jackal.

Lupus pilum mutat, non mentem.

A jackal in the course of its nightly peregrinations visited the house of a certain dyer and tumbled into the blue dye-pot, and its fur became as blue as blue can be. In this ridiculous state it went away, but was afraid to return to its companions. Eventually it took up its abode on the top of a very high rock. In the course of time the news spread that a new beast was to be found in a certain place every night at such a time. The bear, the tiger, the lion, all were informed of this new animal, and a big council was held in which it was decided to invite the stranger and to make him their king and head. The blue jackal came and was duly crowned by the lion; but at evening-time when all the other jackals began as usual to scream and to howl, this blue jackal, also, instinctively screamed and howled. Now the mystery was discovered. This king was only a painted jackal! When the lion and bear and tiger heard this they went at once and killed the blue jackal. (This story slightly changed is in the Pañca-tantra.)

Shálih tárak háwuni.

To show stars to a (sharp) woman, (in order to try and frighten her).

She knows well enough what you are up to, you will have to try some other plan.

Shálin byol chhuh hihúi.

Shol seed is like shol.

Like father like son.

Shol is millet-seed (*Pennisetum italicum*).

Shámah gaṭah tah rot arafah.

The evening darkness is the vigil of the night's festival.

Quoted when any one pushes on work into the late hours of the night in order that little or none may be left to be done on the morrow.

Shámah tsutur tah mandini bĕhwál.

Sharp (enough) at evening, but lazy and sleepy at noon.

Quoted against wives and unemployed sons, &c.

Shamásui tal chhĕh gaṭah.

There is a darkness under the candle.

A good king, but bad ministers; a good master, but bad servants.

Hindí.—*Chirágh ke tale andherá.*

Sharákuts hanz deg chhĕh khemuts honev.

The dogs ate up the partnership saucepan.

Two partners quarrel and go to law, and lose everything.

Persian.—*Du morg jang kunand fa'ida-i-tirgar.*

Sharahas sharmúi kyah!

What, is there shame in "The Law!"

Right as the Bible.

Shayih ástan tah lúkanuí toshtan.

Live thou and do good to others.

This is a line from one of the verses composed by the clever wife of the celebrated Munshí Bahwání Dás, who lived in the time of Akbar. He was a Kashmírí, a great poet, and some of his works remain in the Persian language; but there is no trace of his house or family.

For some reason Bahwání Dás separated from his first wife and married another. This second wife became very devoted to him, and one day in a fit of jealousy she composed the following lines:—

Tanahdai vĕsie sunah chham asán.
Yanah yári travanam karní kath.
Sheyah ástan tah lukanuí toshtan.
Totih chham dilasuí sat.
Chhamah ládan akih laṭih yiyih ná!
Wandahsuí haṭikuí rat.
When my husband does not speak to me;
Then, O friend, the other wife laughs at me.
O let him live and do good to others!
And there will be comfort to my mind.
If he would but come to me once.
I would offer unto him the sacrifice of my throat's blood!

Wĕs is a woman's female friend. (Hindústání—sahelí.)

Sun, a rival wife. (Polygamy is not very common among Kashmírí Hindús).

Shĕh tah trĕh tah nav tah kah.

Six and three and nine and eleven.

> "Black crows have been thrown up, Three, Two and One;
> And here I find all comes at last to none"!
> "The Three Black Crows."—Byrom.

Shekhah bahí kúlah sahíh, pagáh nahín.

The Shekh's custom is "Yes" to-day, and "No" to-morrow.

A fickle person.

Shekh Imám-ud-dín was the last of the ten Sikh governors, who tyrannised over the valley for about twenty-seven years (1819 to 1846 A. D.) Report represents him to have been a very fickle monarch, and tells the following anecdote concerning him:—

One day the Shekh appointed a Pandit to some office and soon after his appointment the Pandit appeared in the palace-yard riding upon a horse with his face towards the beast's tail. The Shekh happened to be there with his retinue, and seeing this ludicrous character laughed loudly. Great was his surprise to find that the man was the very Pandit, to whom he had just given an appointment. "Why are you making such a fool of yourself?" said he. "I am riding thus," replied the Pandit, "in order that I may see quickly who is to be appointed in my place!"

Afterwards Shekh Imám-ud-dín did not change his servants so frequently.

Shekhah royih Shaitán.

A Shekh in appearance, but a devil in truth.

Appearances are not always to be trusted.

Shenkaruni makuz, nah phalán tah nah galán.

Shenkar's axe, neither wears away, nor melts.

Cited concerning a hale and hearty, old wicked person.

Shenkar (Sanskrit, Shan-kara) was a very famous Hindú fakír of the grand style.—His dress was of pashmína, (a very fine silky cloth), and he always rode upon a handsome horse. He lived at Chhatsah-Bal, where there is a small temple erected to his memory. He died about two years ago, at the age of sixty.

Shenkar used every day to climb the Takht-i-Sulaimán (a big hill overlooking Srínagar), to perform his devotions in the ancient temple there. Another name for this hill is Shenkarátsárí, an ancient Hindú philosopher. after whom this Shenkar was called. (Cf. Śankarácárya. Monier William's Dicty.)

Shenkar's popularity was chiefly derived from his celebrated charmed axe. It was so, that whenever he heard that any one was in trouble or sickness, he would visit them, and after saying a few words, would wave the axe above and around the distressed person's head and body, and should he be indisposed, or the weather be inclement, he used to send the axe with especial directions how to manage it. Report says that large numbers were thus healed and comforted. The axe was a very strong and handsome one.

Shenkar's family are still living in Srínagar, and are very much respected. Rám Chand seems to be the principal member of this family now alive. He is a very clever munshí, and in receipt of about Rs. 200 *per mensem*. Every year, on the anniversary of Shenkar's death, his two hundred special followers, all of whom belong to the *dar* class, visit Rám Chand and make special presents to him in recognition of their intense respect for his father and their saint.

Sheṭh gav zih breṭh gav.

Sixty years become, stupid become.

Once a man, twice a child.

Sheṭhah wuhur káv tah shítah wuhur káwah-pút.

Sixty years a crow and eight years a young crow (*i.e.*, in the matter of wisdom and experience).

Foolish father, wise son.

The Kashmírís tell a story of an old female crow, who was once giving advice to her young ones. She warned them especially to beware of man. He did not care for their forwardness, nor was he charmed by their "caw-caw"; but on the contrary, he would certainly kill them, if he had the chance. "Now, listen," said the old crow. "When you see a man bending his body down to the ground, and putting forth a hand, take heed; because the man is about to pick up a stone wherewith to strike and maim you." "Very well, very well," said the young crows, and there was a general "caw-caw" of approval. But one of the young ones, who was sharper than the rest, did not quite agree. "Suppose," enquired he, "that the man has already a stone under his arm, what shall we do in that case?" Cf. "Folktales from the Upper Panjáb." Rev. C. Swynnerton, *J. R. A. S.*, 1884.

Sheyav pírav khutah chhuh be-pírui ján.

Better to follow no saint than (to try) to follow six saints.

A man cannot serve many masters.

Sheyih manih nah shábásh, wupasas nah laz.

No praise if one cooks six maunds of food, and no shame if there is nothing cooked

A too lenient, indifferent, father or master. If the child, or the servant does well, he has no praise for him; and if the child or the servant neglects or spoils his work, he has not a word of blame for him.

Shikas'ah náv Shád!

Broken-hearted yet called Gladness!

Shín díshit yih gagur karih tí chhuk rupeyih díshit karán.

What the rat will do when it sees the snow, that you are doing when you see rúpís.

The Kashmírí says that rats can tell from the quantity and character of the snow upon the mountains whether the winter will be a very severe one or not. Should it augur badly, then each rat will gather for himself as much as six sers of rice-grain.

Shínah pĕto! báyih yito!

Fall, O snow! Come, O brother!

Yearning for the absent one's return.

A bird called Shínah-pípín was going away much to the sorrow of his brother-Shínah-pípín, who asked him with tears in his eyes, when he intended to come back again. "When the snow falls I shall be here again," he replied. Time passed, the snow fell heavily, but no Shínah-pípín came back.

Shínah shart.

A snow concern (or arrangement).

No practical jokes, please. This is not Shínah shart (or "April fool's day.")

The Kashmírís are very glad to see the snow; and they have a custom which allows them to play jokes upon one another with impunity on that day, when the snow first falls. Sometimes they will take a piece of the new snow and wrapping it up in paper give it to a friend as if tobacco, or snuff, &c.

Should this friend take and open it, then he is very much laughed at, and has to pay a forfeit. Amongst the educated it is customary to write the following Persian couplet upon paper, and give it to their friend as if it were an important letter or parwána, &c.

Barf i nau aftád sad mubárak bád,
Án chi shart ast zúd báyad dád ?
The new snow has fallen, a hundred congratulations to you.
What is the agreement— (but a trifle !)— so you must pay up quickly.

Should the friend read only one word of this, he is caught and has to pay a trifling forfeit.

A Pandit has just remarked that the animals, too, are rejoiced to see the snow, but especially the dogs. On being asked "Why?" he said, "Because all the dogs look upon the snow falling as their maternal uncle coming from Heaven to visit them." On further enquiry as to where he heard this, he replied that. "All children in Kashmír were so taught. He did not know any reason for thus thinking."

Shír-i-mádar chhuí.

A mother's milk to you.

A proper arrangement, &c.

Shírahpúrih pírah yeniwol áv.

The wedding-company of saints from Shírapur has come.

The arrival of any great man.

Shírapúr is a little village about two miles from Islámábád, and abounds in Muhammedan saints, who marry their daughters in grand style. Horses and music, and sometimes as many as a hundred singers, attend the wedding-company.

Shistarah suĕti chhuh shistar phaṭán.

Iron is cut by iron.

Set a thief to catch a thief.

Persian.—*Ki áhan ba áhan towáṅ kard narm.*

Shíyas shíyá tah Míyas Míyá.

Shías with Shías and Míyás with Míyás.

Caste with caste ; like with like.

Shiyá—Míyá, (Shí'a and Miyáṅ) the one is a Muhammedan and the other a Hindú sect.

Shodah sanz kalah hír, yután dazuk,
Tután karuk nah pánahwáni kat.

Until the head of the Shodah is burnt,
They will not speak to one another.

Five friends chanced to meet, and all having leisure they decided to go to the bázár and purchase a hír, and have a great feast in the house of one of the party, each of whom subscribed four ánás. The hír was bought, but while they were returning to the house it was remembered that there was not any butter. On this one of the five proposed, by way of having some fun, that the first of them, who should break the silence by speaking, should go for the butter. Now it was no light matter to have to retrace one's steps back to the butter-shop, as the way was long and the day was very hot. So they all five kept strict silence. Pots were cleaned, the fire was prepared and the hír laid thereon; now and then somebody coughed and another groaned, and one even was so filled with a sense of the ridiculous as to laugh aloud, but never a tongue uttered a word, although the fire was fast going out, and the hír was getting burnt, owing to there being no fat or butter wherewith to grease the pot.

Thus matters proceeded until at last a policeman passed by, and attracted by the smell of cooking, he looked in at the window and saw these five men perfectly silent and sitting around a burnt hír. Not knowing the arrangement he supposed that either these people were mad, or else they must be thieves; and so he enquired how they came there? and how did they obtain the hír? Not a word was uttered in reply. "Why are you squatting around the burnt hír in that stupid fashion?" shouted the policeman. Still no reply. Then the policeman full of rage that these wretched men should have thus mocked at his authority took them all off straight to the Police Inspector's office. On arrival the Inspector asked them the reason of their strange behaviour, but he also got no reply. This rather tried the patience and temper of this man of authority, who was generally feared and flattered and bribed. He ordered one of the five Shodahs to be immediately flogged. The poor Shodah bore it bravely and never a sound he uttered; but when the lashes fell thick and fast, and whipped the already whipped and wounded places, so that the blood appeared, he could endure no longer, and so shouted, "Oh, oh, why do you beat me? Enough, enough. Oh, is it not enough that the hír has been spoilt?" His four associates now cried out, "Go to the bázár and fetch the butter. Go."

The Police Inspector was still more surprised and annoyed when he heard of this further contempt of the court. and ordered a thorough investigation of the whole matter. Everything was now, of course, fully and clearly explained, and great was the amusement of every body, not excepting the Police Inspector. Cf. "Story of the Twenty-five Idiots" in "The Orientalist," Vol. I., p. 136.

Hír is the head of any animal used for food.

Shok͟h tah punahsund.

Happiness and more (children) to you.

A Kashmírí blessing.

When the piece of flaming birch-wood is being passed around the head of the child and company present, the midwife repeats the above words. Cf. custom "*sutuk*" in note to "*Lántshah garih sutuk.*" There is a division of opinion regarding the meaning of these words, even among the highest class of Bráhmans. The balance of favour seems to be for the above rendering, deriving *Shokh* from the Persian and *punahsund* from the Sanskrit पुनः "again," and *sund* from सन्तु, "may these be."

Shrákih tah mázas chhuá wád?

What answer will the meat give to the knife?

The tyrant will not receive any reply.

Shukr, zát-i-pákah, nah áyam yad nah lugum phákah.

Thanks, O holy one, neither was my stomach filled, nor had I to fast.

"Give me neither poverty nor riches; feed me with food convenient for me."—Prov. xxx. 8.

Shungit báng dapuni.

To cry the báng when asleep.

A lazy, dilatory, fellow.

Báng is the Muhammedan call to prayers.

Shupi kánih wachhas zarí nál.

A golden nál over a fan-like bony breast.

A gaudily-dressed ugly person.

Shup is a flat basket used for winnowing grain.

Nál is the border of the garment called the kurtah, round the neck and down the breast.

Shur gav bror; wulah wulah kurus tah yiyih.

A child is a cat, tell it to come and it will come.

A child cries and runs for food.

Shur nyuv pázan tah shistar khyav gagaran.

The hawk took the child and the rat ate the iron.

Tit for tat.

Persian.—*Ki mosh áhan khorad kodak barad báz.*

A man about to start on a journey entrusted several maunds of iron to the care of a merchant-friend. After several years he returned and sent to this friend for the iron. The merchant, in whose charge it was, being a rogue had sold the iron; and now sent to say how sorry he was that the iron had been eaten by rats. This reply somewhat astonished the other merchant, he could not understand how the iron could possibly have been broken and masticated by rats. However, he did not argue the matter in words, but went straight off to the place where the lying-merchant's child was playing, and decoyed the little fellow away to a very secret place. The merchant on discovering the loss of his child, became almost frantic with grief. He went tearing his hair and shrieking everywhere, "My child, where is my child?" The other merchant seeing him in such distress enquired what was the matter, and was told that the little boy has either strayed or been stolen. "Alas," said he, "I observed a great hawk hovering over the head of your boy. The bird must have flown away with him." "You mock me in my sorrow," said the bereaved merchant. "How could a hawk carry off my boy?" "As easily as rats could devour iron," said the other merchant.

The result was the exchange of the lost boy for the lost iron.

This proverb and story is evidently translated from a Persian work, "Chihil qissa," (*i. e.,* Forty stories,) but it is very well known among the common folk of Kashmír.

Shuri chhur kuṭhis.—Shur máronah kih náh kuṭh tsaṭon?

The infant wetted the lap. What shall be done? Shall the infant be killed? or shall the knee be cut off.?

Parents in doubt as to whether they shall, or shall not, help a profligate son out of his difficulties.

Shúshas tih pushí.

Not enough even for a lung.

A small income.

Sikah nílu tah bánḍah begári.

Like a Sikh obliging one to buy what they have to sell, and compelling the musician to play without hire.

Oppression.

A Muhammedan saying. The Muhammedans tell dreadful tales of the oppression which they suffered during the rule of the Sikhs in Kashmír.

Síkh tih bajá tah kabáb tih bajá.

If the spit is right then the meat is right.

Sikandar-Náma.—*Miyán-jí chinán kun baráe sawáb.*
Ki ham síkh bar já buwad ham kabáb.

Sínas támat shínas gái, ; suád kyah zániov toe kariov.

We got breast deep in the snow; whatever inducement was there to get married on such a day as this (*lit.,* what taste did you feel that you made a feast).

A very clever Hindú Persian scholar was once invited to a wedding feast in a certain village during winter-time. It happened that much snow fell just about the time of the wedding, and those guests who lived at a distance experienced much difficulty in attending. On arrival this Hindú was heard thus to remonstrate with the parents of the wedding-party.

Notice the play upon the names of the four Persian letters sín, shín, sád, and toe.

Sína, (Persian) breast.
Shín, (Kashmírí) snow.
Suád, (Kashmírí) taste, flavour, &c.
Toe, (Persian) feast, festival, &c.

Sír gav sírdan ; aḍ sír gav guzrán ; páv chhĕh páwán.

One ser is enough ; half a ser a man can live upon ; but a quarter of a ser prostrates a man.

Sírah sán pírah mahárázah áv.

The wedding-company of saints came along secretly.

A great man travelling in a humble way. The very respectable people have their marriage processions at night. Only the poor and uneducated classes have large demonstration-processions by day.

Sini muhimah suṯsal tah rani muhimah khanḍahwáv.

If there is not a plate of meat and rice there is a mallow, and if a husband is wanting, one can get a shawl-weaver.

Anything is better than nothing.

Shawl-weavers (Muhammedans) are to be found in abundance all over the valley. They are a sickly, immoral, ill-paid race.

Siryas hyuh nah prakásh kune ;
Gangih hyuh nah tirt kaṅh ;
Búyis hyuh nah bándav kune ;
Ranih hyuh nah sukh kaṅh ;

Achhin hyuh nah prakásh kune ;
Kuṭhĕn hyuh nah tirt kaṅh ;
Chandas hyuh nah bándav kun
Khanih hyuh nah sukh kaṅh ;

Mayas hyuh nah prakásh kune ;
Layih hyuh nah tirt kaṅh ;
Dayas hyuh nah bándav kune ;
Bayas hyuh nah sukh kaṅh ;

Sĕd Báyú was one day sitting down with his famous female disciple, Lal Dĕd, when the following questions cropped-up :—

"Which was the greatest of all lights?" "Which was the most famous of all pilgrimages?" "Which was the best of all relations?" "Which was the best of all manner of ease?" Lal was the first to reply :—

"There is no light like that of the sun;
"There is no pilgrimage like Gangá;
"There is no relation like a brother;
"There is no ease like that of a wife."

But Sĕd did not quite agree. "No," said he—

"There is no light like that of the eyes;
"There is no pilgrimage like that of the knees;
"There is no relation like one's pocket;
"There is no ease like that of the mendicant's cloak."

Then Lal Dĕd, determining not to be outwitted by her master, again replied :—

"There is no light like that of the knowledge of God;
"There is no pilgrimage like that of an ardent love;
"There is no relation to be compared with the Deity;
"There is no ease like that got from the fear of God."

I have seen something like a part of the above lines in Rev. C. Swynnerton's "Adventures of Rájá Rasálú," but not having the book at hand I cannot say in what connection they occur there.

Gangá or *Gangabal* is one of the great Hindú places of pilgrimage. Hither go all those Pandits, who have had relations die during the year, carrying some small bones, which they had picked from the ashes at the time of the burning of the dead bodies. These bones are thrown into the sacred waters of Gangabal with money and sweetmeats. The pilgrimage takes place about the 8th day of the Hindú month Bádarpĕt (August 20th *cir.*) Cf. "Vigne's *Travels in Kashmír*," &c., Vol. II., pp. 151, 152.

So zan bozih isháráh suĕti.
Ko zan bozih damálih suĕti.
A hint and a good man hears.
Threatening and fuss before a bad man hears.

Gulistán.—*Ánchi dáná kunad kunad nádán.*
Lek ba'd az kabul i ruswá,í.

Sonawári sában.

The soap of Sonawár (*i.e.*, the washing of the people of Sonawár).

Something wrong in the arrangement.

Sonawár is a little village close to the Takht-i-Sulaimán, Srínagar. The inhabitants have got a name for wearing either a clean pagrí and dirty garment, or else a clean garment and dirty pagrí.

Sont chhuh tshali tah harud chhuh bali.

Spring is a matter of inclination, but the Autumn is whether he will or not.

H. H. the Mahárájah gives a certain amount of seed to each zamíndár about seed-time, the sowing of this seed depends very much upon the will of the zamíndár. But when the seed has been sown, the harvest ripens and the crops are ready to be gathered, then, *nolens volens,* the zamíndár must cut it and give the usual State allowance.

Sopúr-i-mázarat.

An invitation from a Sopúr man.

Nearly all the Sopúr people are most inhospitable. Ananta-nág (*i.e.,* Islámábád) and Pámpúr folk have got a name in the valley for hospitality.

Sorah rag melih tah worah rag melih nah.

There may be a vein of affection in a pig, but not in a step-child.

About fourteen years ago Hindús were permitted to keep swine. Since then the city has been entirely cleared of them by the order of the present Mahárájah. His Highness' late father, the Mahárájah Guláb Singh, is said to have introduced swine into the valley.

Sorah sanzih wudih morah sund táj.

A peacock's crest upon a pig's crown.

A place for every man and every man in his place.

Soruí chhuh dúr tah marun chhuh nazdík.

All things are far-off, but death is nigh.

In the midst of life we are in death.

Soruí chhuh muli, kath chhĕh muft.

All things are at a price, but conversation is *gratis.*

Srandah srandah tsuwán har ; yután nah ak chhuh marán, tután chhih nah path rozán.

A buffalo quarrels with another buffalo; until one of them dies the fight is not over.

When Greek meets Greek then comes the tug of war.

Srug, sift, tah panáhdár.
Cheap, nice, and broad.
Hot, sweet, and strong.

Srugui chhuh drug tah drugui chhuh srug.
Cheap is dear and dear is cheap.
It is better to pay a little more and have a really good article than to buy an extraordinarily cheap (?) article, and presently discover that it is not worth having.

Subhuch chilam chhai tíl charágas;
Subhuch chilam chhai bágas híi;
Subhuch chilam chhai nárah pháh Mágas;
Subhuch chilam chhai drágas zíi.
The morning pipe is like oil to the lamp;
The morning pipe is as jessamine in the garden;
The morning pipe is as the heat of a fire in January;
The morning pipe is as employment in the time of famine.
Chilam is that part of the hukkah which holds the tobacco and the charcoal-ball.

Subhuk batah ai nákárah pyos doh neris pandi;
Pheran ai nákárah gos wahrí neris pandi;
Zanánah ai nákárah peyas umr neris pándi.
If the breakfast is bad then all the day will go wrong;
If the dress is bad then all the year will go wrong;
If the wife is bad then all the life-time will go wrong.

Suchhuk garwol tah máh-i-ramazánik nemázi.
A householder (only) in time of abundance, and prayers only during the month of Ramazán.
An unreliable character.
Ramazán is the name of the ninth Muhammedan month, during which every orthodox follower of that religion abstains from eating, drinking, &c., between the morning dawn and the appearance of the stars at night. On the 27th day of this month the Qurán began to descend from heaven, and every prayer offered up on that night (called lailatu'-l-qadr) will be answered. Also prayers offered up on the 19th, 21st and 23rd days of Ramazán are thought to avail much.

Sudámun kum bus.
Sudám's handful of chaff.
A rúpí to a poor man is as much as one thousand rúpís to a rich man.

Sudám was a great friend of Krishna. He at one time was in such great distress, that only a handful of chaff was left to him, which he purposed to eat and then die. However he thought the better of this and went to the Rájá instead with the handful of chaff. Rájá Krishna was so touched with the man's poverty and simplicity, that he himself ate the chaff and gave the Bráhman Sudám whatsoever his heart wished for.

Suh tih dohá Nasaro.

That day also passed, O Nasar.

Come good, come evil, there is an end.

A quotation from a list of conversation between Shekh Núr-ud-dín and his favourite disciple Nasar. Conversation between these two saints often took the form of poetry according as they were inspired. Here is the piece of poetry :—

Maidán wáwas tsakuj nani ; suh tih dohá Nasaro.
Tun wugarah tah sĕni pani ; suh tih dohá Nasaro.
Nishi rani tah wurani khani ; suh tih dohá Nasaro.
Wurah batah tah gáḍah gani ; suh tih dohá Nasaro.

When the back was bare upon the bleak plains ; that day also passed, O Nasar.

When we had wet rice and dry vegetables only to eat ; that day too, has gone, O Nasar.

When the wife was near one and warm clothing covered the bed ; that day, too, went by, O Nasar.

When boiled rice and sliced fish were provided for us ; that day also passed, O Nasar.

There is something similar to this in Persian, but who is the author of it, or where it is to be found, is not known :—

Munam ki kabáb mekhorad :
Meguzrad.
War báda i náb mekhorad ;
Meguzrad.
Daryozah ba kashkol i gadáí nán rá,
Tar kardah ba áb mekhorad ;
Meguzrad.

The wealthy man eats roasted flesh :
Passing away.
Should he drink pure wine ;
Passing away.
The beggar eats the alms-bread,
After having soaked it in water ;
Passing away.

These lines were probably known in the days of Akbar, for when that monarch asked his favourite minister Bír-Bal to do something for him, which would be a source of happiness to him in time of adversity as well in the time of prosperity, Bír-Bal replied by sending to the emperor a few days afterwards a beautiful ringstone upon which he had caused to be engraved in Persian character the word "Meguzrad"; he also sent a nice letter with it advising the king to look upon the ring whenever he was tempted to be over-elated by prosperity, or over-depressed by misfortune.

Another Persian saying from another unknown source is frequently quoted by the Persian-speaking Kashmírí :—

Shab e samur guzashto ;
Shab e tanur guzasht.
That night, when we had fur to cover us, has gone ;
That night, when we had the fire to warm us, has gone.

Sukhas ḍes.

A stick to peace (or striking his peace).

A man, who really has nothing to complain of—he has health and wealth and friends, but he says that he is never well, not rich, and that every body is against him.

Sumis sum niámat tah be-sum kiyámat.

Like with like is blessing, but unlike is confusion.

Birds of a feather flock together ;
Birds of a different feather tear one another.

Shírín-o-Khusrau.—*Kunad ham-jins bá ham-jins parwáz*
Kabútar bá kabútar báz bá báz.

Sun chhuh pánai kahwachih pĕṭh málum sapunán khuṭ chhuá yá khur.

Gold is known upon the stone, whether it is alloyed or pure.

A man is known by his work and walk and conversation.

Kahwaṭ is a touchstone. (Persian.—Mihakk-i-zarrín.)

Gulistán.—*Mihakk dánad zar chíst.*
Gadá dánad mumsik kíst.

Sunah sunz shrák, nah wár thawanas tah nah wár tráwanas.

A golden knife is neither fit to keep, nor to throw away.

Sunas gayam sartal kanas chhas nah batah ladán.

To me gold has become as brass. I do not load my ear with food (*i. e.*, and I am not such a fool as not to know it). Cf. "*Kanas chhas,*" *&c.*

My position is altered and I know it.

Sunas mul kanas tal.

The worth of the gold is in the ear.

Possession is everything.

Sundari tsah pari mai tráv hukai; tsĕh káli sorí chikah cháv.

O pretty woman, don't step so haughtily, you will lose your youthful pride in time.

A silly, conceited, young woman.

This is evidently a line from one of the Kashmírí songs, but it cannot be traced as yet.

Sunur nai sunah tsúr karih tah káts gatshĕs.

If the goldsmith did not steal the gold he would get káts (*i. e.*, a subtle disease, hectic fever).

The suspicion with which the goldsmith is looked upon is not peculiar to the people of Kashmír.

Cf. Kalíla o Damna; the story of the Bráhman Thephasavámi in Herr Adolf Bastian's German collection of Siamese tales; "The Orientalist," Ceylon, Vol. I., p. 180; the Rev. C. Swynnerton's appendix of folk-tales of the Panjáb to his book on Rájá Rasálú; and the Tamil story told in p. 184, Vol. I. of "The Orientialist." But in "The Book of Were-wolves," by S. Baring-Gould, it is stated on the authority of a gentleman who resided in Abyssinia for ten years, and published an account of his experiences afterwards, "that in Abyssinia the gold and silversmiths are highly regarded, but the iron-workers are looked upon with contempt as an inferior grade of beings. Their kinsmen even ascribe to them the power of transforming themselves into hyænas, or other savage beasts. All convulsions and hysterical disorders are attributed to the effect of their evil eye."

Súr malit tsúrah jamáat.

Rubbing ashes over his body (like a saint) and yet belonging to a company of thieves.

Súrah banih wuth nah káv.

The crow did not rise from the dust-heap (although stones were thrown at it).

A man taken into court, but bribes were paid and so the matter was kept secret.

Súrah phalih balái dúr.

From a speck of dust misfortune flies.

A word, and the thing is done.

Suranai gatshih wáyini, gali gatshanas nah khasuni.

The lute should be played, but the checks need not be blown out.

When a man does a good work there is no necessity to send someone with a trumpet to advertise it.

Sutí dugah bah trak.

Slowly, slowly, twelve traks (*i.e.*, 114 pounds) will be pounded.

Rome was not built in a day.

"*Sutsal kami rani?*" "*Amí chánih pránih.*"
"*Míthuí chhĕh gámuts.*" "*Myánih khalani suĕti.*"
"Who cooked the mallow?" "That old woman of yours."
"Ah! it is very nice." "Yes—I stirred it."

Anxious to avoid the blame, but to get the praise.

Sutsalih manzah gushtábah nerun.

Soup comes forth from the mallow.

"Despise not the day of small things."
Gushtábah is a rich soup composed of mince-meat, &c.

Sutsan dapán panahdáwih "Sárí chhih gámuti akí náwih."

The needle says to the piece of thread "We are all in the same boat" (*i.e.*, where you go I go, for we are fastened together).

All the people appear to know this saying, but no one could tell me its origin. It is very strange to meet with such a peculiar expression in this country, and to find that it has the same meaning which it has in England, viz., Both treated alike; both placed in the same conditions. The reference in England is, as is well-known, to the boat launched when a ship is a-wreck.

Suwun tah gĕwun tagih prat kánsih, magar suwun chhuh suwunuí tah gĕwun, chhuh gĕwanuí.

Everybody can sew and sing, but let him sing who can sing (properly), and him sew who can sew (nicely).

Suyih suĕt mandul chhalun.

To wash the back with a nettle.

The harm of keeping bad company.

Syud sádah chhuh sháhzádah.

A plain, simple man is a prince.

T

Tábah Ṭásal nah mandachhán nah chhuh mándachhanah diwán.

Tábah Ṭásal is not ashamed nor does he put any one to shame.

A shameless person.

Tábah Ṭásal was a Paṇḍit, who, contrary to all rule and custom, hired himself out for weddings and other entertainments. He was a good singer and jester, and used to accompany his songs with a-clapping of hands. He struck them together in such a peculiar way that it is said the sound could be heard one mile off (?) He would visit all sects and sexes, and would sit by the hour in all society, never feeling any qualms of conscience, or noticing any wickedness in others.

Tábah was surnamed Ṭásal from the word ṭás, which means clapping of hands.

Tal talí taláv khanán pádsháh garas lúṭ karán.

Apparently digging a very deep well; but, really, robbing the king's house.

A traitor.

A Gosá,ín once visited a king and said that he had a matter for him. "Would his Majesty listen to it, and give his servant one hundred rúpís for it?" The king consented; and this proverb was told him, which he was to repeat aloud every night three times in succession before going to sleep. Now it happened that this king, like most other kings, had his enemies—and enemies, too, in his own household. One of his ministers hated him intensely, and was ready to do and bear anything, so that he might bring about the king's death. Amongst other plans he had a subterranean passage made from his house to the king's, and one night, when the work was almost completed and but a foot more remained to be dug, he himself went along this passage, which communicated directly with the king's bed-chamber, with the intention, if possible, of removing the little earth that remained, and getting close enough to murder the king in his bed. On such a dreadful errand, and in such a dark dangerous place, we cannot imagine this wicked minister's feelings when he heard the king with a loud and distinct voice say, three times in succession, the words which the Gosá,ín had taught him. "I am discovered," said he, and hastened back.

This saying has also been turned into a riddle, of which the answer is a rat.

Talah, dadi talah pati pĕṭah daz tál ; Yá Bár Sáhibo rúdá wál.

Below the sole of the foot is burnt, above the crown of the head is burnt ; O Great God, let it rain.

A favourite prayer for rain.

Yá Bár Sáhibo.—Great God. (*Bár*, participle of *báridan.*)

Talah, talah palah bah shet.

Down, down, twelve hundred rocks down.

A Stoic—hard, deep, and mysterious.

Tálawas dah lurih tah jangah wizeh nah ak tih.

(Usually) ten sticks in the roof, but not even one there in time of fighting.

Abundance of servants, rúpís, &c., but not one at hand when especially wanted.

Támír chhuh kár-i-amír.

Building is the work of nobles.

The wealthy build houses and poor men buy them.

Tanúras nakhah kunḍal.

A little earthen pot beside the oven.

A little man in the company of the great.

Kunḍal is the inner earthenware part of the kángrí.

Tas chhuh nah gáṭul wazír.

He has not got a wise minister (*i.e.*, a good wife to advise and help him).

A certain king was one day sitting with his wife in the verandah of the palace, when a poor miserable-looking and almost nude peasant passed by, carrying a big load of wood for sale in the city. "My dear," said the king to his wife, "how sad it is to see a man in that wretched condition, and in this cold weather too. What a sorrowful existence he must eke out from the pittance which he receives from his wood every day!" "He has not got a wise minister," replied the queen. The king did not understand this remark; he thought that, perhaps, it was meant as a sort of side-hint for himself; hence it would have been a reflection upon his own chosen ministers, and so upon the arrangement of his country. He brooded over these words, until he became in a furious rage, and going to his wife ordered her to prepare to leave the palace at once and be that poor wood-seller's servant. The queen obeyed, though with a sorrowful heart. However, she did not despair, but determined that through her wise counsel and management this poor man should prosper and become great, and then she had a conviction that by some means or other she would again be united to the king her husband, and that both would derive profit from, and be happier for, this temporary separation.

On arriving at the wood-seller's hut she made her salâms, and explained the reason of her visit. "I have come to serve you," she said, "but let me sometimes advise you, and you will be the better for my counsel." The wood-cutter was so surprised at the humble demeanour of the queen, that he fell upon his knees and stammered out something to this effect: "That although the king had given her to him to be his servant, yet he felt himself to be her slave, and that whatever she commanded, that he would try to perform."

The days passed pleasantly enough; now and again, not suddenly but as if quite naturally, little changes were made in the house; this room was regularly cleaned and things began to be arranged in their right places; and one day when the wood-seller's wife was sitting idle, she advised her in a kindly manner to spin; another time she prevailed upon the man to eat his dinner in the city instead of coming home to eat it, because oftentimes, when by evening he had not sold all his load of wood, he had been tempted to take little or nothing for it, in order that he might be rid of his load and get home to his longed-for dinner; and again on another occasion she was able to say something about saving a quarter of his earnings. In these and other different ways the presence of the queen-servant worked quite a revolution in the house. The man became rich and was much respected, and the woman his wife was his true help-meet.

Many years had elapsed since the queen had been separated from the king, yet she had not forgotten him or decreased in affection for him. She was always planning, in order to bring about her return to her husband. One day she heard that he, attended by several of the courtiers, would go to shoot in a certain jungle, so she went and told the wood-cutter her master (now a man of property), to take a small vessel of water and some bread with him, and follow the king's company into the jungle, and when the chase was over, at which time the king would very likely be hot and thirsty, he was to go forward humbly and present his bread and little vessel of water for the king's acceptance. No doubt the king would receive of the offering, and would make some present in return. Should he ask what he would have, he was to say—"I have wealth in abundance. I do not wish for any more money. I only desire that the king will grant me an interview in the palace." The man agreed to carry out the queen's wishes. He went to the jungle and finding opportunity he respectfully presented the little water and bread, which he then happened to have, to the hungry and thirsty king. The king gladly received the gift, and asked what he could do for the man. "Ask what you will," he said, "and I will grant it you." The man answered, "I want not anything from your Majesty, but that you will grant me a few private interviews within the palace." The king was surprised at this strange request, but nevertheless promised that it should be so.

Great was the rejoicing when the queen heard of this, the beginning of her triumph, as she thought.

Frequently did this man visit the king privately, and the king appeared to welcome his visits. When the nobles and courtiers saw this they were very jealous, and afraid lest this "risen" wood-cutter should impeach them; and so they got to know this man more intimately and began to give him handsome gifts by way of a bribe to check his tongue concerning themselves.

The wood-cutter had now become the king's great companion, and having amassed still more wealth, the queen thought that it would not be inconsistent, if he made a great feast and invited the king and many of the nobles to grace it by their presence. The king readily accepted the invitation. The dinner was served on a most magnificent scale, and everybody seemed pleased. Before the company retired the queen went up unperceived to the king, and told him that his host was the poor wood-cutter of former years, and that she was his "wise minister."

A reconciliation was then and there effected between the king and his wife. They retired to the palace together, and ever afterwards lived together most happily.

Tasbíh cháni chham gunasá hisho, muríd díshit karán kham.
Shĕh chinih khĕyitham hisham hisho, tsuh ai pír tah rahzan kam.

Your rosary is like a poisonous snake to me; when you see a disciple you twirl it.
You ate six full dishes of rice, O if you are a saint, who is a robber?

Shekh Núr-ud-dín, a very famous saint in Kashmír, during the end of the eighth century was accustomed to wander about teaching and preaching as he went. At night he would frequently sleep in a mosque. One evening he arrived at the mosque of another very holy man, concerning whom it was said that the angels often came to converse with him during the hours of darkness. This report obtained credence everywhere, and to such an extent in the village itself that the people subscribed together and brought him every day six full dishes of food to feed the angels with. The truth, however, was that he himself ate the food.

Now when this saint saw that Núr-ud-dín intended to lodge there that night, he was afraid that something of his wicked ways would be discovered; and so Núr-ud-dín was advised to depart because of a great monster which sometimes came and troubled the place. Núr-ud-dín, however, declined to go, saying "that he was not afraid if God watched over him." The evening wore away until at last Núr-ud-dín laid down to sleep. The other pír was by, and when he thought that his unwelcome visitor was fast asleep he began to take out the six dishes of food, which had been brought to him that day, and to eat them. He ate them all, and then lay down as if one dead.

At early morning he arose, took out his rosary, and began to mumble. But Núr-ud-dín had seen all that had transpired during the night, and telling the man so, said also to him the words of this saying and left.

Talisuí katas wasih muslah.

The skin will come off from the warm sheep.

Now is the time.

Butchers flay the sheep quickly after killing it; because if the flesh were left to get cold, the skin would not then come off without great difficulty.

Tavit wovmut.

Like roasted-corn sown.

Good words and deeds are wasted upon some people.

Táz-Baṭ-i-kán.

Táz-Baṭ's arrow.

A wind-fall.

Once upon a time a king placed a ring upon a wall and sent forth a proclamation that whosoever could shoot an arrow from a certain distance, straight through the ring, should receive two thousand rúpís as a reward. The best and bravest archers in the kingdom tried, but none succeeded. At length a man called Táz-Baṭ, a poor ignorant fellow, was one afternoon passing by that way and firing his arrows in all directions in a most reckless fashion, he came to the place where the ring was hanging, and more from a playful feeling than from any thought of accomplishing the difficult feat, he let go an arrow, which to his great astonishment passed clean through the ring.

Táz-Baṭ was at once taken to the king, who praised him and gave him the promised reward. Cf. "*Garih yĕlih,*" &c.

Baṭ is commonly met with both in Hindú and Muhammedan names. (Táz-Baṭ in the saying was a Muhammedan.) Very probably it is derived from Baṭah, which means a Hindú. Whenever a Muhammedan has this name it would seem to prove that his ancestors where Hindús, who were converted *per vim* to the faith of Muhammed during the supremacy of the Mughals in "the Happy Valley."

Telah andrai chhuh tíl nerán.

From the sesame-plant oil is expressed.

Fruit according to the tree, and wages from labour, &c.

Tĕlih há-málih ásan kiyámatik keran yĕlih tsuṅṭi papan tseran suĕt.

When apples ripen the same time as apricots ripen, then, O father, will come the day of resurrection (*i.e.*, the resurrection will happen at a most unlikely time, when men look not for it).

Tĕlih tosh, yĕlih nosh garah wátí.

When your daughter-in-law reaches home then be glad (and not before, as you may rejoice to no purpose).

Don't count your chickens before they're hatched.

Tĕlikih, Zai Ḍárah bĕyih yihlah doh tárah.

O Zai Ḍára of former times, come again and stay a few days.

Mourning over the weaknesses of old age.

Zai Dára was a very strong man, who lived to a very great age. He used to say in his declining years, "O Zai Ḍára of former times," &c.

Táre nah situr tah merá nah katah-wani.

You have not got your cotton and I have not the price of my spinning; (we are quits).

Quoted to those who are lax in paying for the making up of any article, *e. g.*, a man gives some cloth to a tailor to make up into a coat, and promises that he will pay him eight ánás for making. In a day or two the man goes and asks the tailor for his coat, but declines to pay the promised money just then. As a general rule the tailor, who has been forced to do so from a past bitter experience, replies, "No, no, you don't get your cloth, and I don't get the price of my labour; we are quits."

Teshal gaikhai peshemán, myániv achhiv ḍeshemán.

O proud woman, you will regret it, my eyes see it.

Cited when from pride any gift or work is refused.

Peshemán (for Pashemán) is always thus pronounced by the female, and very uneducated male, population of Kashmír.

Tĕṭis láras zan tsuṭanas kalah.

He was beheaded like the bitter end of a cucumber.

A speedy punishment.

The Paṭhán rulers were famed for their quick justice (very often injustice). No sooner was the order given "Behead the man," or "Take out his eyes," or "Cut off his nose," than the executioner left and did the cruel deed.

Tham hale tah ham nah hale.

The pillar may move but I shall not move.

A fixed, determinate character.

Tharih posh chhih nah warih gatshan.

All the buds upon a bush do not blossom.

Every child in a family does not thrive.

Thukah nĕchuv mukaddam.

A stammering sputtering son as the headman of an office or of a village.

A man not fitted for his position.

Timah gorih gayih dud kanit.

The milkmaids have sold their milk and gone.

After noon it is almost impossible to get milk in Kashmír, as it is generally all sold by that time.

Persian.—*Án kada bishkast o án sákí na mánd.*

Titshúí tsuwai har yut matinai khar; tah luk wuchhanai tamáshih.

I will have such a row with you, that it will be as if the asses had gone mad; and the people will come out to see the sight.

If I do quarrel with you, I will quarrel.

Toṭ marit tah koṭ taiyár.

The dear one dies and the gallows are ready.

Better to die, for the world is as a gallows set up, constantly troubling and destroying.

Vigne and others of his day speak of having seen bodies "swinging" from the bridges, &c., as they passed up the river through Srínagar. Now-a-days, however, capital punishment is not permitted in the valley as it would be contrary to the Hindú law. (It is very seldom that one hears of a murder in Kashmír.)

Trah zih sah; tsatají zih patají; sheṭh zih breṭh.

A man of thirty years of age is like a lion; a man forty years old is like a torn, worn, mat; and a man sixty years of age is a fool.

Shírín o Khusrau:—

Nasháte 'umr báshad tá ba sí sál
Chihil ámad faro rezad par o bál
Pas az panjáh na báshad tandurustí
Basar kundí pazírad pái sustí
Chu shast ámad nishast ámad ba dewár
Chu haftád ámad aftád álat az kár
Ba hashtád o nawad chun dar rasídí
Basá sakhtí ki az gítí kashídí
Waz anjá gar ba sad manvil rasání
Buwad marge ba súrat zindagání.

Balthasar Gracian, in his "Oraculo Manual," has a similar saying: "Reason makes its appearance after seven years, and every seven years the disposition alters. At twenty years of age one is a peacock; at thirty years of age, a lion; at forty years of age, a camel; at fifty years of age, a snake; at sixty years of age, a dog; at seventy years of age, an ape; and at eighty years of age, nothing."

"Three things make a prodigy, and are the highest gift of Heaven's liberality—a fruitful intellect, a profound judgment, and a pleasant and elevated taste. At twenty years of age the will rules; at thirty years of age the intellect rules; and at forty years of age the judgment rules."

Trakas wukhul pársang.

A mortar as an equipoise for one trak ($4\frac{3}{4}$sers).

An incorrect weight.

Trámahwĕn bánan chhuh tsuk ámut.

The copper vessels have got their bottoms burnt.

Only the wealthier classes use copper vessels; hence the meaning is, that trouble visits the great also sometimes.

Tran chízan chhĕh nah yets kál tán káimí rozán, 'ilm be-bahs, mál be-tijárat, tah mulk be-siyásat.

Three things have no long continuance; knowledge without argument (exercise); wealth without commerce; and a country without law and management

Cf. Gulistán Ch. viii.—*Se chíz ast ki bilá se chíz nĕme mánad, 'ilm be bahs, mál be tijárat mulk be siyásat.*

Tráwamuts thuk ningalani.

To swallow one's spittle.

Taking back a divorced wife, or dismissed servant.

Treh hat nah bahai puntshí.

Three paisás not twelve mites.

Six, not half-a-dozen.

Three paisás are equal to twelve mites, but there was once a very stupid fellow who would not see this. Hence the above saying is sometimes quoted on receiving any stupid answer.

Trukis kathá mudas lorih hatá.

To the sharp a single word; to the dull a hundred stripes.

Trushis gará fushis.

A spirited person angry for an hour.

Tsah dap "beni," buh dapah "báyih;" panani kath chhĕh pananih jáyih.

You say "sister," I will say "brother." Each one's matter is in its own place.

We are both guilty. The only thing for us both to do, is not to go and peach one on the other, but to smother our feelings and keep quiet about it.

Tsah tah buh tah Lúṭah kák.

You and I and Mr. Plunder.

A secret between two people; let both of them take care not to inform against each other!

Kák is a term implying intense respect for the person thus addressed, and is common both to the Muhammedans and Hindús. A son will thus address his father "*Hatah, sah, Kák.*" The younger members of the family will thus address their eldest brother, "*Walah, sah, Ánand Kák.*" And any very respected person outside the family may thus sometimes be addressed, "*Boziv, sah, Naráyan Kák.*" Notice that only the father is called simply Kák.

Kák is also the name of a Hindú sect in Kashmír.

Tsalanas ṭak.

Running instead of fleeing.

Trying to overcome a difficulty in a "half-and-half" sort of way.

Tsalawunĕn bonṭh tah lárawunĕn path.

In front of the runners-away, but the last of the pursuers.

A coward.

Tsam tah nam wuthit rukhsat.

After wearing one's skin and nails away in hard work to be dismissed (without pay)!

A tyrannical master.

Tsar chhĕh akí phalih bápat hairán.

A sparrow is in distress about one grain.

A poor man's need, just a mite will relieve.

Tsarĕn zuwan ṭuphuí kyah?
Tsaris gamas gamuí kyah?

What is a little more irritation to a woman whose head is full of lice?

What is grief to a person already overwhelmed with it?

This proverb is sometimes also thus interpreted:—

When there are many lice where is the sting?
When there is much grief where is the grief? (*e. g.*, A famine, a war, or any other general calamity.)

Sikandar-Náma.—*Ki marge ba ambuh rá jashan khund.*

Tsarih chhuh kanḍi-tharih pĕṭhuí ráhat.
There is rest for the sparrow upon the thorn-bush.
Each man finds rest in his own proper state and station.

Tsarih hund wánṭhuí kyah chhuh?
What is inside the paunch of a sparrow?
No help from a helpless man, and no mercy from a merciless fellow.

Tsarih kashanah chhuh rat yiwán.
Blood comes from much scratching.
From much teasing, a quarrel; from much work, exhaustion; from much reading, madness, &c.

Tsaris gúṭas chhuh tsur khur.
The wiser the man, the greater the blame (if he errs).

Tsaṭit hĕndawand tsahit sodá.
Cutting a water-melon, and tasting the things (before purchase).
Advice on going to the bázár.

Tsachamatsih ungajih nunah phĕṭ.
A pinch of salt to a cut finger.
A sharp word, a mean trick.

Tsei hishih gabih chhiá nyár khasán!
What a ewe like you climbing up to the meadow!
An expression of contempt for another person's powers.

Tsentah Dewahnih wadiwih.
Tsentah Dev's congratulations.
Tsentah Dev was a very poor man with a very large family. Children were born so quickly that it seemed as if the people were always coming to congratulate him on the introduction of another member into his already numerous family. He got very angry and unhappy about affairs; but still his family so increased that now his numerous household and constant congratulations have passed into a proverb.

Tshalas tal chhuí hust tih band.
The elephant also is caught in the trap.
A great many things that are left undone as being impossible might easily be accomplished if people would only think a little.

Tshĕnimuts yĕni hish.
Like broken warp.
A weak, useless fellow.

Tshoṭuí chhuh muṭ.
A little is good (*i.e.*, a little dinner, pride, money &c.)

Tshuche tshuche kánine, zyuṭhuí waharum hák ;
Yuthuí ausum karamah lon tithuí pyom grák.
I spread out my fine vegetables under the roof ;
And as was my lot so the buyer fell to me.
A bad day's business.

Tshun paijámah khas larih pĕṭh, tshun kúńsh tah kar ṭhas, ṭhas.
Put on trowsers, climb the house, put on the kúńsh and tap on the ground as you go.
A boasting fop.
Kúńsh is a kind of shoe worn by women in Kashmír, having high iron heels, and the uppers lessening towards the heels.

Tshupih chhui tyut pháidah yut sinis pákah suĕt.
As much profit from silence as there is profit to the dinner from cooking.

Tshupah chhai wupah-kár.
Silence is profitable.

Tshupah chhĕh rupah sunz.
Silence is silvern.

Tshupuí gupun gudámi kháv ;
Dándai zánih, yas pihun tsáv.
The silent heifer eats the tether ;
That ox will know who has to bear the yoke.
Experience teaches.

Tshur athah chhuh nah atsún ásas tih.
An empty hand does not even enter the mouth.
Be liberal and generous wherever you go, and into whosoever's house you enter ; if there is nothing in your hand you do not think of putting it to your mouth as though to eat, &c.

Tshurui phar tah gontshan war.
Empty boasting and twirling of moustaches.
You may take his price from the worth of his clothes.
Three Kashmírís on account of their poverty went to Dĕlhí, to see what they could do for themselves there. They do not, however,

seem to have bettered themselves very much, for after some years when they had paid all their bills, and the expenses of a return journey to their own country, they found that they all three together were only worth one gold ring, a gold tooth, and a gold-worked turban tail.

One day in the course of their perambulations they stopped outside a butcher's shop in the village of Drugjan with the intention of buying something. The man with the ring pointed with his jewelled finger to a piece of goat's flesh, and asked the price, "*Yĕta bakha kĕtá káwe?*" "What is the price of this goat's flesh?" The man with the gold tooth, lifting his upper lip in speaking, said, "*Das takke, das takke.*" Two ánás, two ánás. The man with the grand turban, shaking his head, said, "*Páwe, páwe*" *i. e.*, "You'll get it, you'll get it." All this time the butcher was silent; but now seeing that they had finished, he quoted the above proverb, "Empty boasting and twirling the moustaches."

The language of these three men is supposed to be bad Panjábí.

T̲shuṭ ai khĕmah kami lubah?

If I eat the remnants of the dinner, with what desire shall I eat it?

Supposing I do this thing, what profit will it be to me?

T̲sithur ai dushih waharas poshih, wahrát ai dushih tah paharas poshih nah.

Should it rain in March-April, then there will be quite enough for a year, but if during August it rains, then it will not be enough for a watch (*ie.*, a space of three hours).

T̲srárah Brĕswár.

T̲srár Thursday.

Any great gathering is so called.

T̲srár is a village about one march from Srínagar. It is the burial-place of Shek̲h̲ Núr-ud-dín, and hundreds flock there on Thursday afternoons, so as to be present at the Friday's prayers and sermon.

T̲suchih-warih andarah neryá anz?

Will a goose come out from the bread?

Not enough for you and me and everybody else.

T̲sunih machih kuluf tah kunih machih búnah kuṭ.

A lock for the charcoal-pot and a store-room for the pot.

Unnecessary carefulness.

T̲súnṭ chhuh t̲súnṭis wuchhit rang raṭún.

An apple gets colour from seeing an apple.

Iron sharpeneth iron; so a man sharpeneth the countenance of his friend.—Prov. xxvii. 17.

Tsúr chhuh be-núr.
Thieves are without light (*i. e.*, they love darkness because their deeds are evil, they are without understanding in their heart, or light of expression in their eyes).

Tsúr chhĕh phak.
Theft is like a bad smell (certain to be detected).

Tsúr gayih nangah hangah-tah-mangah.
The theft became known by chance (*i. e.*, somehow or other it was made manifest).

Tsur gav zih khur gav.
Too much is despised.

Tsúr mah kar tah tsrális mah khots.
Don't steal and don't fear the mahalladár.

" Rulers are not a terror to good works."

Tsrol is the ancient name of mahalladár, the watchman or spy appointed over every village in the valley.

Tsúr tswanzáh khúrd u raft o man shudam ambárdár.
Fifty-four thieves ate and went, and I became the man in charge.

A man is appointed over a work rather "against the grain," and loses by it.

A saying of Shiva Kák's concerning whom a story is given. Cf. "*Kisar láríáyí,*" *&c.*

Tsúrah kapras dánguv gaz.
A walking-stick is the yard-measure for stolen cloth (*i.e.*, a thief cannot expect to get the full price for his stolen goods; sometimes he loses a part of it; sometimes he has to bribe to keep the matter quiet; and generally he has to dispose of the things quickly from danger of discovery, taking whatever receivers may offer him).

Tsúrah kukur.
A stolen cock.

A forbidden work.

Tsúran niyih zanánah, ṭhagan khyav mukhtahár.
Thieves took away the wife, and sharpers ate the necklace.

Ṭhag, a class of thieves and sharpers who prowl about the city by day and by night, and are especially on the *qui vive* on Fridays, the day when crowds of country people come into Srínagar for trading, and worship in the different mosques.

Tsúras nai múr ásih, san kĕthah páṭh shrapĕs.
If the thief is not sharp, how will he digest his theft.

Tsúras phuṭ khor tah píras múrok muríd.
The thief broke his foot and the pír's disciple was killed (for it).

The innocent punished and the guilty acquitted.

Once upon a time when unjust rule, tyranny, and all manner of wickedness reigned in the valley, a thief clambered up the high wall of a house with the intention of stealing whatever he could lay his hands upon. Now it chanced that the wall, being old, and perhaps loosened a little, also, by heavy and continuous rain, had become very weak, and so tumbled down breaking the thief's foot in its fall. The thief was very much annoyed at this interruption of his purpose, and at once limped along to the house of the Deputy-Inspector of Police, and took out a summons against the owner of the tumbled-down wall. The man accordingly appeared in court and pleaded his entire ignorance of the fragile nature of the wall, saying, that he had not built it, and that the bricklayer should be summoned. Accordingly the bricklayer was brought into the court and ordered to show reason why he had built the wall in such a way as that it had fallen down with a very slight knock. He, too, pleaded "Not guilty," saying that there were many coolies there at the time, and that they prepared and gave him the plastering. If any one, surely these coolies ought to be summoned. Accordingly the coolies, who had prepared the mud for plastering, were sent for; and duly presented themselves at court. They also said that they had not done any wrong, but that perhaps the fault lay with the water-carrier, who might have poured too much water over the earth, so that the plastering became thin. Undoubtedly the water-carrier was the man to be punished. And so the water-carrier was summoned. Poor man! The downcast, hopeless, expression of his countenance as he entered the court betokened his case. "Why did you pour such a profusion of water," said the Deputy-Inspector, "as that the mud for the plastering of the wall was thin and feeble?" "I acknowledge my fault," said the water-carrier, "and am very sorry. The reason of it all was, that when I was pouring the water out of the skin upon the earth, it happened that a pretty woman passed by and I took a look at her, and was so enraptured with the sight, that I forgot for the moment what I was doing. I do trust that you will have mercy upon me and forgive me, because it was not my fault, that that beautiful woman just then went by." The beautiful woman was then sought out and brought into the court,—and truly she was very beautiful, but her good looks failed to impress the hard hearted Deputy-Inspector, who charged her with passing by that way at the time of the erection of the wall, and finding that she had nothing to say in defence, ordered her to be hanged with the greatest possible speed. Dumbfounded with fear and astonishment the woman suffered herself to be led along to the place of execution without saying a word. Thither the Deputy-Inspector and many others (for the matter was quickly blazed abroad over the city) were already assembled. On seeing the man who had issued the dread and unjust order for her death the woman begged to be allowed to ask one favour before the deed was done. "Look," said she, "at that large heavy beam (the gallows), and look at me so thin and feeble. The two are not compatible. Better that you seek for one fatter and stronger than I am; and let me go free." The Deputy-Inspector touched with the humour of the request, and not really caring so long as somebody was executed by way of a tamáshá, granted it. Search was at once made for a strong, corpulent, person.

* * * * *

In those days there was a very famous pír in Kashmír, who used to reside in the jungle with no other companion than a faithful, loving, disciple. Now this disciple frequently had occasion to visit the city for the purpose of purchasing little articles, which he himself and his master required. One day this disciple returned to his jungle-home with the alarming news that there was *bebúj* in the city, *i.e.*, bad government had commenced, and that every one and everything were in a state of rampant confusion. On hearing this the pír advised his disciple not to go again to the city until order and rule were re-established there; otherwise he would certainly get into trouble. The disciple, however, made light of this counsel; and on the very next opportunity went to the city. Sorry time for him! He found the place and neighbourhood in the greatest state of anarchy, and had not proceeded far along the noisy, crowded, bázár, when he, being a fine, strong, stout, young fellow, was accosted by the Deputy-Inspector's messengers and informed of his fate. A short time after this he was a corpse; a victim to his own rash curiosity.

Very, very sad was the pír when he heard of his disciple's death. "A thief broke his foot and my faithful follower got killed for it," he cried. "Henceforth alone and friendless I shall have to wander in the woods and desert places." First, however, he determined to go to the Deputy-Inspector and avenge his disciple's unjust death. Immediately on reaching the city he commenced to distribute alms and pretended to be most happy. On the way he met the Deputy-Inspector and told him who he was. The Deputy-Inspector was astonished to find him so glad and joyful, and asked the reason of it. "My disciple," replied the pír, "has reached heaven more quickly through this cruel execution; why should I not be happy and glad?" Hearing this the miserable Deputy-Inspector said within himself, "I, also, will be executed, that I, too, may arrive at bliss quickly. This certainly is the better way." And so he executed himself, and there was an end of the matter.

Tsúras tah tsrális bájwaṭ.

A partnership between the thief and the watchman.

"Can two walk together except they be agreed."—Amos iii. 3.

Tsrol. For their origin, *vide* note "*Kashírih kahai garah.*"

Tsuṭ gayih kolih tah rúh-i-padar.

The bread has tumbled into the river and "for the father's sake."

A man does not give anything to God willingly, but if he loses any money, &c.; he professes not to mind—"May God bless it to my deceased father," says he.

Tsutal shahras trěh pal páv.

In the sodomitish city three pals to a páv.

A badly-managed city.

Páv, a weight of half-a-pound, in which are five *pals.*

Tsyap laj tah tíras, ponṭak gayih tah grístis.

The sheep got a wound and the farmer got a piece of wool.

To harm another person by stealing that which is of the greatest importance to him, but of not the slightest use to the thief.

Tuhas dug dini tah páni mandun.

To pound chaff and churn water.

To plough the seashore.

The Kashmírí has a very ingenious way of making butter. When the milk is ready for churning, it is placed into a big vessel, in the cover of which there is a hole. In this hole a stick is placed. The part of the stick which is inside the vessel is thick, and the part outside the cover is thin; to this thin part a piece of string is attached, and the ends of it the man or the woman holds in their hands, and putting one foot upon the cover to steady it, twirls about the stick with the string, first pulling one end and then the other until the butter is prepared.

I believe a slightly different custom prevails in India.

Tul khěni honin suět.

To eat mulberries with dogs.

To degrade oneself.

Tul palav wuth tsalav.

Gird up the clothes, rise, and away.

A wandering life.

Tumalah síras yĕlih shikmas andar batah sharpí kat wĕpî ná?
When the ser of rice is digested in the stomach does the matter remain?

Scandal at the dinner is blazed abroad as soon as the meal is over.

Turah ba kadr-i-'ilm.
The length of the tail of a man's turban according to his knowledge.

A very wise and learned man called Shekh Challí visited Kashmír, greatly desiring to know to what extent the people had been educated, and whether they were a clever and thriving class. The Kashmírís got wind of this visit and gathered a council to consider how they might entrap this inquisitive foreigner in his speech. The result of their deliberations was, that they sent a most uneducated man named Malah Dupiyáz to meet the learned Shekh at Báramula, a town at the north-west end of the valley.

Malah Dupiyáz went in very grand style; he was beautifully attired and looked of a most serious and meditative disposition, whilst to complete the deception, a man walked behind him with a plate upon which was rolled in a coil the end of his turban.

The Shekh was much surprised at meeting so learned a Kashmírí as this man appeared to be. In the course of conversation he asked him why he wore such a long tail to his turban. The Kashmírí replied, as he had parrot-like learnt, "*Turah ba kadr-i-'ilm.*" Then the following dialogue in Persian and another unknown tongue passed between them:—

Suwál-i-Shekh. *Kabk chíst?*
Suwál-i-Malah. *Mabk chíst?*
Jawáb-i-Shekh. *Kabk dar kohsár sang-rezah mekhorad.*
Jawáb i-Malah. *Mabk dar mohsár mongrezah memorad.*
Question, Shekh. What is the meaning of "kabk?"
Question, Malah. What is the meaning of "mabk?"
Answer, Shekh. "Kabk" is the name of an animal which eats gravel upon the hillside.
Answer, Malah. (Cannot be translated, as it is a language made up for the occasion, in order to *non-plus* the Shekh.)

Mabk also was a word coined for the moment and means nothing. In this way Malah Dupiyáz thoroughly frightened away the Shekh, so that he did not venture any further into the country.

Kashmírís are very fond of carrying on these conversations in imaginary tongues. No entertainment is complete without them.

U

Unglas pĕṭh bungalah.
A bungalow upon an inch of ground.
A good bargain; a cheap concern.

Un dúnd ráwarih súsas dándas wat.
One blind ox will lead a thousand oxen astray.
One fool makes many.
Gulistán, Ch. II.—*Na mebíní ki gáwe dar 'alafzár*
Biyáláyad hama gáwán i dih rá.

Un kyah zánih prun batah?
Will a blind man know white rice?
A fool knows nothing.
There are fourteen varieties of rice grown in the valley.

Un khuts̲ih nah anigaṭih,
Kani phaṭih nah vĕdrih zah,
Húnis aḍij roṭih nah haṭih.
Níkí karit ráwih nah zah.
A blind man will not fear the darkness;
A stone will never be broken by the ice;
A bone will not stick in a dog's throat;
A good deed will never be lost.

Ur mah gats̲h tah yuri wulah.
Don't go there but come here.
Do not interfere in a quarrel or any wickedness.

W

Wabúhas Kalimah nah dar kunih tah nah dĕwár.

The Kalima in time of plague is neither a door anywhere nor a wall (*i.e.*, is no protection; you should have repeated it before).

Pray betimes.

Kalimah is the Muhammedan confession of faith. *Lá iláha illa 'lláh, wa Muhammad Rasúlu'lláh.* There is no Deity but God, and Muhammad is the Apostle of God.

Waguvi dandarih pĕṭhuí gos pĕnjih chhamb.

The edge of the mat became as a precipice to him.

A man who becomes a bad character from a very little matter; or who dies from a very little sickness; or who is in despair because of a very little discouragement.

Wahathor kálah gupan tah pagah sor.

O Wahathor, last night a cow, and to-morrow a pig.

A fickle disposition.

Wahathor, a village in the Yĕch pargana.

Shekh Núr-ud-dín once cursed this village, because one day he went there expecting to be hospitably treated as in former times, and the people would not at all entertain him.

Wájih sán athah pĕṭh thawun.

To put the jewelled hand upon another's shoulder.

Words from the wealthy man fail to comfort the poor man. Why does he not back them up with a present of money?

Waktas nah wĕtsán mŏchhih tah waktas nah wĕtsán kuchhih.

Sometimes it is contained within the hand and at other times it cannot be held within the bosom.

The fickle world.

Persian—*Ki áyín e jahán gáhe chĕnín gáhe chĕnán báshad.*

Waktuk kár gav takhtuk pádsháh.

Work done at the proper time is like a king's throne.

Wanah wálit wĕthi, wahras rachhit, wálanih wizih, dab.

After having tended a tree for a year to cut it down and take it to the river; and at the time of taking it down to throw it with force upon the ground.

After showing a man much kindness, and considerably helping him, to turn the back upon him.

Wanah wálit Wĕthih tshunizih Sirun wazum dizih nah zah; mandini gar khĕnih gatshzih Mungah-Hum sálas gatshzih nah zah.

Better to bring it from the jungle and throw it into the river than to lend anything to the people of Sirun, (for they never pay back); and better to eat the flesh of the sacrifice than to accept the invitation of the people of Mungah-Hum, (for they are very bad hosts).

Sirun is a village in the Dachhanpór pargana. Vessels of stones are hewn there. Sometimes this place is called Siram Khira Hum.

Mungah Hum, a village in the Chhirát pargana.

Wanánuí aut tah ranán nah kĕnh.

For a long time saying only, but not cooking anything.

Actions speak louder than words.

Wananwálih tsĕh nai chhai akl tah bozanwálih tsĕh tih chhai ná?

O talker, if you have not got understanding, you have, O hearer, haven't you?

Never listen to idle tales and scandal.

Wandas chhuh jandan pháh.

In the winter-time there is warmth from an old patched-up garment.

Sikandar Náma—*Maiyafkan kawal garchi 'ár áyidat, ki hangámi sarmá ba kár áyidat.*

"*Wángujo garah ho dúdúí.*" "*Wagĕvi han pilanyum.*"

"O Wánguj, here the house is on fire." "Give me my little piece of matting."

Every man for himself, and especially in time of trouble.

Bústán, Ch. I—*Shĕbe dúd i khalk átashe bar farokht*
Shĕnidam ki Baghdád nime bisokht.
Yĕke shukr guft andar án khák o dúd.
Ki dukán i márá gazande nabúd.

Wání chhĕh bawání.

The sound is as a goddess (= to our "Amen").

Wáni chav sharáb tah suh gav sharmandah;
Tílawáni chav kúnz tah tas lug mad.

A shopkeeper took a little wine and was ashamed of himself;
The oil-expresser drank some rice-water, and he became intoxicated with pride.

A respectable man is ashamed of a very small fault, while the man of low degree is made proud by a very small matter.

Woni, shopkeeper, one who sells sugar, rice, oil, &c. He thinks himself immeasurably above the tílawoni in position, and would not intermarry with his people on any account.

Wani, wani kani pati.

Speaking, speaking behind the ear.

Forgetfulness. Inattention.

Wani, wani tsandun.

Jungles upon jungles of sandalwood.

A life of supreme ease; peace and plenty everywhere.

Tsandun. Natives say that there is a jungle of a kind of sandalwood in Wamá Díví in the Kúṭahár pargana. Large quantities are imported from the Panjáb.

Wanichĕn yáren Khudáyah sund saq.

The water of God for the pines of the wood.

God will provide.

The pine is very common on the Himálayas. The most widespread species is the *Pinus longifolia*.

Wánis chhih grák wĕdí.

The customer is known to the shopkeeper.

Wánṭis ḍunis khĕzih kĕnh tah tshotsis kyah khĕzih?

A man can get something out of a wonṭ walnut, but what can he eat from a tshots.

As good as nothing.

There are four kinds of walnuts :—(i) *Wonṭ*, a walnut with a hard shell, from which the kernel is separated with great difficulty. (ii) *Burazul*, a walnut with a thin shell, and the kernel is easily separated. (iii) *Khokhur* or *Tshotsah-kon*, which is without a kernel. (iv) *Tsú-shákal, Trĕhshákal* or *Suskokul* is a walnut having eight divisions, and very rare. Whenever one is obtained it is readily purchased by the Hindús, who never eat it, but keep it as a dainty morsel for the gods.

Wányo dĕgalis nai chhuí tah zĕvih tih chhuí ná?

O shopkeeper, if you have nothing in your pots, you have a tongue, haven't you?

If one's dinner is meagre, his speech need not be so.

Warah-mulih Tulah-mul.

From Báramula to Tulamul (about twenty-four miles distance).

A good walk or ride.

Warah-mul is the correct name for the town commonly called Báramula, where visitors change horses and coolies for the boats on their way into "the Happy Valley." The lower class Kashmírís, and perhaps residents of Panjábí extraction, have changed the *w* (wáv) into *b* (be), as also in the case of other words, *e.g.*, *Wernág* is changed by them into *Bernág*, Achhi*wal* into Achhi*bal*, and *Wij*biárá into Bijbihárá, &c.

Mul or *Mulah* is a common ending to Kashmírí names of places. Besides Warah-mul and Tulah-mul, there are Drugahmul, Kuchihmul and others. Mul means root, foundation, creation, &c., Hence the creation of Warah or Waráh, the root of the mulberry tree, and so on. Warah-mul, the creation of Wárah or Waráh or Waráha, the hog or third incarnation of Vishnu. So called, because in ancient times the place is said to have been terribly troubled by a Rákshasa called Híranák, who had fortified himself against all attacks of man or beast by asking the deity to protect him against these. He had, however, forgotten to include the name of the boar amongst the others which he had enumerated as wishing to be protected against; and so when the people of Warah-mul cried unto their gods in great distress their petition was heard, and Vishnu, assuming the form of a boar, came down and slew the Rákshasa. Cf. Sanskrit *Hiranyáksha*, Monier Williams' Dicty.

Tulah-mul, the root of the mulberry-tree. It is supposed to have been a lake at first, and having connection with the great Ánchár Lake, about four miles distant from Srínagar. Three hundred and sixty Nágs (or snake gods) are said to have resided there, and in their midst the goddess Rágniá; but no one ever saw them, except a Paṇḍit, Krishna Kár by name. He was one of the goddess' devotees, and he worshipped her so regularly and earnestly that the goddess deigned to manifest herself to him. She appeared unto him in a dream, and told him to go to the Ánchár Lake, because there she would show herself to him. The Paṇḍit enquired how he should find her Nág, whereupon she told him to go there in a boat, and on his arrival she would under the form of a serpent lead him to the place. All happened as the goddess had said. The Paṇḍit was guided to a spot where a mulberry tree had grown; and the place was quite dry. There and then Krishna Kár worshipped Rágniá, and afterwards left and told all the people of the wondrous vision and gracious words which he had seen and heard. Cf. Sanskrit *Rájní*, Monier Williams' Dicty.

Warah mulik wáv.

The wind of Báramula.

Jánbáz Sáhib, a Muhammedan religious mendicant, lived at Báramula in olden days, when the place was noted for its great heat. At one time for a whole week the sun shone upon the town with such increasing vigour that the people were being struck down with fever in large numbers. Then it was that Jánbáz prayed, and the air was at once changed, and a good wind sprung up, which has continued to blow around Báramula ever since. Jánbáz Sáhib's tomb is to be seen in the town, and is much venerated and visited.

Warhajih mundare par nai ásie,
Noshi nai ásie hash tah zám,
Mukaddamas patah nai phukaddam ásie,
Gámas tulihe shámas tám.
If there were not an axe for the crooked log,
If there were not a mother-in-law and sister-in-law for the daughter-in-law,
If there were not a phukaddam after the mukaddam,
Then he (or she or it) would trouble the village until the evening,

No rule—no peace, and no country.

Mukaddam, the headman of a village, called lambardár in the Panjáb.

Phukaddam, an officer under the authority of the mukaddam.

Warí chhuh treh hat tah sheṭh doh.

A year is 360 days.

Lay by for the morrow.

Wárini nishih shur thawun khaṭit.

To hide the child from the midwife.

Perfectly useless to try to keep the secret.

Wom :—Dái se peṭ nahín chhuptá.

Wáriní prasun hĕchhináwán.

Teaching the midwife how to deliver a child.

Teaching one's grandmother how to suck eggs.

Teaching a shopkeeper his tables, &c.

Wast chhih dubi sandih ṭukah talah sáf gatshán.

The clothes become clean beneath the washerman's stick.

"There is a great want in those people who have not suffered."
McCheyne.

Watah wĕlai tah jorah judáí.

May you miss the way and be separated from one another.

A Kashmírí curse.

Wátal Baṭwárah.

A sweeper's Saturday (*i.e.*, no time—I shall never get it).

There are several classes of wátul or mihtar log. Some who make winnowing fans and are called shupi-wátul, some who do regular mihtar's work and are generally called duwanwol: and others who make boots and shoes and are called simply wátul. Like people of other crafts the bootmaker invariably wants something in advance, and promises the boots on the following Saturday, which promise is renewed for two or three Saturdays, until the order is fulfilled. Hence the proverb.

Wátal Braswárah.
The sweepers' Thursday.
Vide supra.

Wátalan tír.
The sweeper's sheep.
Money or property in the hands of a man of low degree.

Watan hund máz latan tah latan hund máz watan.
The flesh of the road to the sole of the foot and the flesh of the soles of the feet to the road.
A man who earns his living with great difficulty.
Some work so hard, and walk so far, that the skin comes off from their hands and feet, and the dust of the ground comes in its stead, and cannot be washed off again.

Watih watí chhuh áb pak án.
The water flows its straight regular course.
No humbug about that man or that arrangement.

Watshen wahrahwud.
A birthday to calves! (there is no need to commemorate their natal day).
Cited when an unworthy man has been honoured, &c.

Watshis gyad tah dándas lov;
Insáf rov tah wanav kas?
Kahan garan kuní tov,
Hĕmmat ráv tah wanav kas?
Six wisps of grass to the calf and only one to the ox;
Justice lost and to whom shall we speak?
Only one frying-pan between eleven houses.
Courage gone and to whom shall we speak?
The reign of injustice.
Cf. note to "*Kashírih kahai garah.*"

Wav, bá, wav, zih lon, bá, lon.
Sow, brother sow, that you may reap, brother, reap.

Wáv kas zih yĕs patah áv?
Who has such trouble that he should lag behind?

Wáv wuchhit gatshih náv tráwuni.
Look at the wind before you loose the boat.
Consider before you act.

Wáwas náwah sail.

To take out the boat when a strong wind is blowing.

An unsuitable time for any work.

Wĕlinjih pĕṭh wukhul.

A mortar upon the clothes-line.

Impossible.

Natives tie lines of string right across their rooms and hang clothes, vegetables, &c., upon it.

Wĕshámitrun surug.

Wĕshámitar's heaven.

To die on the completion of any great object.

Wĕshámitar was a rikhis, or arch-saint, among the Hindús. He made a heaven for himself, and when he had finished it and had just set foot on the doorstep to enter therein, he died.

Wĕth poshih nah athah chhalanas.

The river-water will not be enough for washing his hands.

A wasteful, extravagant, man.

Wĕth is the Jhelum river in its course through Kashmír.

Wĕth tshenià zih panun tshenih?

Will the dividing of the river be as if any of your own relations were going to be hurt?

Your own is your own, another's is another's.

Wĕthí kati chhak grazan zih ágarah?

O Wĕth, whence are you roaring? From the spring.

The spring of a woman's happiness is her husband's love, the spring of a man's prosperity is a friend's help, the spring of a nation's distress is the ruler's mismanagement.

Wĕthih nábad phul.

Some sugar-candy for the river.

A little gift lost in the vastness of the receiver's need.

Wĕtsár-Nágai marutsah nábad.

(Eating) the sugar and pepper at Wĕtsár-Nág.

To break one's journey for rest and food, or to eat at home the food which was prepared for the journey.

Gangabal is a stream tributary to the Sindh river. Hither go those Pandits bearing the ashes of dead relations who died during the previous year, which they throw into the sacred stream with great reverence. Cf. note "*Siryas hyuh nah,*" *&c.* When going to this place, while ascending the Barut mountain they sometimes fall sick either from the effects of the rarified atmosphere, or else from overtiredness; and so the pilgrims are advised to take some sugar and pepper with them and eat these as medicines, if they should feel ill. These sugar and pepper are not on any account to be eaten at Wetsár-Nág. On one occasion a little boy about six years old, not having been well instructed in the manners of the pilgrimage, began to eat some of his sugar-candy at Wĕtsár Nág, a march or so too early.

Woni budih tah parmánah thurih.

The shopkeeper will grow old and throw about the scales.

A useless, old servant.

Woni chhuí poni kisarih talí.
Hárih hastis hĕwán mulí.

The shopkeeper is like water below rice-chaff.
He buys an elephant for a cowrie ;—(sharp, cunning fellow!)

Woni gav suí yus pánis bozih hisáb.

He is a shopkeeper, who understands (even) the worth (of a drop) of water, (so that he does not waste a trifle of anything).

Woni gav suí yus machh tsahih.

A shopkeeper is he who will lick up a fly (*i.e.*, will not waste a scrap).

A shopkeeper married his daughter in very grand style. During the ceremony he placed some very valuable pearls upon her veil. Everywhere his name became distinguished because of this splendid wedding.

Some days after the wedding was concluded two merchants came to him bringing some honey for sale. He bought it, and while he was storing it away in his shop he noticed a fly in one of the pots, which he extricated, licked the honey off from it, and then threw away. His daughter chanced to see him do this dirty trick and despised him for it. "Father," said she, "how could you be so vulgar after having spent so much money over my wedding and appeared so grand!" The girl was so upset by this act of her father's that she got ill, and only became well again when it was proved to her that this extreme care, which her father manifested, had alone enabled him to spend such an enormous sum of money over the wedding.

Wuchhit un tah búzit zur.

Seeing, yet blind, and hearing, yet deaf.

See all and hear all, but say nothing.

Wuchhto kyah pyav husnas wâv; rántasih kuruk Sháh Mál náv.

Look, what a misfortune has happened to beauty; people have given the ugly woman the name of Sháh Mál.

Sháh Mál is the name of a great and beautiful woman.

Wudah-Púruk be-garaz.

The independent, lazy people of Wudapúr.

Wudapúr is a village in the Utar pargana. The people are as they are proverbially represented. No person, if they can help it, will take a servant from the village.

Wufawane ratanih.

Catching (birds or) things as they fly.

"Credulous fools."—Shaks.

"*Wuntá khasun kuthú zih wasun?*" "*Har-dú lánat.*"

"O camel, how do you going up and coming down hills?" "Oh, both are a curse."

There is a touch of the curse about everything down here.

Wunth budyov tah muthar karun hĕchhun nah.

The camel has become aged and has not learned how to help himself.

Old age is second childhood.

Persian.—*Shutur pír shud sháshidan na amokht.*

Wuntah natsun tah khar áhang chhĕh mashhúr.

A camel's dancing and an ass's braying are well-known.

A work out of time and out of place.

A camel and an ass were grazing in the same meadow together, when suddenly the ass brayed very loud. "Be quiet," said the camel, "you will disturb the whole neighbourhood and the people will come out, and catch us and bind us, and we shall henceforth have to carry burdens. Be not so foolish, I pray you." But the ass did not desist; on the contrary he brayed the louder, and the consequence was that some men hearing the noise came forth and caught both the animals. The camel was filled with rage, but kept his counsel, determining to revenge himself upon the ass at the earliest opportunity.

One day both the camel and the ass were walking together carrying loads, when they arrived at a bridge, upon which the camel began to dance with all his power.

"Steady, steady," cried the ass, "you will break the bridge and we both shall be precipitated into the deep river." But the camel did not hear; on the contrary he seemed to dance more clumsily and with greater vigour, until presently the beams of the bridge snapped into two pieces and they both fell into the water and were killed. Cf. Journal, Asiatic Society, Bengal, Vol. LII., Part I, p. 90, the Rev. C. Swynnerton's tale of "The Four Associates."

Wunuk tám thuktam suzahárih sun chhum ;
Ajih hárih kanahwáj drúyí no.
Wunuk tám thuktam málin kronuí ;
Az nai dún tshutsah-konuí droí.
Up to this day you boast about the gold in your purse ;
But never so much as an earring of half-a-cowrie's worth has appeared.
Up to this day you boast about your father's house and people ;
But to the present day not an empty walnut even has come out of it.

Empty boasting.

Wupar mahalluk gav kukar tsúr.
A man from another district is a thiever of fowls.

Srínagar is divided into several mahallas. People of one mahalla dislike very much to have anything to do with the people of another mahalla. The people of the one will not receive the people of the other ; the children of the one will beat and abuse the children from the other ; and the very dogs also will not recognise one another in a friendly way. It is a constant occurrence to lose fowls, &c., as a natural consequence of this estrangement.

Wupasladas chhuh kún patai.
A dog following after a fasting man.

One trouble after another.

Wurah-gabar chhih sorah khyul.
Wurah-mális torih dab zangih.
Wurah-mális khorah rut.
Step-sons are like a herd of swine.
A stroke with the chisel upon the feet of the step-father.
A chain for the feet of the step-father.

Wurun wuchhit gatshih khor waharun.
A man should stretch out his feet after looking at the bed-clothes.

Marathi.—*Hátrun páhun páya pasaráve.*

"*Wushini bĕni, yuharin wulah,*" "*turuni bĕni uharin gatsh.*"
"O warm (*i.e.*, rich) sister, come here. O cold sister, go there."

Cupboard love.

In Kashmír a wealthy man is called a warm man, *ak garm mahynuv* ; a rich tomb (place of pilgrimage,) is called *ak garm ziárat.*

Wushneras khal khish ; turneras mal mish.

To a warm (*i.e.*, a wealthy) man, his heart's desire ; but to a cold man (*i.e.*, poverty), filth and repulsion.

Khal khish, lit., slaughter of beasts.

Mish is a general word said with a drawl for urging cattle along, &c.

"Wuth nush kuṭ khas." "Áyas kyah karanih ?"

"Rise, O daughter-in-law, and get up to your room." "What else have I come for ?"

One's duty.

People are married very early in the country of Kashmír, if their parents can afford it. The custom of Hindûs at the first marriage is to make the bride and bridegroom sleep together in the husband's house for one day only. After which they are separated until the bride attains the age of puberty. Among Muhammedans the couple sleep together for a whole week, and then are separated. In the saying above the bride is supposed to have reached her mother-in-law's dwelling, and immediately on arrival she is told to go to her room. "For this very purpose I have come," says the girl.

"Wuth nikah kám kar." "Nikah chhus tah hĕkah nah."
"Wuth nikah batah khĕh." Ḍul myon katih chhuh ?"

"Get up, youngster, and work." "I am weak and cannot."
"Get up, youngster, and eat something." "Where is my big pot ?"

Wuthiv koṭhĕv bihiv koṭhev khĕyiv shikár máz.
Wuthiv nai bihiv nai tah khĕyiv panun máz.

Get up knees and sit down knees and eat the flesh of the prey ;
If you wont get up and sit down then eat your own flesh.

Work is health and life.

Wuṭih wulah, madano.

Come, O friend, and be tempted ; (not I, I know better).

Wutini baláyih tut.

Another gets his punishment.

The wrong man.

Wuvur matyá zih wunah t͟súr karih bĕyih ?

Is the weaver so mad that he will again steal wool ?

A burnt child dreads the fire.

Panjábí.—*Ag dá jaliá titáne te dardá haí.*

Wuvuri sundi dyáran dah sás.

A weaver's wealth is ten ánás.

A stupid man with a little money who wishes to be thought a great personage.

There was a poor wretched weaver who had only ten ánás, which he hid in the dust under his feet. He put five ánás under one foot and five ánás under the other foot, and while he was weaving he used to work his feet up and down (as if at a treadmill) and say "*Is phallih pánch, us phallih pánch*," which translated is "Five in this place and five in that place." News of this got wind, and one day the poor weaver lost all his ten ánás. He then continued to say. "*Is phallih toh, us phallih toh*," of which the interpretation is, "On this side chaff and on that side chaff."—It appears that the thief had put some chaff in the place of the money stolen.

Wuzalih kanih tsup kadun.

To bite on the red side (of an apple, &c.)

A gaint share in the partnership.

"*Wuzamuí, nats nats tai ai panziai.*"

"O monkey, dance upon loan."

A debtor's reply to a hard creditor.

Some of the natives earn their living by training monkeys to dance and do other tricks. They take them about, as they do in England, to the people's houses, and some of the people give them money, while others promise to give on the morrow.

"*Wuzamyo kutú guk?*" "*Horĕr ráwaranih.*"

"O debt, whither gone?" "To increase the debt."

Keep out of the clutches of the money-lender.

Y

Yá púr nah tah dúr.
Either altogether, or else be at a distance.
The whole hog or none.

Yá tai kaj nah tah laj "Huri" wanane.
At first she was dumb, but afterwards she began to say "Huri."
Time will make mention.
Huri is a sound for driving away cows.

Yá tsalun nah tah tsálun.
Either flee or else suffer.

Yá zurav nah tah burav.
Either suffer or else go. (*Vide supra.*)
"Go, you rascal, or I will smite you."

Yaḍ chhaní táh chhiṭ naní.
The stomach empty but the dress displayed to view.
Stinting the stomach to support the back.

Yaḍ chhuh nah wuchhán kaṅh tah tanih chhuh wuchhán parat kaṅh.
No one sees the stomach but everybody sees the body.
An argument for dress.

Yaḍ dag chhĕh boḍ dag.
The stomach pain is a great pain.
"In the sweat of thy face shalt thou eat bread."

Yaḍ tsharuí tah gontsan diwán táv.
An empty stomach, yet twirling his moustache.
The would-be gentleman.

Yaḍal chhui be-ímán.
A fat man has no religion.
"Jeshurun waxed fat and kicked."

Yájih ai phuchhih tah kúchih chhĕs ati.
If the biscuit is broken, the pieces are here.
Here are the items of the account, we will add up the total again.

Yak tan tah dú kas.

One body and two persons.

A married couple.

Yakar chhánuni kukar pachih-baran.

Yakar, the carpenter's fowl-house.

An unfinished work.

Fowl-houses, garden-walls, &c., in Kashmír are frequently made of a loose rough kind of wooden railing called *pachah-baran.*

Yakar, a carpenter, is said to have built a fowl-house for some person, which tumbled down directly one of the fowls flew upon it.

Yakur márit athan phak.

Lay hold of (lit., kill) the yakur plant and your hand will smell.

You cannot touch pitch without being defiled.

Yamah, yitam tah nitam.

O angel of death, come and take me.

Quoted in a most piteous tone when any person begs to be let off any difficult or unpleasant work.

Yapárih bál bakar tah apárih bál lakar.

On this side of the hill (he promised to give me) a goat, but (when he had reached) the other side (by my help, he gave me) the stick, *i.e.*, he beat me.

Yár kyah layih zih tsarih bachih.

What is the worth of a friend that you will not give him the young sparrow.

A request refused.

Yár gai batah-mar.

Friends are rice-stores.

"Make to yourselves friends."

A king had three sons, to each of whom when they were grown up he gave a lákh of rúpís to profit with as they each thought right. One of them tried trade and became exceedingly rich, another went and founded many caravanserais for pilgrims and travellers; and the third travelled everywhere lavishing gifts upon the people and entertaining them in large numbers, and in grand style. In course of time they all met together again and recounted their several experiences. When the king had heard these he praised the first two sons; but was angry with, and despised, the youngest.

* * * * *

The king's country was in a state of great confusion; an enemy with a very strong force behind him had appeared against it. What was the king to do? He was weak and friendless. He called his wise ministers, but they could not help him out of his difficulties. At length he sought the advice of his sons. The first son advised yielding in the most honourable way possible; the second son said that he could not help his father; but the third—who had been sent for, it was true, but without any expectation of real help or wise counsel from him—he said, "O king, my father, command me to go against this enemy and I will overcome him." The king consented. "Go and do better with your men when you get them, than you did with your money when you had it." The youngest son went forth with a glad and hopeful heart calling together his friends on the way. The people remembered his generosity and amiability and answered readily to his call, until at last he had with him a very large force of most enthusiastic followers, by whose help he thoroughly routed the enemy, so that they returned no more to trouble the land.

The king had a different opinion of his youngest son after this. Instead of despising him he esteemed him the most worthy of all his sons, and appointed him to the greatest honour.

Yár zágán tshalas tamáki chilim chat tah tsalas.

The friend lies in wait to deceive; after smoking the pipe he will run away.

A heartless servant or friend, &c.

Yáras moj muyih tah lukah sásáh, yár múd tah kunih nah kanh.

If a friend's mother dies a thousand people remain (because the friend is alive), but if the friend is dead, then there is nobody left.

"All the wealth of the world could not buy you a friend, nor pay you for the loss of one."

Yas gov hund dud tah gurus khězih tasund pětshur tih gatshih tsálun.

One must take the cow's kick as well as her milk and butter.

We cannot afford to quarrel with a good servant or good horse, &c.

Yas korih nethar soh kúr lubaran!

A daughter about to be married gathering dung!

A person who is everywhere and doing everything except in the right place and doing the right thing.

Yas lug "karah karah" suh karih;
Yas lug "marah marah" suh marih.

He who says "I will do, I will do," he *will* do;
He who cries "I shall die, I shall die," he *will* die.

Where there's a will there's a way.

Yas mahnyvis bĕyih sund bad yiyih tas gats͟hih panun kámuni.

He who wishes evil to another man, will suffer his own loss.

Harm hatch, harm catch.

Yas nah wats͟h nar tas gayí garasuí andar phar.

He whose arm is not raised (in labour), to him a dried fish has become in the house.

Industry begets wealth.

Phar.—During the winter months the fishermen go out with their boats in companies of ten or twelve after these little fish, which they catch in a cast-net. Half-a-dozen boats will spread themselves across the river sideways and beat the water with their paddles, to frighten the fish into the half-a-dozen nets, which have been thrown for them by the other boats a little way ahead. In this way sometimes a mile of the river is scoured in an evening, and maunds upon maunds of fish are frequently caught by one company. When it begins to get dark the fishermen fasten their boats to the bank and collect all their fish together into one place. Then they spread a layer of leaves or grass, and over this a layer of fish and a sprinkling of salt, then another layer of leaves or grass and so on, until a great mound is raised. Everything ready they now light big fires on all four sides of this mound to dry the fish, and sit by and watch, until the fires go out. On the following morning the fish are taken out and strung upon sticks ready for sale. Only the poorer classes purchase them, as they are not very savoury or wholesome.

Yas wandas hammám tah rĕtahkálih gáv, suí há-málih dunyahas áv.

That man has come into the world, O father, who has got a warm bath for the winter and a cow for the summer.

Blessed is the man who has everything in its season.

A saying of Shek͟h Núr-ud-dín.

Yas wat ráwih tas háwan dah ;
Yas kath ráwih tas háwih nah kaṅh.

Him, who loses his way ten men will direct ;
But he who loses a word,—who will direct him ?

"Each sacred accent bears eternal weight,
And each irrevocable word is fate."—Pope.

Yas wats͟h nar tami khĕyih lukah hanz lar.

He who raised his arm (*i.e.*, in labour) ate the house of the people.

Industry begets wealth.

Yas yus gatshih suh tas gatshih muhará dit.

Let that man who wants anything give a gold-mohur (as a bribe) for it.

Money commands even the gods.

Yat bawah-saras áyai kahtí !
Kańh nai dyuthum kánsih suĕti.

How many people came to this lake-like world!
But I have not seen anyone (going away) with anyone (*i.e.*, we die separately and alone).

This world is called lake, or sea like, because it is so difficult to cross over it with safety—*Vide* note "*Samandaras manz,*" &c.

Yat nam atsih, tat shistar kyah lágun.

Where a finger-nail will enter (will do it), there is no necessity for iron.

When one can accomplish the matter easily, what is the good of creating a noise. When it can be done very economically, what profit is there in spending much money over it, &c.

Yath gámas nah gatshun ásih, tamih gámuk náwui hyun kyah chhuh ?

Is it necessary to ask the man of that village whether you have to go, or not?

Useless speech.

Yath núrah butisui mai dí núruye.
Dur nai latiye rozih samsár.
Wuchhtai Pándawan hund dih duruye ;
Tím králah garanui chhapane tsái !
Timanui kyah aus lyukhmut Hariye.
Dur nai latiye rozih samsár.

Don't hide your light face in your sleeve, dear.
The world will not always remain.
See how firm were the bodies of the Pándus ;
Yet they had to hide themselves in a potter's house!
According as Hari had written in their lot.
My dear, the world will not always remain.

"Nothing in this world can last."

The above is the poetry of a very holy fakír woman (neither Muhammedan nor Hindú) named Habbah Khotan, who used to live at a village called Pándachhuk, where there is a wooden mosque, which she erected from the savings of her spinning-wheel earnings. The people say that she was accustomed to cross the river upon a lion, which beast God gave her as a special present.

Páṇḍus. Yudhishthira, and four other princes, sons of Páṇḍu, a sovereign of ancient Delhí. For a full account of these demigods and of their great enemies the Kurus, cf. any classical Dictionary of India. Here I will only explain the above lines. Yudhishthira, the eldest son, was installed as heir-apparent, and soon became reuowned for his "justice, calm passionless composure; chivalrous honour and cold heroism." The people wished Yudhishthira to be crowned king at once, but the Kurus tried hard to prevent it. First of all the Páṇḍus and their mother were sent to a house built of combustible materials, with the intention of burning the whole family in it. The Páṇḍus, however, were informed of this, trick and escaped to a potter's house in another city, &c., &c.

Hari or *Harí* is a name of Vishnu. Kashmírí Hindús believe that he inscribes upon the foreheads of human beings their several destinies. The following is a quotation from the *Hitopadesa* (with Johnson's translation) :—

स हि गगनविहारी कल्मषध्वंसकारी
दशशतकरधारी ज्योतिषां मध्यचारी ।
विधुरपि विधियोगाद् ग्रस्यते राहुणासौ
लिखितमपि ललाटे प्रोज्झितुं कः समर्थः ॥

"Since even the moon sporting in the sky, destroying sin, possessing ten hundred beams, marching in the midst of the stars; from the influence of destiny is swallowed by the dragon :—who then is able to avoid what is written on his forehead by the finger of destiny." Cf. "*Sáfah khutah,*" *&c.*

Yath tílawán zachih, yih phyúr tih.

Let this drop also fall upon the oilman's dirty clothes, (what difference will it make?)

A little more trouble to a man already overwhelmed with it. Some oilmen have been known to wear the same long smocklike garment for the space of three years without once having it washed or changed all that time. The quantity of grease which collects within a few months, even, is almost incredible.

Yath tumbis tih hugḍai.

This piece of wool also for dried fish.

"On the verge of bankruptcy—what can matter a shilling or so more."

Persian.—*In lakad ham ba gor i Hátam i Tai.*

Yatsan gagaráyan rúd nah, tsarĕn kathan súd nah.
There is not rain from much thundering, and there is not profit from much speaking.

" *Yatsarih, raneyih khĕtsarih mĕtah.*" " *Wulo kánṭarah.*"
" *Boh dai lugus wálah-barí.*" *Tsĕh dai mutsuí* " *tah ati khĕh.*"
" O zealous woman, you have cooked a handful of curry." " Come, O cock sparrow."
" I am fastened, O woman, in a net." " It is left over for you; eat it there."
Misfortune.

Yelan jel tah mawásan khalat.
A prison for the royal and obedient, and a robe of honour for the rebellious.

Khalat (Khil'at in Arabic) is generally a robe of honour with which princes confer dignity on subjects, and visitors of distinction. Sometimes a sword or a dagger, or a rare jewel, or some other valuable, is given together with a turban and shawl.

Yĕlih ausum lukachár tĕlih ausum nah mukajár.
When I was a child then I had not any leisure.
Time hangs heavily upon an old man.

Yĕlih ḍal darwázah wut gatshán, tĕlih chhuh nah kánsih hund bozán.
When the flood-gates of the lake open, then they do not listen to any one.
The word of the ruler—no alternative.

Ḍal darwázah, lit., the door of the lake. The Ḍal is a large lake close to the city of Srínagar. When the river is low the gates, called "*Ḍal darwázah,*" remain open; but when the river rises to a certain height, they close of themselves, thus preventing inundation of the land around the lake.

Yĕlih diwán Khudá tĕlih kaṭas nún zan;
Yĕlih niwán Khudá tĕlih kaṭas mún zan.
When God gives then it is as salt for the sheep;
When God takes then it is as wool from the sheep.

(*i. e.,* when God gives, he gives to profit—the gift is as salt, which preserves and fattens the beast; and when God takes, he takes but His own—what He himself has given, *i. e.,* as wool from the sheep, which fattened from the salt, which God gave it).

Yĕlih píran hisáb mangan, kuṭah píran naṭ atsih zangan.

When the pírs' accounts will be taken, counterfeit pírs will tremble.

A wicked steward, a dishonest servant.

Gulistán of Sá'dí, Chap. I.—*Har ki khyánat warzad dastash dar hisáb bilarzad.*

Yĕlih sun tĕlih nah kan, yĕlih kan tĕlih nah sun.

When there is gold (for the earring), then there is not an ear; and when there is the ear, then there is not the gold.

A wife and expense, or no wife and save; a son and expense, &c.

Yĕlih tsah ásak pádsháh tĕlih ásah buh wazír.

When you become king then I will be minister.

"I'll be up with you."

Yĕlih yih shúbih tĕlih tih kar.

When it is proper then do it.

A time for everything.

Yĕmi daulat jamá kar, yá niyas tsúr yá ráwis zamínih tal, nah khyon pánas nah nyun athih nah ditun bĕyis.

He who gathered together riches, either a thief will take them from him, or they will be lost under the ground; the gatherer neither partakes of them himself, nor does he take them with him, nor does he give them to another.

Yĕmí dits noshih suí dapán "Garah bigaryov."

He who commits incest with his daughter-in-law says: "The house has become bad."

Every bad man suspects every other person of being bad likewise.

Yĕmi dits wani tas suí wani, yĕmi tsaṭ wani tas suí wani.

He who plants a grove of trees, may God do so to him; and he who cuts the grove may God do so to him.

"Whose end shall be according to their works."

Yĕmí herih khatsos tamí herih ai wasahah, yemí ṭapah ai lasahah tah lĕjih wasahah nah zah.

I came up by this ladder and if I get down again by it and am free of this misfortune I will never steal from the pot again.

Poor people's children are constantly pilfering from the pot. One day a little child was seen in the very act, and was caught at the top of the ladder, which generally runs up outside a Kashmírí hut, and by which she sought to escape, perhaps, over the roof. While her mother was beating her on the top round of the ladder, she shrieked out these words, which have passed into a proverb, and are now constantly cited by other and bigger children, when they are discovered doing anything forbidden.

Yĕmi hov tami nyov ; yĕmi khuṭ tami ruṭ.

He who made the thing manifest caused it to be taken away, and he who concealed the matter, held it.

Keep your own counsel.

Yĕmi hyut suh hut.

He who took grief (into his heart) rotted away.

Yĕmi khani gang tas gayih tati andar panuni zang.

He who dug a pit for others has got his own legs into it.

Persian.—*Cháh kan rá cháh dar pesh kardah i k͟hesh áyad pesh.*

Yĕmi kur ár suh gav k͟hwár.

He who does shame comes to shame.

Yĕmí kur gungul tamí kur kráv.
Lukah hanzih láganaiyih pĕṭh mo bar cháv.

He who began the harvest reaped the end of it.
Do not be covetous over other people's fields.

Yĕmi kur lawah hat suh tih tutuí ;
Yĕmi zol lawah hat suh tih tutuí.

He who made a hundred bundles of grass, to him so much ;
He who burnt a hundred bundles of grass, to him so much.

A master who does not praise the good servant and reprove the bad, but serves all the servants alike.

People gather the long lank water grass which grows by the river-side in the Autumn, tie it up into bundles, and sell them during the Winter at the rate of sixty bundles for an áná.

Yĕmi lukah hanzan michan tah ṭukran pĕṭh nazar thav suh gav hairán.

He who keeps his eyes upon the pieces of rice and bread of other people is in a wretched state.

A loafing, wandering, fellow.

Yĕmi Sáhiban ás ditus suh diyas ná khos tih khyun kyut?

Whom God has given a mouth, to him will not He, the same God, give a little pot for his dinner?

Bustán of Sá'dí—*Yake tifal dandán baráwurda bud,*
Pidar sar ba fikrash faro burdah bud.

Mukhor gam bará e man ai be khirad—
Har ánkas ki dandán dihad nán dihad.

Yĕmi sháli chhih wuchhmati yiti kahtyáh rúd!

This jackal has seen plenty of rain like this!

An old experienced man.

Yĕmi wuchh naris tah dalis suh gav khwár;
Yĕmi tshun akis khoras pulahur, bĕyis paizár.
Suh chhuh barkhurdár.

He who paid attention to the sleeve and border (of his garment) was ruined;

He who wore a grass shoe on one foot and a leather shoe on the other, he was prosperous.

The man who wishes to succeed must not mind a little dirt sometimes.

Yĕmis "Nannawárih" náv dráv tas tsalih nah zah.

If a man has got nicknamed "Bare-footed," the name will never leave him.

In olden times there lived in Kashmír a very great man named Khwájah Karím Dín. He once visited the 'Íd gáh in time of snow. On arriving at the common he noticed the nice level ground and said to his attendant "Take off my shoes. I wish to run on the grass for a few minutes with naked feet." His servant obeyed, and Karím Dín ran about for a long time to his heart's content.

From that hour the people called him Karím Nannawor. Of course he was very angry at this, and tried every means in his power to check it; but all to no purpose. To the very hour of his death, and since, whenever his name has been mentioned, people have spoken of him as Karím Nánnawor (*i.e.*, bare-footed Karím).

Yĕmukuí dár tah tamukuí pun.

Whence the timber, thence the wedge.

Set a thief to catch a thief.

Yĕnan wĕnah tah wanan hí; suh kami chháwai hápatí.

Wĕnah upon the river-bank and jasmine in the wood; and who plucked the jasmine? The bear.

Good things in the hands of the bad.

Wénah is a non-edible plant with a smell like mint.

Yĕni nah kunih, wonun nah kunih tah kats gaz yerav?

Warp not to be found anywhere, woof (also) not (to be found) anywhere, and how many yards shall we sort?

An order but not all the requisites for fulfilling it.

Yĕtí bĕhĕ Nági Arzun tatí bĕhá Bági Parzun?

Will Bág Parzun (a poor, ignorant, fellow) sit in the same place with Nág Arzun (the great)?

People should know their rank.

Yĕtí pahalis khyul tatí sahas guph.

Where the shepherd's flock there the leopard's lair.

Where riches there thief, where glass there stone, where a man of high position there envious, covetous persons.

Yĕtih ai ásih mengun suh tih hĕyih tsĕngun.

If there were a little boy here he also would be amused.

Cited to a forward, impertinent, little fellow.

Mengun, lit., sheep and goats' ordure, which being small, a little boy has been likened to it and called after it.

Yĕtih áb tatih áp.

Where there is water, there is a god.

Hindustání.—*Jahán áb wahán áp.*

Rivers and springs as sources of fertility and purification, were at an early date invested with a sacred character by the Hindús, who are thoroughly in their glory, living in this land of Kashmír, a land of rivers and fountains and lakes, &c. The Muhammedans are constantly twitting their Hindú neighbours concerning the number of their water-gods.

Yĕtih kon tatih nah hájat myon.

Where there is a one-eyed man there is no necessity for my presence.

The natives declare that the Devil said this.

Hindustání—*Káná ṭerhá bad-fiạlá.*

Persian.—*Yak chashm gul, digar na bilkull.*

Panjábí—*Káná káchṛá hoch-gardaná: yeh tínoṅ kamzát!*
Jablag bas apná chale, to koí na puchhe bát.

Yĕtih nah balawír tatiá wugarah ṭír?

Where that great man is not able, there will that poor, weak fellow be able, to do anything?

Wugarah ṭír, lit., a handful of cooked-rice, but here means a poor, weak man.

Yĕtih Rájá Bhoj tatih Gangá Tílí.

Where Rájá Bhoj there Gangá Tílí.

Money is oftentimes the only patent of nobility besides lofty pretensions. Rájá Bhoj was the celebrated sovereign of Ujjain, the great patron of learned men, and to whose era the nine gems or poets are often ascribed; the "Singhásan battísí" describes his virtues. But Gangá Tílí was an oil-merchant whose only claim to sit in the great Rájá's presence was his great wealth and a little kindness once shown by him to Rájá Bhoj's predecessor, Rájá Vikramáditya.

Yĕtih táp tatih shuhul.

Where sunshine there shade.

"There is compensation in this world even."

Yĕts gav zih mĕts gav.

More than enough is as dirt (no use to a man).

Yĕtsan zanánan poni kámuni, tah tsarĕn mardan batah kámuni.

Many women, little water; and many men, little rice.

It is the custom both among the Muhammedans and the Hindús for the women to fetch the water from the river. If there should be more then one woman in the household, there will probably be frequent quarrelling as to who shall perform this duty, and sometimes both having refused to go for the water, the members of the household will "run short" of this necessary commodity. On the other hand, if there should happen to be more than one husband or man in the house, there will probably be constant wrangling amongst them as to who shall pay the baniyá's bill.

"Yí bandah yatshán tí no sor. Há wulo bála-yáro lo."

"What the servant wishes cannot be had. Come, O my young friend."

Man proposes but God disposes.

Yí wuth haṭih tí khut maṭih.

What has gone down the throat has ascended as a charge to keep.

A promise is a charge to keep.

Yih chhuh bich yut rachhihan, tut diyih ṭuph.

This is a scorpion, as many as cherish it, so many will it sting.

An ungrateful, malicious person.

Yih chhuh khush-khowúr tah ulaṭah. Dapahas, "Daryávas gatsh," tah gatshih hĕnaras.

He is a left-handed, contrary fellow. Say to him, "Go to the river," and he will go to the drain.

Yih chhuh huni—wushkah tah máṅshi gúh hyuh, nah lagán lĕwanas tah nah zúlanas.

He is like dog-barley and buffalo-dung, which are of no use for plastering or burning.

A worthless fellow.

Yih gámas tih mámunis wutshis.

What (happens) to the village also (happens) to the uncle's calf.

Famine, &c., bad for all; every one suffers more or less.

Yih gav likhit tih gav hukhit.

What is written is dried up (no smudging it out).

"*What is written.*" One's fate.

"*Dried up.*" An allusion to the native custom of smudging out an error. A Pandit has been sitting by me for the last eighteen months, writing for an hour or so nearly every day. He always used to rub his forefinger over any mistake he had made; and it was with the greatest difficulty that I got him to use a penknife. Of course, if the writing had dried there was no daubing the error out, it either remained, or else another sheet of paper was used.

Yih hakímas dizih tih konah dizih bĕmáras?

Why cannot that be given to the ordinary sick person, which is given to the doctor?

Native doctors are sometimes very strict over their patients concerning their diet. A youth is now squatting on the floor by my side, who has just recovered from a long and sharp attack of fever. "For a whole fortnight," he says, "the doctor would not allow me to have any thing but rice water and a little *hand* (*Cichorium intybus*). But these doctors are not always so particular as to their own diet when they themselves are ill."

Yih hánzani purnih pĕṭh wuchhih tih wuchhih sáwĕni tsarnih kini.

Whatever the boat-woman sees in the open that the sáwĕni sees through a crack or little hole.

Sáwĕni is a *parda-nishín* woman, *i. e.*, one who remains behind the curtain and is not seen of men.

Yih kákanih tih báyinih tih.

What is the eldest son's that also is the youngest son's.

Show no favouritism in the family.

Yih khĕzih bukris tih khĕzih nah pyúwali gov.

What a man eats from rudeness and gruffness that he would not eat from a cow with young.

Muhammedans do not drink the milk of a recently-delivered cow until the fourth day after the birth. Hindús wait till the eleventh day, when the Bráhman comes and the owner of the cow worships and makes presents. If the calf should be born on a Friday, then both Muhammedans and Hindús have special arrangements according to their different religions.

Yih mallah wanih tih gatshih karun;
Yih mallah karih tih gatshih nah karun.

What the Mullá says you must do;
What the Mullá does you must not do.

"Do what I say but not as I do," says the parson.

Yih nah bánas lárih tih lāriá pánas?

What will not stick to the pot, will not stick to the body.

Thin rice or weak soup, &c.

Yih pron guyun karih tih karih nah nov gásah?

What old manure-grass can do that new grass can not do.

Wisdom and experience are on the side of age.

"*Yih rasas suĕt wasih tih gav halál*" *píran aki chhuh wunamut.*

"What came out with the soup is lawful," a pír said.

Pharisaism.

A certain stranger's goat wandered inside the door of a pír's house. When the pír saw it he said to his wife: "Look here, there's that goat trespassed into our place again. What shall I do? Bring the 'Book of the Law' and I will see what is right to be done." After some little searching he discovered that it was necessary to stand at his door and cry for three times, "Who has lost a goat?"

Accordingly the pír went to the door and cried with a very little voice. "Has any one lost any thing?" This he did three times, and then went back into his house and told his wife to kill the goat at once, as he had shouted three times. He also told her to cook the meat in a separate vessel and separate place, in order that the ordinary cooking vessels and places might not be, perchance, defiled.

When the meat was cooked and ready for serving-up, he ordered his wife to tip the pot a little and let out some of the cooked soup, but to be very careful lest her hand should touch it; for, said he, "there is no sin in drinking the broth, but we must not eat, or even touch, the flesh." However, while the woman was tilting the pot, her hand shook and some meat escaped with the broth. "Never mind, never mind," said the pír, with ill-disguised pleasure, "what has come out with the soup is also legal."

Yih shahruch sáwĕni khĕyih tih khĕyih gámuch gáv.
The rich city woman and the village cow fare the same.
The rustic fills his stomach but the city-man feeds his back. *Sáwĕni* is a *parda-nishín* woman, as all the wives of the wealthier classes are in Kashmír.

Yih tsŏh chhuí wundas tih chhuh mih chandas.
What is in your heart is in my pocket.
"I have your secret. Beware!"

Yih zĕwih zĕwih karizih tih konah karizih zangi zangi?
What you can do with your tongue you can do with your legs (can't you? then do not be afraid, but go and do it).

Yihunduí rat yimanuí mat.
Rub their blood upon their bodies.
A man gives a present; but it costs the receiver as much as he gets.

Yim gai sukhas ḍus dini.
These things are disturbers of peace.
Riches and honor to an unthankful, unsatisfied man.

Yimah há-málih chhai wuzmalah tah traṭai gaṭahkár tah gagráyih path kun.
O father, there are lightnings and thick thunderbolts; and mists and thunder are behind.
No end of trouble ahead.

Yiman gabar timan nah batah, yiman batah timan nah gabar.
No food to those who have children, no children to those who have food.

Yimawui mári imám tah timawui kur samah.
They who killed the imám lament his death.
To do a man an injury and afterwards be sorry for it.
Samah—a song of lamentation. An allusion to the mourning of the Shí'as for the two sons of 'Alí, Hasan and Hosain.
Imám is a Muhammedan priest.

Yindar chhas katán; tsandar ḍíshit batah ṭok; nindar chham nah yiwán; sindar gayam pánas.
I spin the wheel and when the moon shines forth I eat my dinner; sleep does not come to me, and my flesh is dried up within me.

A favourite song in time of trouble.

Munshí Bawání Dás excommunicated his first wife *a mensâ et thoro* on account of some fault of hers. She used to sit at her wheel every day in an adjoining house singing this song, and one day her husband on hearing it sent for her and took her into his house again.

Yírawani náv ; chírawani dali.
A boat afloat (before the wind) ; a wrung garment.
A Kashmírí curse "May you be like," &c.

Yitui tsángi titui gásh.
As many lamps so much light.
The more, the merrier.
Tsong—is a little earthen lamp called dípá in Hindústán.

Yiwawani daulat pĕwawún shín ;
Tsalawani daulat, galawún shín.
Wealth comes like the falling snow (*i. e.*, slowly).
Wealth goes like the melting snow (*i. e.*, quickly).
Persian.—*Kuráza, kuráza biyáyad nukhust*
Rubáyad azo chúnki gardad durust.

Yizmanbái dārih kini wuchhlai,
Púnah chhĕk buchh tai kas kyah dik ?
O mother of the wedding-party, look out of the window.
You yourself appear hungry, to whom will you give ?
A meagre, wedding-feast, or dinner.

Yupis shup dakhah.
Like trying to keep back the water-floods with a fan.
Large expenses and small income.
Shup is a small fan used for cleaning grain.

Yúri kun rĕh túri kun tĕkar.
Where the flame there the pot.
Money commands everything.
This is only the last line of a verse of poetry concerning the rich man :—

Ásanwális chhĕh ásanach tĕh ;
Watih pĕth myulus kentsháh khĕh ;
Tsángij tshuninas yatití bĕh ;
Yúri kun tĕkar túri kun rĕh.
A wealthy man has the pride of wealth ;
If any one meets him on the way it is eat something (O friend).
Then the mat is spread and he is asked to "sit down."
Where the pot is there the flame will be also.

Yus akhúh khĕyih tah chéyih tah kánsih diyih, suh chhuh ján tasandih, khutah, yus anih tah jamá karih.

He who eats and drinks and gives to another is better than he who brings and puts together.

Yus dandav nishih gav suh gav bandav nishih.

What went from the teeth went also from the body.

The value of good teeth.

Yus gav Lás suh zah nah áv.
Áv ai tas nah zah wáv.

He who went to Lhassa (Tibet) never returned.
If he did come back then he was a rich man for ever.

Yus gelih paras, tas gatshih garas.

He who slanders a stranger, will be slandered in his own house.

Yus khĕyih harah han tah tarah han, tas chhuí suĕt suĕt zarah han ;
Yus khĕyih húkah han tah wugarah han suh chhuí ḍugarah han hyuh.

He who eats cream and spices and other rich things, will always have sickness.
He who eats unstrained rice and vegetables is like a Ḍugra.

Ḍugra—"A mixed race, (descended from a Rájpút father and low-caste mother) of reputation in the Panjáb. The reigning family of Kashmír is of this tribe Its members speak of themselves as Rájpúts. The Ḍugra are land-holders and cultivators."—"Sherring's Hindú Tribes and Castes."

Yus mazah phalis suí mazah gurnas.

What flavour there is to the grape there will be to the whole cluster.

A sample.

Yus nah dúnas pĕwih suh konah rĕwih púnas ?

He who cannot (afford even) to light a fire, why will he not adorn himself ?

"He has got all he is worth upon his back."

Yus nah gabah phaṭih suh dapiá "Babah."

Will that boy say "Father" who did not burst the womb (*i.e.*, who was not born to me) ?

An adopted child.

Yus pherih suh krerih.
Yus ajih suh gajih.
He who turns (from his promise let him fall) into a well.
He who (fulfils only) half his promise (let him fall) into a furnace.

Striking hands with his creditor the debtor will quote these words.

Yus phul suh phul gunchai.
What bloomed, bloomed when it was in the bud.

The child is father of the man.

Yus yas zánih sui tas mánih.
He will obey him whom he knows.

"One of themselves" would have more influence.

Yus yuth karih suh tyuth surih.
Yus yuth wavih suh tyuth lonih.
As he does, so will he receive;
As he sows, so will he reap.

Hindustání—*Jaisá doge waisá páoge.*

Yúsuf Júah! wutsh rat.
O, Yúsuf Jú! take hold of the calf.

A dependent character.

A sharp fellow would fix the calf under one arm and milk the cow, but Yúsuf wanted another man to hold it. Cows in India always have their calves by them when they are being milked.

Yúsuf Jú is a Muhammedan Hindustání name. *Yúsuf* is from the Arabic for Joseph, and *Jú* is by way of respect and means lord! master! sir!

Yusuí khĕyih ser suí sapunih ser.
He who eats a ser (*i.e.*, lbs. 2 English) will be satisfied.

Ser is the Kashmírí and Hindustání word for a weight=2 lbs English; it is also the Persian word for satisfied.

Yusuî ruchhum tasi nish rachhtam Khudáyo.
O God, preserve me from him whom I cherished.

An ungrateful protege, offspring, &c.

Yusuí ruchhum yiman athan, suí yuván netharah kathan.
He whom I brought up with these hands is coming to me with words of marriage.

Money and position frequently shake hands.

Yut guris yiyih raṭanah wag tyut pakihbarábar.
The horse will go according as he is held by the bridle.

Yut kur tami mih tyut karas buh tih.
As he did to me so will I do to him.
Lex talionis.

Yut wírih ṭak dik tyút chhus yáwun.
As much as you cut the willow so much will it grow strong.

Yut wustád titi tsáṭ ásan.
As (is) the teacher so will the scholars be.

Yutáni nah hakím ak zah már karih tután sapanih nah hakím.
Until the physician has killed one or two he is not a physician.

Yután nah ranj tulih tután labih nah ganj.
Until a man takes trouble he does not get treasure.
Persian.—*Tá ranj na kashí ganj na yábí.*
No pains, no gains.

Yután puz pazih tután álam dazih.
Until the truth appears the world will burn (with anger).
Let them fight it out.

Yután tshuṭ pilan karih tután zyúṭh yaḍ barih.
While the short man is reaching up to a place, the tall man fills his stomach.
To which the short man replied :—

Yután zyúṭh jái tshánḍih tután tshuṭ nindar karih.
While the tall man is seeking for a place wherein to repose, the short man sleeps.

Yutuí zuwah tyutuí suwah.
As I earn so will I sow.
Dress according to position.

Z

Zabán chhĕh shamsher.
The tongue is a sword.
Tongue is a sharp sword."—Psalm lvii. 4.

Zachan pachah phur.
To turn and mend old clothes.
Making an old coat look new.

Zágun tah zuwun, tshúndun tah melun.
Expect and live, seek and find.

Zah thazah tah gádah dazah.
Two persons high (-minded) and the fishes burnt.
Somebody in the house must bend, or the work will not be done.

Zainak Kadaláh pĕṭhah thuk gayih hó!
The spittle has gone from Zaina Kadal!

A man came from India to see Kashmír and enquire about the inhabitants. In the course of his ramblings he went and stood on the fourth bridge and spat into the river; and then looked at the spot where his spittle had fallen, and said, "Where has it gone? Where has it gone?" The passers-by asked the meaning of this. He did not reply, but continued saying, "Where has it gone?" More people crowded around, until at last a vast assembly had gathered, and there was great danger lest the bridge should break. Then he told them that his spittle had gone, and the crowd scattered; and the man from India went back to his own countrymen and told them what stupid people those Kashmírís were.

Zaina Kadal, the fourth of the seven bridges spanning that part of the river Jhelum, which flows through Srínagar, and forming the principal means of inter-communication between the two sides of the city, is the principal thoroughfare in Srínagar. It is said that whatever news there may be it will certainly be known some time or other during the day on Zaina Kadal. There is a story illustrative of this:—

Ázád Khán (1763 A. D.) was a most tyrannical ruler. Even in his own palace he was a very hard master. One of his wives was about to be delivered of a child; just before her confinement he went to her lying-in room and said, "If it is a boy that be born, I will give you many presents; but if it should be a girl, I will slay both you and the child." A girl was born, and as soon as the king heard of it he slew his wife and threw the infant into the fire-place. Uneasy as to what report might be spread concerning this dastard act, he sent his servant to Zaina Kadal to see whether the people had got wind of it, and if possible the report was to be traced and the originators seized. The servant went and in a little while four or five persons were seized, and the report traced back to one man. This man was carried before the king, who asked him how he had obtained the news. The man replied, "I saw in a dream Sháh Hamadán (cf. note to '*Áyas wate*,' &c.), or one like unto him, coming to me and saying that such was the case in the king's house. Accordingly I told the people, whom I met, of my strange vision, and on Zaina Kadal there was quite a little company of strangers to whom I related my strange experience." "True," said the king, "Zaina Kadal's news is correct concerning the ruler also." Then going at once to the bridge he had all the houses, which Zainu'l-ábadín had erected on either side of it, destroyed, lest they should prove dangerous treasuries of scandal.

Even now authorities are afraid of the bridge, and the police have special orders to prevent any gatherings there (?)

Zálih surinam tah kánih sárinam.

It goes off from my fingers, but rolls on in to the ball.

The father loses but the son gains; it remains in the family. Sung by the women dozens of times in succession very often, as they sit at the spinning-wheel.

Zám ai ásih gám tatih pěthah ladih pám.

If the sister-in-law should be in a village, thence even she will send reproaches.

Few enemies go so far as that they out-distance their enmity.

Zám is the wife's husband's sister. She is generally a great stumbling-block to the wife's happiness.

Zámatur ai hangas manz rachhzěn totih mandahchháuěs rangas manz.

If a son-in-law be brought up in the best way, and with the greatest attention possible, still he will put you to shame in the assembly (*i. e.*, he will not respect or love you).

Hangas manz, lit. in, the centre of the head or turban, the place of security and honour.

Zámatur gav pámatur.

A son-in-law is a giver of reproach and curses.

Zamín chhai dusi dusi sun.

Land is like beaten gold.

Zán chhĕh jahán.
Acquaintance is the world.

Zán nah tah pachhán nah, tah "Khálah jí salám!"
Nor known, nor recognised, and "Good morning, uncle."
Said of a stranger claiming friendship or relationship.
Marwari.—*Ján na pahchán, "Khálá barí salám!"*

Zánai nah kaum nah krám nah nám.
I will not know your sect or class or name.
Refusal to inter-marry.

Zanánah chhĕh prasanih wizih taubah karán, prasit chhĕh bĕyih wátán tutuí.
A woman in the hour of travail repents, but when she is delivered of the child she again arrives at the same state (of lying, &c.)

Zanánah gayí khoran hund pulahor ak trov tah byák tshun.
A wife is like the grass shoe on one's feet—one is left and another is put on (*i.e.*, a wife easily got rid of, if she should prove disagreeable).

Zanánih akis parutshuk rĕtsar chhuyih. Dupanak "Kĕnh nah. Shuris ám kut."
It was asked of a woman "Are you well?" She replied, "No, not at all. The child can just walk."
A mother's anxieties are increased by her child being able to toddle about and get into mischief.

Zanánih hund asun chhuí mardas manzimyor.
A woman's laugh is a go-between herself and the man.
Manzimyor, Match-makers, called *Ghatucks* or *Ghatkís* down in Bengal. As a rule these people are utterly without principle, *vide* "Hindús as they are," by Bose, Ch. v.

Zanánih hund yáwun gandun tah chháwun; Wethih hund yáwun wubaláwun; wírih hund yáwun ṭak dáwun; mardah sund yáwun dan.
A woman's beauty is her dress and jewels; the river derives beauty from its waves; the willow gets beauty from lopping; and a man's beauty is his wealth.
Weth, the river Jhelum in its course through Kashmír. Hindú priests call it Vedastá.

Wír, the white willow. If a big tree, the top branches are lopped every year; if a small tree then it is lopped after three years. During the winter the leaves of this tree are stored up as fodder for oxen and sheep and goats.

Zangah rúdi un tah zĕwih rúdi nyuv.

The runner brought it, but the gabbler took it away.

The talker often gets the praise due to the worker.

Zangih yiwán tsunḍ tah nar dárán, narih yiwán tsunḍ tah zang dárán.

If the hand gets hurt we put out a leg, and if the leg gets hurt we put forth a hand.

An alternative is generally at hand in time of trouble.

Zánit tah mánit karun.

He knew (his work), attended to it, and did it.

A good, honest workman.

Zari búz bahih wahari zih Baḍsháh mud.

The deaf man heard twelve years afterwards that Baḍsháh was dead.

A man with no news.

Baḍsháh, great king, a name given to Zainu'l-ábadín, the eighth and greatest of the Muhammedan rulers of Kashmír.

Zari sunz suranai.

The sound of a flute to a deaf man.

An incomprehensible tale or remark.

Záris wunuk, "Moj, há, mui." Dupanak, "Yapárí anton."

Some person said to the gambler, "Oh! your mother has died." He replied, "Bring her by this way."

The gambler was so engrossed in the game that he could not leave it, even to bury his mother's body.

Zaṭ jilawih wazah guris tah mĕhmánah shuris Rahmánah náv.

A piece of ragged cloth as a bridle is dignity to a horse, and Rahmána is a name for a poor boy.

The would-be gentleman.

Mĕhmán, first meaning is a guest, hence the poor orphan, who is always somebody's guest, has come to be so called, and thus the word frequently means any poor person.

Rahmán is one of the greatest names that can be given to a Muhammedan. It means compassionate, and is the first in the list of the ninety-nine names of God.

Zĕnun gatshih kharah sandi púṭh tah khyun gatshih narah sandi páṭh.

One must work like an ass, but eat his dinner like a man.

Zeṭhĕn narĕn mod.

Honour is given to long sleeves.

"And ye have respect to him that weareth the gay clothing."

One day Shekh Núr-ud-dín went to a wedding feast with nothing but his ragged faqír dress on, and the consequence was that the people would not receive him. He returned quickly to his abode, and changed his ragged garment for some new and costly clothes, and went again to the feast. This time he was received with great honour. He first quoted the above proverb at the dinner.

Zĕv chhĕm karán lukh lukh ; luk chhim tshanán thuk thuk.

My tongues does talk, talk ; the people do spit, spit upon me.

A man of many words is despised.

Zĕwui chhĕh márán tah zĕwui chhĕh tárán.

The tongue kills and the tongue saves.

Zíi chheh híi.

Pay for work done is like jasmine.

Sweet are the fruits of labour.

Zindah nah súr nah sás tah marit atlás.

Alive—neither dust nor ashes, but dead—satin.

Undutiful offspring.

Hindustání.—*Jíte na púchhe mue dhaṛ dhaṛ píte.*

Zorah, zorah nashih zú, tah wárah, wárah nashih koh.

From "zorah zorah" life wears out, but from "wárah wárah" the mountain wears away.

Zorah zorah, "Go on, work man," said to a man working in a casual, listless fashion.

Wárah, wárah. "Carefully, not so fast," said to a man working in a quick, reckless way.

Zú gav tsángi rĕh, tílah han gatshias ásuni.

Life is like the flame of a lamp ; it needs a little oil now and again.

Zú ur tah jahán ur.
The spirit healthy and the world healthy.
Health is everything.

Zuí zĕwih tah ryuṅz láyih tah adah páwih shikár.
Zuí will be born and will shoot and will receive his prey.
Building castles in the air.

Zulih gayí zih kulih guyí.
He became drowsy and it fell into the river.
Carelessness is ruination.

A faqír was sitting by the fire-place cooking his dinner as the boat was being towed along. Owing to the great heat he became very drowsy, and so bending his head, he began to sleep. Suddenly the boat struck the bank and the plate of rice and meat tumbled off the fire into the river.

Zuwal boguni zachal dái; yih kusah myáni ágah-bái?
Lousey mistress, ragged nurse; which is my mistress?
General reply of a female servant, when blamed by her mistress because of her dirty appearance.

Zuwalih hund gatshih khyun tah zĕwalih hund nah.
It is better to eat with a dirty-headed woman than with a garrulous woman.

Finis.